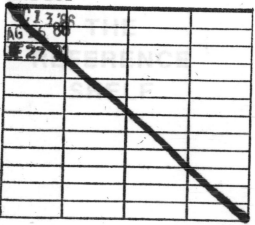

CENSORSHIP
AND EDUCATION

edited by ELI M. OBOLER

THE REFERENCE SHELF
Volume 53 Number 6

THE H. W. WILSON COMPANY

New York   1981

THE REFERENCE SHELF

The books in this series contain reprints of articles, excerpts from books, and addresses on current issues and social trends in the United States and other countries. There are six separately bound numbers in each volume, all of which are generally published in the same calendar year. One number is a collection of recent speeches; each of the others is devoted to a single subject and gives background information and discussion from various points of view, concluding with a comprehensive bibliography. Books in the series may be purchased individually or on subscription.

Library of Congress Cataloging in Publication Data

Censorship and Education
  (The Reference shelf; v. 53, no. 6)
  Includes bibliography.
    1. Education and state. 2. Education—Censorship. 3. Libraries—Censorship. I. Oboler, Eli M.
II. Series.
LC87.C45   379.1'56   81-19732
ISBN O-8242-0658-4   AACR2

International Standard Book Number 0-8242-0658-4
PRINTED IN THE UNITED STATES OF AMERICA

CONTENTS

III. Censorhsip in the Schools and Libraries

IV. Censorship Court Decisions

There is general agreement that everyone in America is entitled to the *best* possible education, one that will equip the child to become a free individual and a useful part of American society. It is also agreed that two of the most effective tools for the education of children are *appropriate* textbooks and library materials. However, there is a great deal of *dis*-agreement on the question of who decides what is "best," and what is "appropriate." This volume will attempt to explore such questions as: Is "the best possible education" to be decided entirely by school boards, school administrators, school teachers, parents or—of late—even by the students themselves? Is the student who never encounters differing opinions about controversial topics—from sexual behavior to the origin of mankind—likely to grow into a "free individual" or a "useful part of American society"? Should selection of "appropriate textbooks and library materials" be made by classroom teachers, school boards and administrators, and local librarians or by politicians and special interest groups?

The first American schoolbook, *The New England Primer*, was, despite its title, a popular textbook in almost every American colony following the Revolution. During the nineteenth century, Noah Webster's spelling book, first published in 1783, became the best-selling American textbook, with a million copies sold from 1807 to 1827. Throughout the period of their greatest influence the *McGuffey Readers*, which sold nearly 122 million copies from 1836 to 1920, became popular nationwide, but especially in the South and west of the Appalachians. The textbooks, written by Webster and McGuffey, had one characteristic in common; they were exceedingly moralistic and taught what might be called "folk" psychology and morality. McGuffey made a practice of quoting only what he called "elegant extracts" from widely accepted authors.

With the sudden flourishing of the American secondary school, after 1900, came a concomitant interest in school libraries. Although the secondary school library was fairly well established in schools (by 1936, 42 percent of all American high schools had centralized library service and 50 percent had classroom collections), the elementary school library lagged; it was not until after World War I that such aids to education came to be desirable, even if not yet required for accreditation.

By the 1950s, instructional materials or the media center concept were coming into being; in fact the first national standards for school library programs of *any* type were called for by the American Library Association of School Libraries in 1960. These standards, which among other things, stress intellectual freedom, clash with the growing feeling among some of the public, namely the taxpayer parents whose children are being taught and who must pay for the library's costs. They claim the right to a part in deciding what goes into the school libraries. This attitude is more pronounced in the 1980s in a conservative and traditional swing, which has elected Ronald Reagan to the Presidency.

American education began with the Puritans who established a conservative, God-fearing educational system aimed at supporting both church and state. By 1981, there appears to be a determined effort to return to such a pattern, for the goal of a pluralist society, redolent of diversity and freedom of opinion, is being openly challenged by traditional forces in our society.

The articles that follow give a broad view of educational censorship and the benefits and drawbacks to intellectual freedom in the school curricula, in textbook choice, and in library collections in the American school system. The first Section in the volume sets the stage for the specific articles following; it discusses different types of censorship and traces censorship through history. Section II is concerned with textbook censors themselves—the publisher, the selector, the distributor, and the user—and discusses specific cases of censorship, the rise of "scientific creativism," the conflicts in "values education," and the amazing power of a two-person lobby to influence national textbook distribution.

In Section III, the articles deal with specific problems of teachers and school librarians, at odds with the censors, attempting to follow and defend the Library Bill of Rights and the First Amendment. At the same time, some teachers and librarians are acting as censors themselves.

Finally, Section IV deals with student rights and the legal aspects of censorship versus intellectual freedom. It reveals the changing and sometimes contrary views of courts on several levels of jurisdiction and in different parts of the country, and describes the struggle by such people as the current president of the Freedom to Read Foundation, William D. North, "to recognize the minimal safeguards required to preserve secondary education from becoming primary brainwashing."

The Editor of this volume is very appreciative of the assistance provided by publishers and authors who have given permission to reprint their articles. He gives more than a conventional tip of the hat in thanks to Mrs. Nancy Anthony, interlibrary loan clerk *par excellence* of the Idaho State University Library. No one library could hold the diversity of resources needed to compile a book like this; Mrs. Anthony provided international access.

November 1981   Eli M. Oboler

I. THE CLIMATE OF CENSORSHIP

EDITOR'S INTRODUCTION

We know that, to a great extent, society and the time in which we live determine the degree and type of censorship in our schools and libraries. We also know that such factors as group prejudice and fear of social change can very often help to determine the course of censorship. However, unlike the weather, we cannot break it down into elements, such as temperature, atmosphere, moisture evaporation, and wind, to forecast when, where, and how it may strike.

That censorship is on the increase in the United States in the 1980s is clear, even if all of its causes are not. Judith Krug, Director of the American Library Association's Office of Intellectual Freedom, which keeps track of reported incidents of censorship said that, in fact, "Attempts to censor books in the nation's libraries have more than tripled since last November's election." Perhaps we can describe the climate of the time as a sort of conservative pattern that cyclically hits the country. The educator on all levels is affected by it, and, to extend the weather metaphor still further, it can have a "chilling" affect on educational decision-making. The schoolteacher, the librarian, and the school administrator who refrains from adding a particular book or film, cassette or magazine to the curriculum, lest it be considered "controversial," is simply reacting to such a climate.

In the first article in this section, Kenneth L. Donelson in *Library Quarterly*, traces the historical tendency of teachers and librarians to censor reading material on literary merit and moral grounds. In 1789 fiction was banned because it was thought to have a corrupting influence on the young. The second article, from *Publishers Weekly*, points out that, at present, there are attempts to ban *Catcher in the Rye* for exactly the same reason. The only difference now is that the censorship group is called the Moral Majority. In the third article, James Alvino bemoans the banning of Salinger's book, which can be compared to *Tom Sawyer*, "a milestone in American literature," and he questions whether this is providing a broad and varied interpretation of life for the young.

In the next article Stephen Robinson, a professional engineer and parent-citizen adviser writing in the *English Journal*, feels that the individual must be taught to think for himself through a wide range of differing reading materials. In the fourth article, Linda R. Silver, a children's librarian writing in the *School Library Journal*, is concerned, however, that value judgment may be overlooked in concentrating on free access. She maintains that in order to give our children intelligent guidance, we must consider literary standards in book evaluation and selection.

LITERARY AND MORAL CENSORSHIP, THEN AND NOW[1]

. . . Most English teachers and some librarians . . . believe that censorship is essentially and almost exclusively a product of our confused modern society, guilt-ridden, fearful, and perplexed by culture shock. For them, the blight of censorship began with the furor that greeted Salinger's *The Catcher in the Rye*. A few might argue that censorship began with the rise of paperbacks, or perhaps the language in some post–World War II novels, or possibly the rising taxes during the 1960s. Whatever the exact cause, those English teachers and librarians bemoan censorship as a modern interruption in an otherwise apparently age-old tradition of academic and intellectual freedom for schools and libraries.

But they are quite wrong. Academic freedom and intellectual freedom are largely modern terms to describe largely modern attitudes. In truth, the word *censorship* comes far

[1] From article entitled "Shoddy and Pernicious Books and Youthful Purity: Literary and Moral Censorship, Then and Now," by Kenneth Donelson, professor, department of English, Arizona State University; co-author of *Literature for Today's Young Adults* with Alleen Pace Nilsen. *The Library Quarterly.* 51:4–19. Ja. '81. Reprinted by permission from the January, 1981, issue of *The Library Quarterly.*

closer to describing the spirit and practices of American schools and libraries from the 1870s through the 1930s. To understand modern censorship, whether justified on literary or moral grounds, we should look back to the last half of the last century. What we find may tell us something about beliefs and practices that persist even today. It may even make us aware that some past teachers and librarians were among the most avid, the most vocal, the most fanatic censors.

Early in the first volume (1876) of the *American Library Journal*, soon to become simply the *Library Journal*, William F. Poole [head of Newberry Library] listed three common objections to public libraries: first, the normal dread of taxes; second, the more philosophical belief that government had no rights except to protect people and property, certainly no right to tax anyone to build and maintain a public library; and third, fear about the kinds of books libraries would purchase and circulate. Concern over library holdings was often phrased as a question: Are public libraries established for scholars or the general public? But, essentially, the question represented a fundamental fear of books, and of librarians as well. Poole argued that the public library existed to serve the entire community, thus justifying a general tax, but his words hardly satisfied critics. In 1879, W.M. Stevenson spoke for many librarians when he wrote: "If the public library is not first and foremost an educational institution, it has no right to exist. If it exists for mere entertainment, and for a low order of entertainment at that, it is simply a socialistic institution."

Articles about the responsibility of public libraries and the dangers of certain kinds of books raged for years in library literature. The debate was almost exclusively about fiction, particularly whether fiction could safely be read by young people; some librarians apparently believed that *fiction and purity* were mutually exclusive terms. One librarian in 1879 believed fiction would permanently befoul the lives of the young:

The school-boy takes his first initiation in insubordination to teachers and parents from the lawless career of "Jack Harkaway," or some one of the boy-heroes of the "Wide-Awake Boys of

America"; while the school-girl, who has not had her taste and sentiment directed aright, imbibes rank poison from the "Fireside Companion," as she follows the absurd freaks of a "Wilful Goldie."

The debate over the problem of using second-rate or tenth-rate books to encourage the reading habit raged then as fiercely as it does now. In 1877, William Kite argued that his eight years' experience in the Friends' Free Public Library in Germantown, Pennsylvania, from which *all* novels had been excluded, proved that readers did not progress from poor books to better books. Twenty years later, W. M. Stevenson echoed that sentiment about "fiction fiends." "The theory advanced by librarians of standing, that readers to whom books of this [dubious] grade are supplied will gradually rise to something better, has proved in the six years' experience of this library absolutely false." "Once the habit is formed it seems as difficult to throw off as the opium habit. Of course, there are many cultivated people who have read in their youth trashy novels, but have they not attained to culture, not by virtue of such reading, but *in spite of it?*" But the opposing camp had its champions. Samuel S. Green wrote in 1879 that exciting stories had at least two virtues: they kept readers from worse reading, and they gave "young persons a taste for reading." James Freeman Clarke agreed that Oliver Optic and Horatio Alger wrote execrable stuff, "false to life, tawdry in sentiment, full of impossible incidents," but reading even this would "lead to something better in many cases." Writing twenty years later in a survey of librarians on reading tastes and interests, two New York librarians maintained that poorer books could lead the young to better books: "Some may doubt whether a liberal allowance of such writers as Alger and 'Optic' would lead to better things, but I do not hesitate to say that, so far as an observation of twenty years in our library enables one to judge, it is the case with the majority of our boy readers." "What harm will they do her [a poor working girl]? The New York girl, however poor, is generally sensible enough to take all she reads with a grain of salt, and is not at all carried away by the supposed 'false views of life' such books are assumed to contain. She reads for amusement, and these books serve that end. By and by she will tire of them and seek something better."

Librarians often appeared horrified by what they called shoddy, sensational, and pernicious (a favorite word of many librarians then) material all too easily accessible, and they vowed to keep such evil out of the pure and innocent hands of the young. Librarians of that time seemed to spend almost as much time worrying about their clients' personal salvation as they did about their own professional responsibilities. Indeed, saving souls seemed both a moral and professional responsibility of some librarians, second only to their drive to remain personally pure, innocent, and naive. During the second session of the 1876 ALA meeting devoted to "novel reading," one librarian announced that his rules allowed no novels in his library. His factory-worker patrons might request novels, but he simply recommended other books. To laughter, he said he had never read novels, so he "could not say what their effect really was." But some critics, driven by the same impulse to eradicate evil, were even more certain about the horrifying effects of novel reading. Reverend J. A. Milburn, pastor of a Presbyterian church in Indianapolis, preached a sermon in 1896 denouncing the city library as a "purveyor of meretricious literature," especially "debasing, meretricious, immoral, pernicious, and destructive fiction."

Much has been written about Mark Twain's censorship problems with *Huckleberry Finn*, both before and after publication. Less well known is the ALA treatment of Stephen Crane's *The Red Badge of Courage*. At the sixth session in Cleveland in 1896, librarians questioned whether they ought to put the novel on the ALA approved list. The dialogue that followed revealed far more about the speakers and the time than it did about Crane or his book.

Mr. Larned—What of Crane's *Red Badge of Courage?*
A. L. Peck—It abounds in profanity. I never could see why it should be given into the hands of a boy.
Miss Tess L. Kelson—I think the *Red Badge of Courage* is an important contribution to the literature of arbitration. I think it

belongs to that. I think that anyone who reads that book will say that it is the finest thing in the world to put into the hands of people to make them converts to the abolition of war. . . .

C. W. Andrews—I have had the pleasure of listening to the comments of men who stood high in the ranks of the army and who declared that the *Red Badge of Courage* is not true. Therefore I should be decidedly against leaving it on the list because of its not being true to the facts.

C. A. Nelson—If we object to the English in children's books I think we certainly should object to the English in this *Red Badge of Courage.*

G. M. Jones—This *Red Badge of Courage* is a very good illustration of the weakness of the criticism in most of our literary papers. The critics in our literary papers are praising this book as being a true picture of war. The fact is, I imagine, that the criticisms are written by young men who know nothing about war, just as Mr. Crane himself knows nothing about war. Gen. McClurg, of Chicago, and Col. Nourse, of Massachusetts, both say that the story is not true to the life of the soldier. An article in the *Independent,* or perhaps the *Outlook,* says that no such profanity as given in the book was common in the army among the soldiers. Mr. Crane has since published two other books on New York life which are simply vulgar books. I consider the *Red Badge of Courage* a vulgar book, and nothing but vulgar.

The majority recommended striking Crane's novel from the list.

It was a time of censorship, a time when Anthony Comstock, America's premier censor, wreaked havoc in lives and books in his fight to save purity and decency, defined as he alone could recognize it. It was a time when the editor of the *Journal of Education* could praise students at Oakland High School for refusing to read an unexpurgated edition of *Hamlet.*

All honor to the modest and sensible youths and maidens of the Oakland High School who revolted against studying an unexpurgated edition of Hamlet! The indecencies of Shakespeare in the complete edition are brutal. They are more than indelicacies, they are indecencies. They are no part of Shakespeare's thought, have no connection with the play, and can be eliminated with as little jar as could the oaths of a modern slugger. Indeed, Shakespeare's vulgarity was, to all intents and purposes, profanity, scattered promiscuously through the lines with no more meaning than so many oaths.

And what does all this ancient history have to do with contemporary censorship? Obviously, the titles under attack then differ from those under attack today. But the two kinds of censorship—and censors—I best know and most fear were rampant in the late nineteenth century, censorship based on literary merit and censorship based on morality.

Many English teachers, school librarians, and public librarians belong to one or both schools of censorship. They ache to control the lives of others, especially young people, to guide others to different books, better books, purer books, and to determine curriculum or policy to eliminate poorer or immoral or dubious or controversial or questionable material.

I met my first literary censor when I was a child in Clarinda, Iowa. The librarian in charge of the children's room made clear her irritation about both my presence and the kinds of books I insisted on checking out. Staring down her very long nose, or so it seemed to me then, she announced that if I really wanted to read *that*, she could not stop me, but she hoped I would turn to something worthwhile soon. For her sake, I hope I never did, but I may have wandered into literary territory she might have approved of. If so, I would prefer not to know it and would plead only that I did it inadvertently.

Years later when I began teaching, I met another literary censor. She was a public librarian in a small town where I taught, though she could as easily have been an English teacher or a school librarian. She announced to me, immediately recognizing an uncertain and unsophisticated English teacher, that she had a small but great library because she "would never buy or circulate anything except the *greatest* literature." When I mustered up enough courage to ask her how she defined *greatest*, she sighed and gazed compassionately down at me as only a god would deign to look at a mortal and spake, "The test of time determines the greatest of literature." Given her rationale, her library certainly contained the greatest literature, since nothing I could find there had been published in the last fifty years.

Later I heard other teachers and librarians maintain much the same position. Each rode into the battle against ignorance and poor readers waving a banner emblazoned with the words, "Literary Excellence." Since I had been a voracious reader since childhood and since I owned a sanctified Master of Arts degree—in that most practical of areas to prepare me to handle rural kids in English classes, late eighteenth-century English drama—I felt threatened by the public librarian and other English teachers and librarians. I should know, I kept reminding myself, what literary excellence consisted of. But like some other mortals, I had no success defining that term so others would know precisely what was meant. That bothered me. Literary censors are not bothered by self-doubts.

Perhaps it is unfair to say that Lillian L. Shapiro, in the May 1978 *School Library Journal,* reminded me unhappily and uncomfortably of my small-town public librarian and her *greatest* literature. After dismissing popularity with young adults as a valid criterion for book selection, Shapiro approvingly cited three criteria, "objective judgments, discriminating taste, and sensitivity to the needs and concerns of learners and teachers." That sounds fine to me. Now if only she had explained precisely what "objective judgments, discriminating taste, and sensitivity" were, I would have been pleased and possibly even enlightened. She did not like Don Bredes's *Hard Feelings* ("which, for sheer vulgarity would be hard to equal"), she was not fond of Paul Zindel's *Confessions of a Teenage Baboon,* and she liked the television production of Judy Blume's *Forever* better than the book. I admired Bredes's novel, felt indifferent about Zindel's bit of fluff, and was bored with both print and TV versions of Blume's book. Shapiro's tastes and mine are clearly not alike, which, I'm sure, is fine with her; but my objections are not about our dissimilar tastes but about the imprecision of her terms. How fuzzy words like "objective judgments, discriminating taste, and sensitivity" clarify Shapiro's selection policies remains an enigma within a riddle to me.

I hasten to add that I admire and use Lester Asheim's 1953 distinction between censorship and selection and admire almost equally the distinction drawn by Julia Turnquist Bradley in the spring 1978 *Connecticut Law Review*. To know with absolute certainty whether a librarian or English teacher was censoring or selecting, one would need to enter that person's mind and psyche and soul, and, in some cases, the librarian or teacher might be honestly unsure whether she or he censored or selected. Waffling or weaseling with words is not unknown, as Marjorie Fiske learned in her seminal study, *Book Selection and Censorship*, when a librarian in a large municipal library said, "We haven't been censoring but we have been 'conservative.' After all, this is a conservative community, and that is how parents here want it to be."

I have no idea how many librarians have read Arthur E. Bostwick's "The Librarian as Censor" in the July 1908 *Library Journal*, but he considers and analyzes three categories of books, the Good, the True, and the Beautiful. In fairness to a worthwhile and much-neglected article, I will agree that he goes much further, and his entire argument is intriguing even today. But the unhappy subjectivity of his labels remains.

Modern efforts by some librarians to define literary merit operationally have been far worse than Bostwick's. Attacked by the press and some parents because she did not stock Nancy Drew books, one librarian stoutly defended her decision by saying: "I disagree most strenuously that there is no harm in reading the Bobbsey Twins and Nancy Drew, etc. There are only six to eight years in which a child can read, *as a child*, and there are so many wonderful books to be read he will never have time to read them all. To waste these few precious years reading the less than worthwhile is really a crime." Then, speaking of better books for the young, she added: "All these books, and the thousands like them, have this in common: they possess integrity and style, and some portion of the fundamental truth of life." There they are, "integrity and style and some portion of the fundamental truth of life," objective and helpful to any neophyte teachers or librarians, the sort of criteria we constantly search for and rarely hope to find, criteria which should help us baffle and buffalo parents and patrons, words just as fresh and exciting and specific as "relevant" and "viable" and "meaningful" and "interaction" and "great literature" and "classics." I am tempted to add to her "fundamental truth of life" that one of the most fundamental truths in all our lives is our need for diversity, for escape, for sheer entertainment, for the trivial but temporarily engaging—Harlequin Romances, James Bond thrillers, soft-core pornography, *The Total Woman*, Harold Robbins's novels, "I Love Lucy," *Jonathan Livingston Seagull*, disco music, "Happy Days," or Nancy Drew mysteries.

Linda Silver's 1979 attack on popular "trash" in libraries seems to me no more compelling. She noted that some parents objected to using mere popularity as a standard and wanted criteria like higher quality, greater discernment, and better taste (and who could dispute the wisdom of those objective criteria?) applied to library selection. Silver then added:

What will librarians have to offer to a public that even now seems to be turning away from the debased and debasing trivia that pervades so much of society? Schools still teach Shakespeare although McKuen is more popular. Art museums buy Rembrandt, not Holly Hobbie. The Cleveland Orchestra plays Mozart, not Mantovani. Popular literature certainly occupies an important part of public library collections and popular tastes should be served, but to pander to the lowest level of popular taste is a flagrant violation of the library's responsibility to the public and its trust.

But the analogies are invalid, and they provide little help for the harassed librarian. The Cleveland Orchestra has no problem deciding whether to play Mozart or Mantovani (though the Boston Pops may). It will almost certainly have problems if it plays nothing but Mozart, concert after concert, year after year. Should it play Dvorak or Schumann or Grieg or Gould or Shostakovich or Raff or Thomson or Saint-Saëns or Fauré or Gershwin? That is the real problem, and some of those composers are, judged by the standards of Mozart's mature music, distinctly second-rate or worse. Indeed, one can easily imagine a musical snob accusing the director of the Cleveland Orchestra of pandering to the lowest level of popular taste if Gershwin's *American in Paris* were announced for a concert. Good teachers and librarians presumably *meet public needs;* bad teachers and librarians obviously *pander to the lowest level of popular taste.* We can all have fun with silly semantic tricks like that, as we do when we sneeringly talk about the shoddy predictability of Nancy Drew stories and worshipfully discuss the grand inevitability of *Crime and Punishment.*

I do not dispute that literary merit exists or that it is unmeasurable in some inexact ways, but my distrust grows as librarians and teachers talk about the "best" or "great" books. Ignoring the judgments and insights of critics and reviewers—and no self-respecting teacher or librarian can afford to fall back on others' views in determining the nature or the quality of any book—teachers and librarians often have remarkably little ability to gauge literary performance and to arrive at honest and independent assessments.

More important, I have no right to inflict my literary standards on an unsuspecting and possibly unwilling public. Parents often cry for higher standards in classrooms and libraries, and I too deeply believe in trying to raise the tastes of my students, but I know that comes slowly and I must work surreptitiously. Standards will not go up any faster because I use only great books and forbid the reading of trash or second-rate material. A frontal assault waving the banner of "I Read Better Literature than You, and You'll Have the Chance to Read Only What I Like and Approve Of" is doomed to failure. Worse, it is nothing but highhanded, pseudointellectual censorship. And I fear it because it is so common and seems so respectable.

I met the second kind of censor, the moral censor, early in life. She was my mother, devoted, loving, concerned, and protective. She vowed that no harm would come to me, and by the time I reached puberty, I knew full well she feared

some books—not, I will add, the books in our Clarinda, Iowa, library, where there was nothing to disturb me and reality was only rarely allowed to enter even the adult collection. I thought my mother's concern for my moral welfare and my reading might wane as I grew older, but I discovered my error when I returned from the U.S. Navy at nineteen. Assuming I was a man and therefore master of my destiny, I foolishly let her see my collection of books acquired during my duty in the dangerous waters off Seattle, Washington. She spotted E.B. White and James Thurber's *Is Sex Necessary?*, made some salient observation about the foolishness of the title (never explained and I never asked her to explain), and tossed it into our potbellied stove.

I met another moral censor much later, again when I began teaching. He was a minister who announced that *The Catcher in the Rye, Brave New World, The Grapes of Wrath,* and *1984* were "pure garbage," indeed, that most modern literature was garbage and filth and "pure evil." He further pontificated that the Lord had anointed him to protect the young from people like me, that is, purveyors of filth, modern teachers full of rot, modern librarians without standards, that is, without *his* standards. Here was a moral censor going into the battle against immorality and permissiveness waving the banner announcing "Spiritual and Emotional Purity Are All—Literature Can Harm You unless I Select It."

Librarians and teachers of this censorial persuasion are, from my admittedly limited experience, less numerous than literary censors, perhaps because moral censorship today seems less fashionable for teachers and librarians. But more practice moral censorship, while preaching liberal views, than we may suspect. I have no idea how many people preach freedom and education while stocking only those books that please the community, placate the censor, ignore modern problems, eschew moral issues, and therefore avoid controversies. Phrases like "space limitations" or "limited time to assess new books" or "high standards" or "budgetary restrictions" *may* be used to mask the real reasons why certain writers with certain views are available in limited numbers in some libraries.

Moral censorship, as we have seen, was more common and direct in the late nineteenth century. In an 1883 report from librarians on reading of the young, William Kite worried about the love of fiction "which is so demoralizing to the youthful mind," while an unnamed representative from the Newton Free Library warned against books of "an exciting and injurious character." The author approvingly quoted from the official report of the trustees of the Fletcher Free Library: "A wise old book says: 'The world is saved by the breath of school-children. It is important, then, the public library should do its part to make the breath of life sane, and strong, and pure.'" And James M. Hubbard, in an almost interminable battle with the Boston Public Library, warned that libraries should avoid circulating any books "injurious" to the young and should give up entirely any circulation of novels for children.

But moral censorship is not all that difficult to find among modern English teachers and librarians. When I edited the *Arizona English Bulletin,* I conducted two surveys of Arizona teachers and librarians to uncover censorship problems and to try to unmask some reasons for censorship. Several responses to my questionnaire disturbed me. One teacher wrote, "We haven't got a damned thing worth censoring," and a teacher-librarian answered: "No censorship problems. No, nobody here would support us. When they hire English teachers in my town, they make sure that teachers are either cowards or pliable. Those that are cowards present no threat to anything (especially literature or kids). Those that are pliable are brainwashed. Nobody here ever taught anything remotely worth censoring. And if you think that's bad, you ought to see our library. The library has even less to offer than the English classes." One librarian espoused a public-servant, public-morality attitude: "The English teacher and librarian are hired by the school board which represents the public. The public, therefore, has the right to ask any of us to avoid using any material repugnant to any parent or student. Therefore, I would not want to recommend or teach or handle any book anyone might object to for any reason." Another wrote: "Our librarian advises that we do not have a problem because she anticipates that if such books as *The Catcher in the Rye* were in our library, we might have a problem, and she does not put them on the shelves. 'It is available in paperback; if they want to read it, let them buy it.'"

Inevitably, we all look at books in terms of our own personal moral standards, all well and good as long as we do not foist them off on other people. A friend I taught with actively disagreed with much that I read. I rather enjoyed her attention, since I never doubted she wished anything for me save my personal good. Our arguments began, however, when she inflicted her own morality on her students, and words became much more heated when she questioned my judgment in allowing classes to read widely and freely in modern literature. More times than I care to remember, I found her camping at my door early before class and late in the day after school had ended. "Ken," she asked, "why do you let your students read Steinbeck, Hemingway, and all those modern writers of pornography? Why let them read filth when they could read *Our Town* or *Silas Marner* or some good, standard poetry?" She was a highly moral censor.

But so is any teacher or librarian who inflicts personal values on students who can neither fight back nor protect themselves. It's censorship, and it's not pure and it's not simple. Mary F. Poole's objections to Johanna Reiss's *The Upstairs Room* because of the "50 irreverent expletives and the one 4-letter word in the book" as "mere excess baggage . . . used for their shock appeal" portray a moral censor at work. Poole adds, in a defense which soon becomes a rationale for social-class censorship:

In exercising judgment—which can be called censorship—in selecting books, I am in no way infringing upon the freedom of the press or a person's right to read. The press continues to publish what it wishes, what it thinks will sell, and people continue to read what they wish. But I am under no obligation to furnish children with questionable materials . . . students have the right to be protected from things that are likely to affect them adversely. Parents have the right to expect schools to protect their children during their unquestionably impressionable years from such influences, and all school personnel have the right, even the responsibility, not to provide such influences.

That same sort of moralistic, paternalistic stance was announced by a high school librarian worried about controversial books that appealed to young adults. "In my library censorship lives, and I'm not ashamed or afraid to say it either. I have books like *The Boy Who Could Make Himself Disappear* on my shelves, but these are few and far between. To all you so-called liberal librarians out there in city or country schools now condemning this letter, I say to you: 'The kids of today are great! Do you want to help give them a boost or a bust?' " Fear of filth permeates the moral censor, and filth can mean virtually anything. Librarians and English teachers convulsed with the fear of the abnormal (or the normal) in sex sometimes worry about *Catch-22, The Adventures of Huckleberry Finn, The Scarlet Letter, The Catcher in the Rye, 1984, Brave New World, The Chocolate War, Wuthering Heights, Moby Dick, Member of the Wedding, Ruby,* and more, much much more. Some female librarians and English teachers have been willing to see normality in youthful female sexuality but unwilling to see anything but disgusting abnormality in youthful male sexuality. Judy Blume found that when she was "accosted by a local mother who was so upset by two pages in *Then Again Maybe I Won't* about wet dreams that she ripped them out of her son's copy." "What if they had been about a girl's menstruation?" Mrs. Blume asked her, "Would you still have torn the pages out?" "Oh no," the mother replied, "that's normal."

One group of moral censors is of particular concern to us, those who would censor out of social conscience, those who would censor for "good" reasons, as a friend once tried to explain to me. Most of us worry about social changes and social inequality. But some otherwise excellent teachers and librarians normally opposed to censorship in any guise would attempt to alleviate social problems through eliminating modern books or materials they see as racist or sexist. Several months ago, the National Council of Teachers of English Committee against Censorship became briefly embroiled with the Council on Interracial Books for Children (CIBC) over the following statement written by the chair of the NCTE committee: *"Racist statements.* The Council on Interracial Books for Children has objected to books that contain racist slurs. The Council has actively campaigned for fairer treatment of all races in textbooks, but it has also listed books, including novels, that should be removed from school shelves." The CIBC argued the statement was unfair and inaccurate, the NCTE representative responded with what he considered evidence, the CIBC counter-responded, and the argument—battle would be too strong a word to describe what happened—went on for a few letters and a few months, and then lapsed. Neither CIBC nor NCTE could add much to their cases, and disagreement reigned. That was sad. The *Interracial Books for Children Bulletin* certainly deserves readers and subscribers, but the CIBC is apparently unable to see any distinction between their book reviews and book reviews in *School Library Journal* or the *Bulletin of the Center for Children's Books* or the *ALAN Review* or *Booklist,* not a difference in quality but in kind. Book reviews in the *Interracial Books for Children Bulletin* are often intriguing and provocative, sometimes frustrating, and often—and I hope inadvertently—a call for censorship based on social awareness. Let me explain it this way. If I review a young-adult book in a national publication, you can read my review and disagree widely and wildly with my opinion of the literary merit of the book. Whether you agree or disagree with me, you are likely to feel free to buy or reject the book. Differences in tastes are commonplace; in any case, teachers and librarians rarely attack one another for using or recommending or circulating books they don't especially like on literary grounds, mostly because literary merit is a fuzzy term.

Using terms like "racist" or "sexist" to label books carries far greater weight today than literary merit, though "racist" and "sexist" might be no more objectively determined than literary merit. If you purchase a book castigated for its racism or sexism by the *Interracial Books for Children Bulletin,* you'd better be prepared to defend it even though you did read the *Bulletin* review and simply disagreed with the reviewer. In most cases, it is easier *not* to buy or even consider buying any book attacked by the *Bulletin.* Many teachers and librarians know that not buying the book in question will create few waves, but buying and circulating or using a book attacked by the *Bulletin* may lead to serious problems. The *Bulletin,* whether it wishes to or not, creates a climate of censorship. The CIBC may have no intention of acting as a censor, and it certainly eschews censorship publicly. But the council carries great weight with many teachers and librarians and school officials, and it is hardly a secret (except sometimes to the CIBC) that the CIBC is viewed by some as a censor. Sometimes, in my more cynical moments, I wonder if readers of the *Bulletin* are believers or merely followers adopting a party line, concerned about selecting the wrong book (or the right book for the wrong reasons). But then I learned long ago to distrust both disciples and converts; they distort the original messages so badly.

I too like to believe in my own moral standards, but I have no right to impose them on any student. I worry about readers generally, but I do not believe that I have the right, much less the responsibility, to serve as their moral leader or arbiter. Parents seek the good of their young, but then so do English teachers and librarians. We are convinced, as some parents are not, that young adults need protection from reality less and less as they mature. Protected and thus protracted innocence all too easily becomes its own rationale for ignorance; extended, it becomes its own theoretical justification for continued ignorance. Ignorance is not only powerless to fight evil or defend good; ignorance gradually but certainly becomes evil's inadvertent ally against good. That is why those who wave the banner of "Read Only Pure Literature, Stay Away from Evils Like Reality, and Only I Can Tell You What Is Pure and What Is Evil" are usually high-minded but terribly dangerous. I sometimes wonder if the moral censor isn't absolute evidence that God has a finely tuned, somewhat sardonic, sense of humor.

Censorship is so common today that we may sometimes ask, What can a book do? We believe that readers may find enjoyment and excitement and fun and satisfaction and challenge. We believe that some readers may find reflections of themselves and their problems in books and may through reading understand themselves a bit better. We believe books can and often do have consequences. We believe books can lead readers to wonder and question and think, and we believe that without proof except for personal testimony, notoriously unreliable evidence to others who do not already share our vision of reading and readers. I believe it, and my life as an English teacher is testimony to that belief, but I know how unconvincing my arguments are to an unbeliever or an unreader.

What can books do? Censors, too, believe books can and do have consequences. Censors believe books can lead to antisocial acts like premarital sex (why premarital sex is called antisocial when it's about as social as we can get at that age remains a mystery to me) or dangerous acts like doubting the wisdom of those in authority or even dangerous practices like questioning the status quo. And censors believe all that without one iota of evidence save that of personal testimony. Censors frequently offer another kind of proof, a cause-and-effect relationship between pornographic or suspect or violent literature found at the scene of a crime (or in the house of the criminal) and the crime itself. But they often destroy their own case, though rarely in the censors' minds, by assuming a simplistic causal relationship—we do not know whether a sex criminal commits a crime because he has read certain material or because he's already disposed to become a sex criminal. God help the librarian or English teacher who supplies or recommends or teaches a book to a person about to commit a crime. If the criminal is caught, it's possible he will be only too happy to give the book full credit for his impure thoughts and actions. More likely, a reporter, a few days after the crime, may gain entrance to the culprit's room, seeking something, anything, to titillate readers. He may find *the* nefarious book. Nothing satisfies a public already secretly convinced that "bad" books create "bad" people more than to find the *cause* of the crime was a book. Heaven help the poor reporter who finds only one book in the room of a child molester–rapist, a Bible (that happened in a small Iowa town, and no one could see any possible connection between the crime and the book). Alfred North Whitehead wrote words that English teachers and librarians accept but that simplistic people ignore, "Seek simplicity and distrust it."

So books harm us? Can they lead to antisocial acts? Can they corrupt the young? Or the old? Or the fat or the skinny? Nineteenth-century moral critics were convinced books could easily corrupt an already easily corruptible girl or boy; "pernicious" was a favorite word of the worriers. Perhaps books can corrupt, perhaps not. We simply don't know. Some books may, as it has been claimed, densensitize readers. Books like Harlequin Romances or pornography or Nancy Drew mysteries or Barbara Cartland tales of virginal love or Rod McKuen's poetry may distort readers' understanding of reality so acutely that habitual readers of these books may be unable to tell what is real from what is unreal. But then habitual viewers of old Doris Day or Loretta Young films almost certainly face the same problem. I have long been certain that anyone who voluntarily watches reruns of "Hogan's Heroes" or "Medical Center" or anything featuring Mike Douglas or Merv Griffin must inevitably become desensitized and suffer from total and permanent inability to recognize reality.

I believe some books and films and television shows are so dreadful they may deaden us to the nuances of life and love and our many pursuits of happiness. But that is a belief, not a fact. I have no right to impose my views or forbid anyone from reading or viewing whatever he or she wants on a belief founded on my small-town, Iowa-Methodist heritage. I have the freedom to operate from any set of beliefs as long as my beliefs do not infringe on my neighbors. That, I deeply believe, extends to the school or library.

As an English teacher, I have no right to impose my ideas or convictions on students. They will learn, or soon guess, what I believe without my saying a word about values. I have the same responsibility as an English teacher that you have as librarians, to help readers find all sorts of materials to allow them to search for their own truth or truths, wherever that search takes them. That responsibility does not merely imply free access to ideas of all sorts. That responsibility demands that we work continually to secure free access and to stave off those who would deny freedom in education. Lao-Tze underscored our joint responsibility in *Tao Teh King* when he wrote, "To know the unknowable, that is elevating. Not to know the knowable, that is sickness."

Libraries and schools should be special places in any community, in some communities the only places where ideas of all sorts and their consequences can be considered and analyzed. Schools and libraries alike exist to educate, not to indoctrinate. To educate is to open minds to many points of view and many thoughts. To indoctrinate is to close minds to all but one thought and one point of view.

Understanding library and pedagogical history will not guarantee we will emerge unscathed from the troubles of our times, but ignoring the past and its legacy of censorship permits us only limited perception of where we were, where we are, and where we may be going. We cannot condone deception, born out of ignorance, in our students, and we cannot condone in ourselves our own ignorance of the past. The nineteenth century provides us with numerous examples of literary and moral censorship, and the arguments advanced then we hear even today.

If history teaches us anything, it is how slowly but certainly we have marched from indoctrination to education and how increasingly we have come to believe that libraries and classrooms should promote no special interests, no causes save the freedom to read and think and wonder and question. Libraries and schools exist so humanity can learn what it wishes. When libraries and schools cease to allow controversy and diversity, then they cease to have educational value and become mere tools in the hands of special interests. When libraries and schools cease to present multifaceted visions of many people of all natures searching for many aspects of truths, then they become mere collections of books and people, nothing more.

BOOK CENSORSHIP ATTEMPTS HAVE TRIPLED[2]

Attempts to censor books in the nation's libraries have more than tripled since last November's election, according to Judith Krug, director of the Office of Intellectual Freedom of the American Library Association.

"We have been averaging over the past several years three to five reports of attempted censorship a week," Krug said in a *PW* interview. "The first two weeks of November, there were about that number per day." And, she said, the increase has continued at a similar level in subsequent weeks.

Krug said the new focus of the would-be censors has been on public libraries, in contrast to the past, when more than 89% of the complaints were aimed at school libraries. Now, close to 65% involve public libraries.

"I think we learn about only one-tenth of the censorship attempts in the country," Krug added. If they are settled on the local level—by the complainants backing down, by the librarian capitulating or, more often, by both sides reaching a compromise—she usually won't hear about them unless they appear in a newspaper.

She cautioned that her figures were not hard statistics and that some of the increase may be the result of a growing ten-

[2] Article entitled "The First Amendment: ALA's Krug: Book Censorship Attempts Have Tripled Since Election Day" by Howard Fields, Washington correspondent. *Publishers Weekly*. 218:32. F. 20, '81. Copyright © 1981 by Xerox Corporation. Reprinted by permission.

dency to report the incidents because her office has received attention in the past few months. On the other hand, she said, all the cases her office receives are not reported because some of the librarians who contact her are afraid of losing their jobs.

Krug said she began getting calls in September and October from librarians asking for advice and educational materials so they could head off the attempts they could sense were coming. At noon on November 4, election day, she received a telephone call from one of them, Kathy Russell, librarian in the Abingdon, Va., public library, saying, "It happened." A local minister, citing the election of Ronald Reagan and other conservatives, had started his campaign against what he considered dirty books, confident he now represented the majority. The minister demanded a list of those persons checking out books on his "hit list"—which included *Goodbye, Columbus*—but Krug was able to advise Russell that Thomas Jefferson's home state was one of five where such records are confidential.

Krug said she had been struck by the increasing numbers of complainants who will say they are members of the Moral Majority or, if not card-carrying members, will say they sympathize with its aims. Well-meaning and concerned, they often introduce the subject with, "I'm not a censor, but . . ." Many of them, she feels, have not been successful in instilling their values in their children, and their grievances against books are no more than attempts to "put a Band-aid over reality."

She also believes the worst is yet to come. Traditionally, she said, March and April are the heaviest months for censorship attempts, and if the current pattern continues, libraries around the nation are about to be flooded by complaints.

Many of the new censorship fights are the same ones that were fought successfully in the 1960s and early '70s, involving such books as *To Kill A Mockingbird*, *Catcher in the Rye*, and *Brave New World*. Also under attack are books as various as *Go Ask Alice* (which Krug believes is a valuable book for turning children off drugs), Judy Blume's books, *One Flew Over the Cuckoo's Nest, The Lonely Lady, Bloodline*—and even *Sylvester and the Magic Pebble* and *Mary Poppins.*

Although the new emphasis is on public libraries, Krug said, she finds those cases easier to deal with than school library complaints because it's harder to censor books for adults and harder to tamper with libraries that serve the public.

The new wave of censorship attempts has not been without its benefits. Years ago, she said, when she'd call a publisher for help, seeking newspaper and magazine reviews of the books being questioned or anything else in the publisher's files that would be helpful in defending the book, she would receive little aid. "But that's not true anymore," she declared.

Publishers, however, could do more. Krug suggested that individual houses should be more involved in the Freedom to Read Foundation, the separate organization that serves as the legal defense arm of the ALA's intellectual freedom program. Calling the foundation "the only insurance policy for librarians involved in First Amendment cases," Krug concluded: "It's absolutely imperative to defend our librarians. I really think the right to read is right up there with apple pie and motherhood."

IS IT BOOK-BURNING TIME AGAIN?[3]

Apparently, it happens in cycles. I mean the attempts at censorship and repression that challenge our constitutional foundations and test the mettle of our system for tolerating the expression of diverse and pluralistic values.

The latest rash of such cases has enveloped communities in Indiana, Vermont and New York, where the banning of

[3] Article by James Alvino, correspondent. New York *Times.* XI, 18:3. D. 28, '80.
© 1980 by the New York Times Company. Reprinted by permission.

controversial books by local Boards of Education is clashing head-on with the First Amendment.

In Vergennes, Vt., and in Warsaw, Ind., the courts upheld the school districts' decisions to remove certain objectionable books from their library shelves and courses. In Warsaw, the court ruling resulted in a parking-lot bonfire reminiscent of scenes from Ray Bradbury's *Farenheit 451.*

The issue is still pending in Island Trees, L.I. There, following protests from a group of parents, a District Court judge upheld the board's right to purge nine books from its academic curriculum. However, an Appellate Court reversed the lower court's decision, reportedly because it was unclear whether specific books or certain ideas were being condemned. The latter might constitute a First Amendment violation.

In the fall of 1977, I "broke" a similar story while serving as a correspondent for a South Jersey newspaper. Also destined to gain national notoriety, the controversy involved parental objection to the use of J. D. Salinger's *Catcher in the Rye* in an advanced high-school course on the American novel.

The school district was Pittsgrove Township, a politically conservative, 5,000-resident farming community in Salem County. The lines of support and opposition were clearly drawn, and on the surface the outcome appeared all but certain.

Supporters of its use heralded the 1951 novel as a "milestone in American literature," comparing it to "Huckleberry Finn." Holden Caulfield, the book's adolescent hero who found coping with growing up especially difficult, was likened to Tom Sawyer. And Salinger himself was listed among the ranks of John Steinbeck and F. Scott Fitzgerald.

Unlike Tom Sawyer, however, Holden Caulfield uses considerable profanity, and it was this that precipitated the move to have the novel banned. Those spearheading this drive described the book's language as "filthy and profane," as promoting premarital sex, homosexuality and perversion, as being "explicitly pornographic" and, finally, "immoral."

But behind the debate on academic freedom, the discussion of the novel's literary merit and the passionate moral confrontation between those who condemned the book and those who defended it stood two basic issues: How the school board and administration viewed the district's students, and how they viewed the teaching staff.

I interviewed Rebecca R., the 16-year-old 11th-grader whose parents had requested that *Catcher* be removed from the course, and remember thinking how mature and sophisticated this young woman was. She hadn't objected to reading the book, although she also found the language distasteful, and said that she didn't identify with Holden at all. Rebecca's teachers described her as "mature and responsible."

For the chairman of the high-school English Department, as well as the teacher of the course, it became a matter of professional credibility. They had recommended *Catcher*, and the Board of Education had previously approved it.

A school board also hires its teaching staff, and supposedly entrusts to it some confidence and autonomy in determining curriculum. So there was much more at stake in the long term than the fate of a single book and the groundswell of controversy and mixed opinions surrounding its suitability in high school.

And these same pedagogical and political issues are apropos in today's cases. It doesn't really matter what the specific texts are, either, or who the authors are. As the president of Pittsgrove's school board put it following its decision:

"I don't know *The Catcher in the Rye* from the man in the moon."

The questions are:

—Are high school students to be treated as young adults or merely as impressionable, nondiscriminating minds?

—Are they to be offered broad and varied interpretations on life, or are they to be protected and sheltered from those views and styles of expression that some of a certain moral persuasion find objectionable?

—Are we not teaching our children, as a basic skill, to

think critically about their experience, or is the educational process, at heart, really just one of indoctrination?

—Are teachers to function and make curriculum decisions freely on the basis of their expertise and judgment, or act primarily as instruments and puppets of most often well-intentioned, but nonprofessional, laymen and community members?

Ultimately, *The Catcher in the Rye* was ruled safe to read in Pittsgrove Township. The Board of Education let stand its original approval of the novel. The district's superintendent, summarizing the board's decision, stated that the book was used for its universal message, not to teach profanity.

He rejected the contention that the novel scars high-school students and adversely influences their actions. But he also acknowledged that parents had the right to request that their children not read it.

In a prudent and well thought-out judgment, and with a tinge of irony, community members and laymen on the board bestowed a dignity on the district's high-school students by acknowledging their ability and responsibility for making their own appraisals of what they read. The teaching staff was vindicated and given a vote of confidence.

Even parents came out winners; they could decide whether their children would or would not be permitted to read *Catcher* in school.

But that case was several years ago. Since then, and with the recent Reagan landslide, the "conservative tide" threatens to create an atmosphere in which censorship cases become commonplace. It has already begun to happen.

Contrary to this growing ethos, however, it should be noted that the opposite of the "moral majority" is not the "immoral minority." This is one aberration that the First Amendment presumably safeguards against.

School districts and board members throughout the country might do well to examine the dimensions and results of what took place in rural Pittsgrove Township, where both the procedure and outcome were exemplary. Repression, in contrast, is always self-defeating in the end.

It's a principle of basic psychology that making something a taboo intensifies its appeal. So it is with certain kinds of literature. This alone should be enough to cause even the most self-righteous among us to think twice.

FREEDOM, CENSORSHIP, SCHOOLS, AND LIBRARIES[4]

The common denominator of all formal governments, whether Jefferson's or Hitler's, is the conviction that the whole is greater than the sum of the parts, and governments, therefore, are justified in pursuing national interests at the expense of individual citizens. Generally, such governments differ only in whose perception of the national interest is used. A government that primarily promotes the individual interests of its citizens is unusual.

There is always a second governing force made up of public opinion, community standards, and individual prejudices. When a nation has a coherent set of informal standards accepted by the citizenry at large and when its formal government reflects this general concurrence, a unity of social purpose exists in which questions of censorship are almost irrelevant. It is in pluralistic societies with strong cultural and intellectual diversities where the suitability of certain educational materials and library offerings is challenged. It is not uncommon for a particular group to ask the formal government to protect its interests or promote its concerns which conflict with the interests and concerns of others. If the demanding group is small and isolated, it can be safely ignored. If it is large and militant, compromises will usually be sought. This reduces censorship, i.e., determining what is suitable and what is offensive, to a political struggle in which might will probably make right.

[4] Article by Stephen Robinson, professional engineer and parent-citizen adviser. *English Journal.* 70:58–9. Ja. '81. Reprinted by permission.

Conflict does not need to lead to social actions like censorship if the fundamental basis of a democracy, whether direct or representative, is clearly stated and accepted. Always easier to state than accept, that fundamental basis is individualism: the individual's right to think and the individual's obligation to let others do the same. Individuals may be convinced they understand hidden truths of the universe and can translate them into a philosophy and morality for everyday living. They may expect others to accept those same beliefs and be surprised if they don't.

Since humanity is incapable of direct telepathy, the only way we can share our inner thoughts is through oral and written language. Experience suggests this never yields complete understanding or agreement. Therefore, the first conclusion to be drawn is that while individuals may be convinced that what they believe is absolute and eternal truth, truth for a democracy is relative and is only the current majority opinion of those present and voting. A second conclusion can be drawn immediately. In a democracy, the more people participating in the public debate and voting process, the better.

If the citizens of a democracy accept the validity of individualism and individual opinions, then certain rules and constraints logically follow.

No opinion, attitude, or point of view can be forced on any individual. Because citizens share many common experiences and influences, there will probably be an underlying similarity in points of view. This can be expected but not demanded. There is no danger in differing points of view, only in limitations on the right to be different.

Danger exists when individualism becomes ruthless self-centeredness. The second rule, then, is that individuals must be prepared to respect and accept the individualism of others. We must have courage to face not only the open-endedness of our own continuing intellectual and philosophical development but also the uncertainty that follows from divergent thinking in the development of others. Doubt must lead to further study, not to the suppression of disagreement.

Government institutions must be organized to promote and support the right of individuals to their opinions and to protect individuals and groups from the oppression of others. Conversely, these same institutions must not support or promote the beliefs of any individual or group, nor protect individuals from ever having to examine their own beliefs.

Translating social principles into operational directives for social institutions is always easier to describe than do, and if done at all never perfectly. The obligation is always to try.

Public schools must resist all notions of the *empty bottle* or *blank page student* who is to be filled with appropriate facts from a reservoir of knowledge. Similarly, schools must resist all attempts to model themselves after factories where students are the equivalents of tractor fenders, rejects and failures ending up on the same scrap heap.

A school system selects, organizes, and controls that which it presents to its students. It does so to meet goals and objectives. A great deal of what is presented is certain and not widely open to question, e.g., spelling and the multiplication tables. On the other hand, much is tentative and students should be prepared to deal with it.

If public schools are for formally directed education, then libraries are for self direction. A library, by definition, is a wide ranging collection of materials to provide opportunities for the pursuit of diverse individual interests. Items should be included in a library not because anybody is promoting them but because they are a valid expression of human experience.

A library's duty is to provide the widest possible range of materials to help people understand and come to terms with themselves and their situations. A library's right is to provide any material which it reasonably believes will help it discharge that duty. Any attempt to limit offerings on political, philosophical, or religious grounds must be resisted without compromise. Any attempt to limit on the grounds of morality or public taste probably can be dealt with on an individual basis. However, we need to remind ourselves that people do not have to check out and read what they do not like.

Censorship is based on the notion that if people can be

kept ignorant, they can be kept pure. The amount of censorship present is usually a tense compromise between the rights of academic and intellectual freedom on one hand and the demands of an outraged and offended group on the other. Nevertheless, guaranteeing the right to know, to learn, and to choose is the first duty of a democratic government and all of its agencies.

It has been said that democracy is the only form of government that must be won anew by each generation. The best guarantee that this challenge can be met is the school, the library, and the generation of intellectually free people both institutions create.

STANDARDS AND FREE ACCESS[5]

If the International Year of the Child has any messages for librarians, it should be to remind us just how far removed we are from the survival edge of childhood. While all of us are aware of the plight of most of the world's children, including some in our own country, there is little we can do through our jobs to change the physical and spiritual misery in which appallingly large numbers of them struggle to grow up.

Books do not ease hunger. Information has no immediate effect on the daily ravages of neglect and ill health. Story hours and other programs provide momentary relief at best from abuse and deprivation. To the children among the world's refugees, whose numbers now are the largest since the second World War, or to the victims of political atrocities, library service must figure very low on a list of needs. Amid all the IYC celebrations creeps the chilling realization that to many of the world's young, life is no less than what Isaac

[5] From article entitled "Standards and Free Access: Equal but Separate," by Linda R. Silver, assistant coordinator of children's services, Cuyahoqa County Public Library, Cleveland. *School Library Journal.* 26:26–8. F. '80. Copyright © by Xerox Corporation. Reprinted by permission.

Bashevis Singer has called it: "a slaughterhouse . . . a nightmare."

This is the somber perspective from which public library service to children, especially during the International Year of the Child, should be viewed. When all the fun and games, the folk dances and nationality crafts programs, the foreign language lessons and foreign book displays are over, time remains to ask: "What are we doing? What are we here for? Does any of it matter?"

Children's Services and Civilization

The "culture of narcissism," as Christopher Lasch terms contemporary society, has trivialized institutional goals and public expectations. But library service to children earned its reputation as the "glory" of the American public library system precisely because its goals were high, its purposes clear and its responses vigorous and effective. Now, as then, libraries are symbols of a civilized society, for civilization begins only after survival needs are met. If children's librarians are removed from the survival edge of childhood, it is because libraries themselves are addressed to needs that proceed from an absence of chaos and a reasonable guarantee of survival. Established by a civilized society, libraries support civilization by preserving and providing some of the resources that humankind needs to hold back the dark.

The "luxury" of books, information, and library services—which indeed are luxuries to children whose very survival is precarious—are some of the essentials needed for civilized existence. Once assured, the *quality* of that existence then becomes important. IIow well do libraries provide the essentials? Are they available to all children or only to select groups? Are they provided with intelligence, tact, and respect? And perhaps most important, what do we hope will be the result of the books and information on the children who partake of them? The late Spanish cellist, Pablo Casals, phrased the question this way:

Each second we live is a new and unique moment of the universe, a moment that never was before and never will be again. And what do we teach our children . . . ? We teach them that two and two make four, and that Paris is the capital of France. When will we also teach them what they are? We should say to each of them: Do you know what you are? You are a marvel. You are unique. In all of the world there is no other child exactly like you. In the millions of years that have passed there has never been another child like you. And look at your body—what a wonder it is! Your legs, your arms, your cunning fingers, the way you move! You may become a Shakespeare, a Michelangelo, a Beethoven. You have the capacity for anything. Yes, you are a marvel. And when you grow up, can you then harm another who is, like you, a marvel? You must work—we must all work—to make this world worthy of its children.

Differently as it may be expressed, one might venture to guess that this ideal is shared by the vast majority of children's librarians. But *how* ideals are translated into action is a thornier matter than it once was and among children's librarians, as among all librarians, philosophies and responses differ.

The Issue of Reevaluation

Glancing back over the library literature of the past ten years, one notices shifts in emphasis and points of view. In the late '60s and early '70s there was much debate about the issue of reevaluation—the removal from library collections of materials that had come to be regarded as socially or morally retrograde. What was seen as the social responsibility of librarians to remove racist and sexist books from their collections was called censorship by others who believed that intellectual freedom perforce allowed all attitudes, no matter how offensive they might be. Answering the assertion that all ideas are equal in the sight of the First Amendment, Dorothy Broderick wrote: "The whole concept of social responsibilities implies value judgments—some things are right and some are wrong . . . In modern jargon, that is known as an elitist point of view, and elitist is a very dirty word, indeed."

From reevaluation—or what to take out of libraries—to

the selection process—or what to put into libraries—requires just a slight shift of focus and both sides of the reevaluation debate found a common target in selection standards. To many intellectual freedom purists, librarians have no right to judge because those judgments sometimes result in the exclusion of books from libraries and thereby violate their authors' rights to be heard. To many social responsibilities advocates, librarians have no right to judge because those judgments sometimes result in the exclusion of popular books, and thereby cast elitist aspersions on people's taste. Despite their differences, both points of view resulted in an attack on selection standards that were already being looked at uneasily by administrators interested in winning taxpayers' approval by hardly ever failing to meet their demands.

Book evaluation and selection has long been considered a major part of the children's librarian's job. Therefore, the multipronged attack on standards, almost all of it spoken in the name of high principles, hit children's services hard. Because the attack coincided with a growing concern for children's rights, the selection process had added to the charges leveled against it another that placed selection standards in opposition to the right of children to free access to library materials.

Books on Demand vs. Judging Books

To many children's librarians who have always believed in standards and in free access and who have tried to uphold both principles, it is difficult to see the two in opposition. But to those who do find them inimical, the argument is as follows: Standards are elitist because they make value judgments about children's reading interests and tastes. To tell a child that the library doesn't own a desired book does damage to the child's self-image and to the library's "credibility as a nonjudgment agency." Children have a right to pursue whatever interests them and adults do not have the right to inflict their own values on children. Even though children are not yet taxpayers, they are citizens and entitled to expect a tax supported institution to supply what they demand. Because, as children, they lack the economic power to buy what the library doesn't have, the children's librarian has more of a duty than ever to provide it for them. Selection standards put the importance of literary quality above the interests of children, and collections based on literary quality tend to be safe, but meaningless. Furthermore, poor quality books have no ill-effects on the child's growth into a mature human being, and it doesn't matter what children read so long as they read something.

Librarians who believe in standards counter by saying that this argument is off the mark. Making value judgments about people is elitist perhaps, but making value judgments about books is a professional responsibility and a fulfillment of the public trust. No one has the right to expect instant gratification for all wants, and part of the children's librarian's challenge is to find books that are interesting substitutes for those not in the collection. Rather than violating children's rights, a librarian who chooses books with regard for their honesty and literary integrity is upholding the child's right to concerned and intelligent adult guidance. Instead of representing a safe or "protectionist" philosophy, selection by literary standards provides books that will help children test values and question the status quo. Furthermore, a steady diet of bad books does have ill-effects on the child's growth into a mature human being and it *does* matter what children read.

Two Points of View on the Child

Although these two points of view may seem like polar opposites, they have their similarities. Both have the child in mind, although their concept of "the child" varies. Both profess a concern for the values of library service, although they interpret these values differently. And both consist almost entirely of articles of faith, assumptions about children and books that have yet to be proved or disproved by solid research. The tone of moral self-righteousness that often marks the first and the tone of fuddy-duddiness that sometimes

marks the second tend to add emotional clutter to a debate
that calls for open-mindedness and hard thinking. Phrases like
"credibility as a nonjudgmental agency" and "meaningful de-
velopmental growth" are but two examples of the jargon that
replaces reason with verbosity and dialogue with table
pounding. "Hier stehe Ich" may have been an appropriate
response to the Diet of Worms but it doesn't make for good
library service to children and young people, who are frequently forgotten amidst all the sloganeering.

The Question of Intellectual Freedom

A question to be asked about the standards versus free access controversy is if it has anything to do with intellectual
freedom at all. There has been little or no outcry among adult
services librarians to admit the likes of *Hustler* or hardcore
porn into their collections, despite the fact that a readership
for such does exist. Here, obviously, principles of intellectual
freedom are moderated by a concern for the public good. Yet
recognition of this has not extended to children's librarians,
whose attempts to serve the "public good" of their charges
have been labeled as a protectionist imposition of moral standards and as censorship. Neither is the concern for the
reader's self-image too apparent when it comes to the outer
limits of adult literature. When sadomasochistic romances or
child seduction novels, both of which are published in abun-
dance, are rejected because they fall below the level of public
library acceptability, do adult services people suffer the same
pangs about damaging their patrons' sense of self when they
lament the effects of excluded books on children? If they do,
they are unusually quiet about expressing them. It is interesting to observe how selectively principles can be applied.

Are Children Served or Betrayed?

Perhaps the difficulty some have with the standards versus
free access issue is because it is not a valid issue. Literary
standards focus on the book: free access concerns which per-

sons may use the book once it is in the library. The latter is an intellectual freedom issue but the former is not. Creating a *cause célèbre* where none exists may be the last refuge of the bored, but it has wasted countless hours that might have been better spent pondering each of these fundamentally important topics in its properly separate place.

The charge of elitism, made against selection by literary standards (i.e., value judgments), also bears scrutiny. What could be more elitist than the assumption that the "silliest, sleaziest or most salacious," in Lillian Gerhardt's words, is the most attractive to the young? The dewy-eyed image of young people as some sort of noble savages, fully capable of applying reason and discernment to every idea and experience, is put into perspective by Christopher Lasch when he says:

> When elders make no demands on the young, they make it almost impossible for the young to grow up. "The betrayal of youth . . . starts from the assumption that (they) are only interested in wallowing in their own subjectivity . . ." In the name of egalitarianism (reformers) preserve the most insidious form of elitism, which in one guise or another holds the masses incapable of intellectual exertion.

Lasch's chapter, "Schooling and the New Illiteracy," in *The Culture of Narcissism* should be must reading for every librarian working with young people, because it reveals some of the myths by which many well-meaning adults have betrayed those whose rights they advocate and purport to defend.

The Responsibility To Set Standards

Although the current standards versus free access debate has emerged from the reevaluation controversy of a few years ago, it may also be traced to more historical roots. "What right have we to judge?," which could serve as a motto for the opponents of selection standards, is generally regarded (at least by those who adhere to it) as a symbol of enlightened library service. Because standards are mistakenly associated on the one hand with a conservative impulse to keep the lower orders in their place and on the other hand with the perpetuation of an obsolete literary culture, the opponents of standards pride themselves on being in the vanguard of progressive or, when it was stylish, radical change. Yet Lester Asheim, in an article in *Library Trends,* suggests that the public's image of librarians as "inoffensive, nonassertive, compliant" is a result of librarians' *traditional* "self-effacing evasion of decision-making responsibility ('Who am I to say what a person ought to read: I'm only a librarian') and their unwillingness to face the consequences if their professional ideals were carried out in practice." The reluctance, indeed refusal, to judge represents a retreat into the timorous past far more than it reflects any great or courageous leap forward.

It remains very doubtful then whether selection standards have any invidious connection with children's rights. Insuring that children are provided with free access to all library materials is a battle that is far from being won, but attacking standards is a diversionary action. With all the genuine injustices perpetrated against the young everywhere, the International Year of the Child provided a good time for librarians to begin to clear their sights, define what the *real* problems facing children's services are, and do all that is within their particular province to make the world worthy of its children.

II. THE CENSORS: GROUPS AND INDIVIDUALS

EDITOR'S INTRODUCTION

A *censor* (a Roman word) is one who objects to or deletes material deemed to be harmful. As we can see from the articles in this Section, book censors today are on the increase, and their dissonant points of view are resulting in an increased number of conflicts. We find that censors can be individual, or in organizations or movements, and from the right or the left of the political spectrum.

Anna Ochoa, a social studies teacher, examines both conservative and liberal censorship movements in her article in *Social Education.* She points out that censors come from different political camps, socioeconomic groups, religious groups, and from both sexes. Next, Professor Jenkinson also provides a very specific and detailed list of protesting organizations and their "targets"—topics, authors, and specific books—in his article from *Publishers Weekly.* While the first two authors briefly describe the successful censorship attempts of the Gablers, James Hefley devotes a whole chapter in his book, *Are Textbooks Harming Your Children?* to a description of the aims and methods of the Texas "husband and wife team working for America's tomorrow—children."

The next two articles deal with the publication of textbooks which influence a child's education from the very start. First, an article by the Council on Interracial Books for Children (CIBC), in *Publishers Weekly,* rejects the idea that censoring textbooks on racist and sexist grounds is censorship, insisting that it is equal protection. In the second article, Lillian Gerhardt, editor of *School Library Journal,* refutes their argument and laments the fact that CIBC censorship on this basis deprives many of us of our traditional favorites.

The final article in this Section by Dorothy Massie, reprinted from *Today's Education,* decries the rightist attitude in the population, which makes demands and exerts pressures

46

on both the teachers and the school curriculum. She claims, "Anyone with enough authority is a potential censor. The list of those who can censor school materials is long."

CENSORSHIP: DOES ANYBODY CARE?[1]

. . . Attempts to censor from one vantage point or another have been—and I think it is safe to predict—will always be with us. Censorship movements wax and wane, but their candle is never entirely snuffed out. Perhaps in a democracy, which permits freedom of expression, this condition is as it should be.

However, in the late seventies the problem appears especially acute. In several ways we are, though perhaps inadvertently, part of the problem. For, during the 1970s social studies educators have embraced a variety of new interests that have bombarded classrooms from many directions. These activities can be subsumed under various labels: multicultural education, consumer education, global education, law-related education, moral (values) education, action learning, etc. Some of these areas have been, and are, targets of the censors. While moving in these many directions, we have, I think, failed to pay attention to the forces eroding the quality of education. Responsible innovative efforts are terribly important, but ignoring the climate of classrooms, schools, and communities is counter-productive to any serious educator.

That dissonant points of view have a right to see the light of day cannot be questioned. Whether all points of view have an equal claim to control the quality and nature of the educational experience is quite another matter, however.

In my remarks . . . I would like to focus on three points:

1. the first is to highlight the nature and extent of censorship currently;

[1] From article by Anna S. Ochoa, associate professor of Social Studies Education, Indiana University, and 1978 president of the National Council for the Social Studies. *Social Education.* 43:304–9. Ap. '79. Reprinted by permission of the National Council for the Social Studies and the author.

2. the second is to summarize the status of the rights of teachers; and
3. the third is to focus on what needs to be done by educators and schools and by this professional association.

Turning first to the nature and extent of censorship, I would like to organize my remarks around the following questions:

Who is censoring?
What is being censored and why?
Where is it happening?

An oversimplified, but not inaccurate, response to these questions is "everybody, everything, everywhere." However, these are global answers. Let me be more specific.

Who Is Censoring?

First, who is censoring? For me, this question divides into two parts: (a) Who attempts to censor? and (b) Who actually censors? Among those who attempt to censor, a most significant voice is an organization called Education Research Analysts. It is operated out of Longview, Texas by two self-styled textbook analysts: Mel and Norma Gabler. It is estimated that they have a budget of about $150,000 per year. They produce reviews of textbooks that have appeared in many places throughout the country. As consultants to pro-censorship groups, they have personally visited Kanawha County, West Virginia; New Orleans, Louisiana; and St. Paul/ Minneapolis, Minnesota. In general, they find many instructional materials to be anti-Christian and anti-American. Specifically, they offer the following statement as a description of their commitment: "Until textbooks are changed, there is absolutely no chance that crime, violence, VD, and abortion rates will do anything but climb." I would like to provide a few examples of what they object to:

1. In the Justice and Urban America Series (Houghton Mifflin), Norma Gabler objected to an over-emphasis on lawbreaking, violence, prejudice and poverty. She noted that the word "poverty" was used 168 times in one of the eight volumes

which happened to be entitled *Poverty and Welfare*. She further objected to the presentation of a welfare application form in this volume, charging that the material did not encourage individual initiative to find work.

2. In Macmillan's *Search for Freedom*, a fifth-grade text, Mrs. Gabler called attention to the fact that six and one-half pages were devoted to Marilyn Monroe while George Washington was only mentioned five times. She concluded her testimony to the Texas Education Agency with a question that received international press attention, "Is Texas ready for Marilyn to become the mother of our country?"

3. In *Inquiries into Sociology* (Allyn and Bacon), two of the issues the Gablers focused on were moral permissiveness and a disproportionate emphasis on parent-youth conflict. The material, they observed, approved of telling of white lies which the Gablers interpret as situational ethics. They further argued that the following passage exaggerated the tensions between parents and youth: "Unintended functions of the family may be to extend the period of dependency too long, and to imprint the child, often unconsciously, with the parents' prides, passions and prejudices."

4. For Prentice-Hall's *Behind the Mark: Our Psychological World*, the Gablers submitted an eighteen-page bill of particulars. One objection was to the following statement: "This process is called sex role development and that means that we are trained gradually in the ways of behavior as a male or female. Put another way, we learn how to be a man and a woman sexually and adopt that role—as if we were in a play—until that role becomes second nature." The Gablers added that "this theory rejects God who stated that He made us male and female. You are either a male or a female and there is no way to get around it."

The Gablers and their supporters have a variety of targets.

1. Adolescent Novels—ones that deal with the problems adolescents face—whether they focus on drugs, juvenile delinquency, or sex.
2. Realistic Dialogue—here the target is substandard English. The Gablers fear that reading such dialect is a way of teaching students to use it.
3. Works by Questionable Writers—e.g., Langston Hughes, Malcolm X, Joan Baez, Ogden Nash.
4. Books by those considered to be homosexual authors—Emily

Dickinson, Tennessee Williams, Walt Whitman, Gore Vidal, John Milton, and Hans Christian Andersen.
5. Another category is books they describe as trash. Included here are such titles as *Native Son, Catcher in the Rye,* and *Soul on Ice.*

A sixth category is teaching methods that represent secular humanism, which the protesters see as a set of ideas that denigrate family, church, and country. Seventh are materials about ethnic studies and drug education. Eighth is role playing. Ninth, the absence of grammar rules. Tenth, materials that make negative statements about parents. Eleventh is phase elective English programs and twelfth is sex education.

Even though the examples given have applied to the middle and secondary school levels, elementary titles are becoming increasingly vulnerable. Whether in the form of textbooks or library books, elementary materials are becoming increasingly realistic.

In addition to the Gablers' organization, there are other national as well as state organizations. The Heritage Foundation, America's Future, Citizens for Decent Literature, the Hard Core Parents of Louisiana, the National Parents League, the Oklahoma Parents for God and Country, Parents Who Care in Maryland, represent a few examples. These pro-censorship groups are well-heeled and well-organized.

By contrast, the educational community has not had a parallel organization. So far I have placed heavy emphasis on the organized censorship movement because evidence of it is pervasive. However, I do not mean to suggest that there are not individuals, be they parents or not, who do not act independently of the movement.

Further, I have been describing censorship from the conservative side. I'd also like to speak to censorship from the liberal perspective. Racial groups, ethnic groups, and women's groups have also called for the removal of certain books from schools, libraries, and classrooms. *Little Black Sambo* is probably the best known example, but there are many others. This, too, is censorship; and let me submit that there is no such thing as good censorship—not if we value freedom of the mind—there isn't. In this instance, I'd like to make a distinction between the selection of curriculum materials such as textbooks on the one hand and library and supplementary materials on the other. If the curriculum of a school aims to strengthen certain core democratic values, such as freedom and equality, as it seems to me it should, then it seems perfectly logical to select text materials that reflect those values. However, adherence to such values—especially that of freedom—requires that we leave all the books on the library shelves. None of us would argue that *Mein Kampf* or *The Communist Manifesto* should be removed (at least I hope none of us would so argue). Yet these books represent repugnant ideas to many. We do not have to look back too many years to find an account of the removal of a children's book called *The Rabbit's Wedding*. The story is about two rabbits who play together and enjoy one another. In the great tradition of many chidren's stories, the book has a "lived happily ever after" ending. The rabbits were married. However, from the standpoint of those who would censor, there was a problem. One rabbit was black and the other white. The conservatives, who succeeded in having the book censored, found the story to be a symbol of miscegenation. I use this example to illustrate the concept of tyranny of the majority. In this case, those in power, ignoring respect for minority rights, used their power to control the minds of children. Right-wing racists felt that they had the right to exercise their power by removing this book. This illustration emphasizes that in a democracy majority rule must be balanced with minority rights. It is important to remember that today's majority may well be tomorrow's minority. If power, rather than respect for rights, prevails, dictatorship, not democracy, exists. For a democracy, it is imperative that we understand that the group in power is transient, but that the principles of the system must be persistent.

Censorship attempts, then, come from different political camps, various socioeconomic groups, varying religious denominations, and both sexes.

If these groups are the ones who attempt to censor, then

who actually censors? The actual censor has to be a person or group that has authority. In 1976, Mel and Norma Gabler were successful in influencing the removal of several dictionaries from schools throughout the state of Texas. The dictionaries, in their view, contained a number of obscene words. The Gablers protested the use of the dictionaries, as did other parents. But they are not the censors. A censor can be a state board of education, a superintendent of schools, a principal, a school board, a teacher, or a librarian. When any of these authorities give in to the demands of protesters and remove books, put them in special collections, cut out pages or passages, darken the controversial parts of an illustration—they are censoring. It may seem unusual to include some teachers and librarians on this list of censors; nonetheless, it is accurate. Further, such action often takes place without a request or directive that a book be removed. As soon as news spreads that parents are protesting a book in one location, that book may silently disappear from use in several other places. One of the typical consequences of a censorship incident is that self-censorship runs rampant.

A word about publishers. In responding to protesters, publishers have been valiant in their efforts to diffuse the attack and diminish its strength. Nonetheless, if the attack persists they often agree to make the desired changes. States that have centralized adoption procedures are especially threatened. To lose the state adoption in large states such as Florida, California, or Texas involves a cost that is too high for publishers to pay. In states that are open territory where decisions are made by local school districts, the situation is far less threatening, and prepublication censorship is not as likely to occur.

At this point, I hope I've made clear why it is fair to respond to the questions raised earlier—Who censors? What is censored? Where is it taking place?—with "Everybody, everything, and everywhere."

I think it is now appropriate to ask: "What rights do teachers have anyway?" "Or principals or superintendents or school boards?" "Why do they give in?" "Isn't the law on their side?"

Significant Cases on Academic Freedom

First of all, there is no specific law or constitutional provision that guarantees academic freedom. What we have is the First Amendment; and the Supreme Court has, from time to time, affirmed that academic freedom is a form of free speech and free expression. The first instance of such a court ruling occurred as recently as 1923. Up until then, academic freedom was only a tradition that applied exclusively to universities and not to pre-collegiate education, where students are less mature and where the emphasis is on transmitting rather than discovering knowledge.

There are several important cases through which the courts have set some legal precedent. I would like to review a few major ones briefly:

1. The Keefe Case, Ipswich, Massachusetts, 1969. Keefe was an English teacher who assigned an article from the *Atlantic Monthly*. The article contained a vulgar term. While students didn't react negatively, some parents did. When asked not to use the term again in class, Keefe said that he could not, in good conscience, agree. He was notified that he would be dismissed and went to court to stop the dismissal. The judge in the case found the article to be a scholarly one and not obscene. He further observed that the use of the term was central to the theme and that most seniors knew the term anyway. He concluded that the "sensibilities of offended parents are not the full measure of what is proper in education." He also made it clear that his decision did not give blanket approval to the use of offensive language. Whether it is proper, he stated, depends on the circumstances.

2. In fact, in another case in Massachusetts in 1971, the U.S. District Court decided the matter differently. In Mailloux vs. Kiley, an 11th-grade teacher was dismissed for using a variation of the same term used by Keefe. Admitting that under certain circumstances, the use of the term might be

acceptable, the judge ruled that on the basis of expert testimony, there were differences of opinion regarding the technique the teacher used. Some experts had not approved of Mailloux's practice and stated that it was not essential to use the term. The judge ruled that for a controversial teaching method to be constitutionally protected, *it was necessary to prove that the method has acceptance by a preponderance of the profession.* He further emphasized the difference between secondary schools and universities. Secondary schools function more clearly *in loco parentis* than universities. Further, he added, some teachers and students in secondary schools have limited intellectual and emotional maturity. He also emphasized that secondary students are a more captive audience. In spite of this reasoning, Mailloux was reinstated. However, it was not on the basis of academic freedom but, rather, due process. Mailloux, it seemed, had not been given any warning and therefore did not know his conduct was prohibited.

Comparing just these two cases begins to indicate the extent to which the rights of teachers hinge on the circumstances and on the judges who sit on the case.

3. The Parducci Case in 1970 focused on one of Kurt Vonnegut's books, *Welcome to the Monkey House.* Three students (high school juniors) asked to be excused from reading it, some parents complained, and Marilyn Parducci was fired. Several vulgarities and a reference to rape was the basis for the criticism. The judge, however, found nothing obscene and further noted that the assignment did not lead to any disruption in the school or classroom. The judge ruled the dismissal to be an unwarranted invasion of the First Amendment. Marilyn Parducci was reinstated. It should be noted that the absence of disruption and the ruling that the material was not obscene were the criteria used in this case. . . .

This brief discussion of significant academic freedom cases emphasizes that teachers at the pre-collegiate level cannot simply do as they please regarding the selection of materials or methods for their classes. Although the use of controversial materials and techniques has often been protected, teachers must, at a minimum, be able to demonstrate that their professional actions meet the following criteria:

1. are relevant to the subject being taught
2. are appropriate for the age and maturity level of students
3. are not disruptive to school or classroom discipline and
4. have the support of their profession.

Of course, the meaning of words like "relevant," "appropriate," and what constitutes "disruption" is determined subjectively by school boards, parents, expert witnesses that might be used, and the judge or judges hearing the case.

It is also important to remember that vulgar language was permissible when it was found to be central to the article and relevant to the subject matter, but not when it was found to be irrelevant. Teachers need to use sound professional judgment in selecting their materials, as contrasted with the example provided by an English teacher who listed Erica Jong's *Fear of Flying* in his elective minicourse: "The Literature of Flight."

Conditions Heightening the Censorship Issue

Currently, a number of conditions are converging to heighten the censorship issue. I have already mentioned the increasing numbers of organizations that have formed to promote the use of educational materials that square with their particular values. Secondly, the 1973 and 1974 Supreme Court decisions making obscenity a concept that is defined by community, rather than by national standards, are another. (Whether the 1969 Keefe case [where the teacher used the *Atlantic Monthly* article containing a vulgar term] would be judged the same way is, in my view, not certain. It may well be that Keefe would be fired if his case were ruled on today. Indeed, the case may not have been admitted to federal court because obscenity issues are matters of local concern.) Thirdly, the back to basics movement carries with it an increased value for the historical versus the contemporary. This emphasis along with support for conventional morality results in turning aside materials that are likely to be controversial. Finally, the tight job market and low turnover of teachers are factors that will cause even the most courageous teacher to be cautious.

What Can Be Done?

I would now like to turn to the matter of what can be done to deal with a difficult problem in difficult times. . . . Teachers can do a number of things: First, they can inform themselves about academic freedom and censorship. Documents such as the NCSS [National Council for the Social Studies] Position Statement on Academic Freedom and NCTE's [National Council of Teachers of English] Right to Read Statement should be in their possession. Second, teachers can see to it that their principals, superintendents, or department heads have copies of these basic academic freedom publications. Third, regardless of which teacher association prevails, teachers can exert influence to provide an academic freedom clause as part of the contract. At the national level both the NEA and the AFT support this position. Fourth, teachers can work at developing good relationships with parents. They can keep parents informed about what their classes are doing. Although elementary teachers have easier access to parents than do secondary teachers, the effort invested is well worth it. Good communication with parents probably constitutes the best insurance policy against angry and unreasonable attacks. Fifth, teachers can be prepared to defend what they teach. A statement of objectives related to the materials used to fulfill them can be an important tool if protests are made. Sixth, teachers can choose their materials soundly. While we don't want a sanitized curriculum, neither can we justify a sensationalized one. Or paraphrasing one writer, "Don't lust after fads in your obsession for relevance." Seventh, when assigning controversial materials, teachers can make it clear that students may select an option if they find the materials offensive. All of us need to recognize and accept the fact that parents do have the right to decide what their own children read; they do not have the right to make that decision for others, however. Eighth, teachers can avoid using the classroom as an arena for their own ideologies. Rather, their role is to expose young minds to all points of view. This caution should not be taken to mean that teachers cannot express opinions. Rather, it implies that, when stated, such opinions are also open to discussion and debate. Ninth, if censorship attacks are directed at others in the school district, teachers can become informed and can take a position. The problem is shared by everyone. Fighting censorship is a lonely business; providing support to those attacked is terribly important.

School districts need to:

1. Conduct a continuing public relations campaign with the community.
2. Establish a strong academic freedom policy at the school board level.
3. Involve parents in the selection process, although the majority of members should be educators.
4. Establish a complaint procedure to systematize protests over materials. Avoid banning books until they have been fairly reviewed.
5. Maintain a standing review committee for materials that are attacked. Involve parents on this committee.
6. Make sure that all teachers have a set of educational objectives to which they relate their materials and their methods.
7. Make it a matter of policy to provide students with alternative assignments if they object to the regular one.
8. Train all administrative personnel and teachers to handle complaints about materials.

. . . School libraries and classrooms are but one arena for censorship efforts. Because the education of young people is at stake, it is a very important one. To the extent that we who are responsible for and concerned with student learning view freedom to learn as one significant factor in the quality of democratic education, to the same extent we become champions of the First Amendment as applied to school settings.

I would like to end this speech with a quotation from one of the few people who has had a hero-like status for me—Justice William O. Douglas. In a dissenting opinion in 1959, Douglas stated:

Ultimately all the questions in this case really boil down to one—whether we as a people will try fearfully and futilely to preserve democracy by adopting totalitarian methods, or whether in accordance with our tradition and our Constitution we will have the confidence and courage to be free?

PROTEST GROUPS EXERT STRONG IMPACT[2]

In a speech at the U.S. Capitol in which he launched a new phase of his Clean Up America (CUA) campaign, the Reverend Jerry Falwell declared that most public school textbooks are nothing more than "Soviet propaganda." He added: "In school textbooks, pornography, obscenity, vulgarity and profanity are destroying our children's moral values in the guise of 'value clarification' and 'sex education.' Our children are being trained to deny their 200-year heritage." Dr. Falwell then urged his followers to "rise up in arms to throw out every textbook" that does not accurately present the American heritage.

According to Patrick Robinson's report in the May 14, 1979, issue of *Spotlight,* five United States Senators (Harry Byrd, Jesse Helms, Gordon Humphrey, Paul Laxalt and John Warner) and two Representatives (George Hansen and Tom Kindness) endorsed Dr. Falwell's CUA campaign by appearing with him at the rally.

Dr. Falwell's influence extends far beyond his congregation at the Thomas Road Baptist Church in Lynchburg, Va. He has a television and radio audience of millions who tune in to his "Old Time Gospel Hour." And since his appearance on the Capitol steps, Dr. Falwell has, in several sermons, told his nationwide congregation about the "immoral textbooks [used in the] atheistic public schools." He has also repeated part of his Washington message in his sermons: the key to U.S. strength is Christian morality and the key to Christian moral-

[2] Article by Edward B. Jenkinson, professor of English Education, Indiana University, and author of *Censors in the Classroom. Publishers Weekly.* 216:42,44. O. 29, '79. Copyright © 1979 by Xerox Corporation. Reprinted by permission.

ity is the expansion of the conservative Christian school system.

Stamping Out "Secular Humanism"

According to the report in *Spotlight*, Dr. Falwell told his Washington audience that in 1961 there were "a mere 1400 conservative Christian academies in the country." Today, he said, there are 14,000 such schools, with three new ones being founded every day. At that rate, Dr. Falwell noted, by 1992 the number of conservative Christian schools will equal the number of public schools.

Dr. Falwell and thousands of like-minded citizens apparently believed there is little hope for the public schools, which stand accused of secular humanism. At least a dozen of the protesting organizations have distributed the same definition of "humanism," part of which is quoted here:

Humanism is faith in man instead of faith in God. Humanism was officially ruled a religion by the U.S. Supreme Court. Humanism promotes: (1) situation ethics, (2) evolution, (3) sexual freedom, including public sex education courses, and (4) internationalism.

Humanism centers on "self" because it recognizes no higher being to which man is responsible. . . . This eliminates coming to Christ for forgiveness of sin. It eliminates the Christian attributes of meekness and humility. Where does self-esteem end and arrogance begin?

Such terms as self-concept, self-esteem, self-awareness, self-acceptance, self-fulfillment, self-realization, self-understanding, self-actualization, body-awareness, etc., are frequently used. All leave the students occupied primarily with themselves and this is wrong. There are others to consider. Self-centered persons are seldom an asset to themselves, to their friends, family or country.

In an article in *Journal Champion*, Dr. Falwell noted: "Textbook writers are humanists and evolutionists. . . . We should be angry with our school textbooks because they push socialism and one-world government. They make democracy look ridiculous and socialism look appealing." The article relies heavily on textbook reviews prepared by Norma and Mel Gabler, the founders of Educational Research Analysts in

Longview, Texas, who proudly announced in April 1979 that
Dr. Falwell "has asked us to supply resource material to alert
Americans nationwide about the damage being done by humanistic textbooks. Since even many committed Christians
do not recognize that the textbook situation is so desperate,
we believe this wide exposure could be one of God's most
powerful instruments to inform the Christian community!"

The Gablers, their paid staff and a corps of volunteers
provide concerned citizens throughout the nation with reviews of virtually all textbooks used in the United States. The
Gablers also provide their followers with strategies for ap-
proaching the schools about objectionable books and with
materials published by other protesting organizations. A person who sends an initial request to the Gablers for reviews
may receive these two paragraphs in their response, since
they seem to be a vital part of the Gabler creed:

Until textbooks are changed, there is no possibility that crime,
violence, VD, and abortion rates will do anything but continue to
climb.

Textbooks mold nations because textbooks largely determine how
a nation votes, what it becomes and where it goes.

The Gablers prepare extensive bills of particulars in
which they object to specific words or passages in textbooks
that have been submitted for adoption in Texas. They are
highly successful with their protests. For example, in August
1978, the Gabler objections helped the Texas Commissioner
of Education decide to reject 18 of the 28 series of textbooks
submitted for adoption. And that high percentage of rejection
is not unusual as a result of the Gabler's extensive homework.

Probably virtually all of the more than 200 national, state
and local protesting organizations are familiar with the
Gabler reviews and strategies. Not all of the organizations
apparently agree with all of the Gablers' objections, but a
high percentage—from coast to coast—rely on the Gablers'
materials when they protest textbooks at the local level or

when they conduct statewide meetings to encourage parents to start their own conservative academies.

The protesting organizations rise at the local level for a variety of reasons. Some form because they are unhappy with a particular book, such as *The Catcher in the Rye* or *Go Ask Alice*, and they may dissolve as soon as that book is removed from a school library or as soon as they learn that the school board will not remove it. Others use a single book as a starting point and expand their scope to attack a variety of school materials. A great number organize to express their complete displeasure with the "humanistic schools" and their textbooks.

Space limitations prohibit listing all organizations that have protested textbooks, library books and reference books; the listing below is limited to 20 representative organizations:

American Education Association (AEA), New York City
American Christians in Education (ACE), Culver City, Calif.
Citizens Advocating a Voice in Education (CAVE), Atlanta, Ga.
Citizens Committee on Education, Pinellas County, Fla.
Citizens United for Responsible Education (CURE), Montgomery Ct., Md.
Concerned Citizens and Taxpayers for Decent School Books, E. Baton Rouge, La.
Concerned Parents of Monticello, Iowa
The Eagle Forum, Alton, Ill.
Guardians of Education for Maine (GEM), Camden, Me.
The Heritage Foundation, Washington, D.C.
Indiana Home Circle, Bloomington, Ind.
Interfaith Committee Against Blasphemy, Wyoming, Mich.
Let's Improve Today's Education (LITE), Peoria, Ariz.
The National Congress for Educational Excellence (NCEE), Dallas, Tex.
The Network of Patriotic Letter Writers, Pasadena, Calif.
Parents of Minnesota, Inc., Bloomington, Minn.
Parents of New York—United (PONY-U), Clarence, N.Y.
Parents Rights, Inc., St. Louis, Mo.
People of America Responding to Educational Needs of Today's Society (PARENTS), Kenosha, Wis.
Young Parents Alert, Lake Elmo, Minn.

What do the protesting organizations oppose? The list below is a compilation of targets gleaned from reading several thousand pages of protest material and reports of censorship incidents throughout the nation. Not all organizations are opposed to all 40 items on the list, but a few oppose all 40 and a score more:

1. sex education
2. drug education
3. values clarification
4. the study of psychology and the use of psychological principles in teaching
5. sociology
6. anthropology
7. the humanities
8. ecology
9. world geography—if there's mention of one-worldism
10. world history—if there's mention of the United Nations
11. ethnic studies
12. literature written by homosexuals
13. black literature
14. novels that deal with conflicts between parents and their children
15. basal readers with many pictures and drawings
16. the so-called dirty words in dictionaries and all books
17. profanity
18. violence
19. books that do not champion the work ethic
20. books that do not promote patriotism
21. books that do not promote the family unit as the basis of American life
22. mythology
23. stories about pagan cultures and life styles
24. books and stories that "defame" historical figures by revealing their weaknesses
25. "trash"—*The Catcher in the Rye, Go Ask Alice, Black Boy, Flowers for Algernon*, etc.
26. works of "questionable" writers, including Langston Hughes, Dick Gregory, Ogden Nash, Richard Wright, Joan Baez, and Malcolm X
27. phase-elective English programs
28. revisionist histories
29. materials that contain negative statements about parents

30. books that contain any print that is not horizontal and reads from left to right
31. role playing
32. sensitivity training
33. behavior modification
34. subjects that cannot be classified as basic
35. assignments that lead to self-awareness and self-understanding
36. situation ethics
37. assignments that help students make value judgments
38. human development programs
39. the occult
40. stories about the supernatural, magic, witchcraft, etc.

The protesting organizations have every right to complain in a democratic society, and they can fully expect to be heard. However, they should also expect to have many of their objections challenged by teachers, administrators and publishers—particularly when their protests are politically and religiously motivated or when their objections lack substance or validity.

Despite protests from organizations and individuals, publishers must continue to publish the best textbooks they can produce, and they must be willing to defend those textbooks in textbook adoption hearings, in school board meetings and in the media. Otherwise, the students of America will be the losers because they will not be able to read a variety of materials and become acquainted with many ideas, including some that might be labeled controversial.

THE FUTURE OF TEXTBOOKS[3]

... Norma and Mel Gabler are continually asked if they believe the current trends in textbooks will be reversed. They are guardedly optimistic. "I think the pendulum is swinging our way," Norma says. "If the movement keeps gaining

[3] Excerpt, Chapter 12, entitled, "Charting the Future," from *Are Textbooks Harming Your Children?: Norma and Mel Gabler Take Action and Show You How*, by James C. Hefley. Mott Media, 1979. p 177–93. Reprinted by permission.

strength, we'll be going back to the basics—learning skills, traditional math, phonics, morality, patriotism, history that is really history, science that is science, and fair play for free enterprise economics. On my speaking tours I've found parents disgusted. No matter what kind of jargon the educators feed them, they see the results."

The Gablers do not believe publishers will stop producing "progressive" texts. "Realistically," says Mel, "what I think will happen is that the publishers will be forced to put out two sets of books if they want to stay competitive."

The spiral of alternative fundamental schools and private, church-related, and nondenominational Christian schools, the Gablers believe, will be a strong inducement for publishers to provide another set of books. They note that *Biology: A Search For Order In Complexity*, published by Zondervan Publishing House, which three major textbook publishers turned down, is in its fourth printing. Creation-Life Publishers are working overtime producing creation books for use in various science courses. Their most important contribution is *Scientific Creationism*, a handbook for teachers. The public school edition is strictly science with no biblical or religious content. Their new world history, *Streams of Civilization*, promises to be a major contribution to public and private schools interested in history presented objectively and in a scholarly manner. A Beka Book Publications has the largest assortment of texts with no humanistic bias, and has started producing texts for secular as well a Christian schools. Other publishers, such as Bob Jones University Press, are in the process of increasing the supply of acceptable texts. Textbooks from these and other publishers are included in the Gablers' "List of Recommended Books."

Because Texas textbook adoption law permits only publishers to press the advantages of their books, the Gablers and other protesters have wrongly been accused of being against all textbooks by secular publishers. "This is not so," Mel insists. "Whenever we can find a good book, we plug its merits in our mailings. We even condone books that are mildly objectionable when we feel they are the best in a particular field."

"We're not out to destroy any publisher," Mel declares. "We believe in free enterprise. We're simply trying to get publishers to see that they're missing a big market by not publishing books that millions of parents want."

Mel and Norma are hopeful that the big textbook publishers will take a cue from their general trade brothers. "Up until a few years ago their religious lines were mostly liberal," Mel notes. "They noticed that the sales of evangelical publishers were booming, and got on the bandwagon pretty fast. Today, publishers like Doubleday and Harper are signing up evangelical authors to write for the evangelical market. Of course, they still publish liberal books, too."

The Gablers don't see an alternate line of textbooks as any threat to public schools, no more than fundamental alternative schools are threats to the public system. "Perhaps the 'progressive' educators see the fundamental schools as a threat to their ideology," says Mel. "But the basic schools are in the best tradition of American democracy. They're tax-supported, integrated, and so popular that some have a long waiting list."

The Gablers list some of the features of these schools which capture parental confidence: Traditional curriculum, phonics beginning in kindergarten; basic math and grammar; spelling bees and math contests; classes grouped according to ability of students; assigned homework; grades that reflect actual achievement; promotion only on merit; high moral standards and patriotism; dress codes and strict discipline; respect and courtesy demanded.

The Gablers hold that education could change rapidly for the best if the progressive educational establishment would stop trying to enforce its own concept of what it thinks schools should accomplish. They do not believe this will happen. They believe that the establishment is pressing for complete control over curriculum and training and certification of teachers, with increased federal financing.

The Gablers would like to see the federal government get completely out of curriculum. They are encouraged by Arizona Rep. John Conlan's success in getting National Science Foundation funding for the *Man: A Course of Study* series (MACOS) cut off by Congress.

The National Education Association is the most visible promoter of the goals of progressive education. The NEA, the Gablers point out, has never denied its program for educator power. At the 1969 annual meeting, NEA president George D. Fischer urged teachers to form the country's most powerful political group to combat "a conspiracy" against education. The "conspiracy," he said, was composed of the Nixon administration, racist governors, private segregated schools, and private businesses offering to teach reading in public schools on contracts for pupil achievement. He predicted that in a decade NEA would grow to 4 million members, each earning $25,000 a year, with annual dues of 1% of salaries going to "elevate the status of educators and education." With that money and power, Fischer said, the NEA would win passage of a federal law legalizing teacher strikes and requiring school districts to negotiate with their teachers. The NEA, Fischer added, would also control who enters and leaves the profession and the training institutions.

Five years later, the NEA endorsed 310 congressional candidates and achieved a win record of 81%, the best among the nation's political lobbies. In 1974, the NEA also lobbied successfully for passage of the $25 billion bill extending the Federal Elementary and Secondary Education Act for school aid for four years.

By 1975, the NEA had grown more bold. At the 1975 convention, NEA president John Ryor called on the organization to get into presidential politics.

The Gablers worry that if the NEA reaches all its goals, an academic-political dictatorship could be established over public schools. Private schools, already hindered by bureaucracy, will be harassed till they fold or conform.

At the heart of this control will be a standardized, federally financed curriculum, administered and written by progressive educators. The Gablers concede that on the surface this sounds good to average parents. "But they need to consider," Mel warns, "that a powerful liberal group will gain even more control over what our children are taught, advance any ideology they wish, and do it in the name of representative democracy."

The Gablers obviously believe there is hope that this situation can be averted. They believe the failures of progressive education are now so apparent that a grass roots revolt is inevitable.

Even the most ardent progressives cannot deny there is much evidence for concern about American education in a society that seems to be retrogressing academically, morally, and socially.

Item: Average high school scores on the College Board Scholastic Aptitude Test have steadily dropped over the past 11 years. Other tests reveal similar trends in reading, writing, verbal comprehension, and math.

Item: Half of 440,000 11th and 12th graders tested in 1960 now say in a follow-up study by the U.S. Office of Education that their high school education has been no help in giving them special skills for jobs.

Item: A Senate Judiciary Subcommittee studying 75 school districts recently announced a "crisis" in school vandalism and violence. About 70,000 teachers are seriously injured in student attacks each year. Senator Birch Bayh, committee head, said "these hallways and playgrounds of fear and terror also account for an estimated $500 million of vandalism damage."

Item: In society at large, major crimes increased almost 50% during the past five years; 58% of all crimes were committed by persons under 25 years of age; up to $5 billion worth of goods are shoplifted each year, mostly by young people.

Item: Unwed teenage pregnancies keep increasing, as do abortions. The divorce rate keeps moving up. A Temple University sociologist found in a survey of 2,300 wives that 50% expected to eventually be involved in extramarital sex; one of every three aged 26 to 30 admitted they already had.

Item: A million American youth run away from home each year. Suicide is the second leading cause of death for youth ages 15–24. One of ten school-age children has moderate to severe mental and emotional troubles. Drug abuse and alcoholism have skyrocketed.

Item: The teaching of American history in our public schools "is in crisis," reports the Organization of American Historians after a detailed study in 50 states and the District of Columbia. The OAH notes that because history teachers and texts have emphasized concepts rather than facts, college professors are "discovering that their students lack a sense of time and perspective about the past."

Item: Businessmen are concerned that 49% of the American people believe that big business is the source of much of what is wrong with the economy. A Gallup poll of 904 students in 57 colleges and universities showed an abysmal ignorance of economics. They agreed 88 to 10 that business is "too much concerned with profits and not with public responsibility"; they thought corporate profits average 45% (the correct figure is nearer 5%); they guessed a corporation with net earnings of $1 million would pay 25% federal income tax (the correct amount is 47%).

The Gablers do not blame progressive education for all of this, but they feel it must take a major share of the blame, particularly because of textbooks that "glorify" violence and lawbreaking, undermine basic institutions, and encourage students to believe that no system of morals is absolute. They note that social scientists almost unanimously agree that children become what they're taught.

When they began their crusade as "babes in the woods" in 1961, it was unpopular, almost traitorous, to criticize textbooks. Today there is a chorus of respectable voices calling for better books.

For example, the *Wall Street Journal* scolded the pro-textbook forces in West Virginia for proposing "that the way to broaden the sheltered, white, middle-class 1950s outlook is to confront it with the amoral, if not criminal, outlook fostered by . . . Eldridge Cleaver and the world of convicts." The

Journal called on the "educated elite . . . to recognize that . . . the Kanawha County parents had a point."

U.S. Education Commissioner Terrell H. Bell frankly told the Association of American Publishers in a 1974 speech that some of their "current" juvenile literature in textbooks "appears to emphasize violence and obscenity and moral judgments that run counter to tradition, all in the name of keeping up with the real world." He called on the publishers to concentrate on "good literature that will appeal to children without relying too much on blood and guts and street language for their own sake."

In February 1976, Treasury Secretary William Simon urged the New York Chapter of the Public Relations Society of America to "counsel your bosses and your clients to take a close look at the [socialistic] teaching policies of schools and foundations being considered for corporate gifts. Otherwise the largess and the generosity of the free enterprise system will continue to finance its own destruction."

The Gablers are glad, as Mel puts it, "that people are waking up to see what the fuss is all about. But words are not enough. If experience is any teacher, we'll have to keep fighting till boards of education, administrators, and teachers demand that publishers give schools what parents want for their children."

Till that happens, Mel and Norma Gabler plan to keep on in the spirit of the logo on their letterhead: *A husband and wife team working for America's tomorrow—children.*

TEXTBOOKS: A SOCIAL RESPONSIBILITY[4]

What constitutes public-interest criticism and what constitutes pressure for censorship? The distinction has been hotly debated, following charges that racism, sexism and

[4] Article by Council on Interracial Books for Children. *Publishers Weekly.* 216:43–4. O. 29, '79. Copyright © 1979 by Xerox Corporation. Reprinted by permission.

other biases are perpetuated by the books children read in schools and libraries. There has been further debate on whether the use of criteria designed to avoid racism and sexism in children's books also constitutes censorship.

The Council on Interracial Books for Children favors the use of such criteria and rejects the contention that advocacy of nonracist, nonsexist criteria for book selection is tantamount to censorship. In the arena of educational and textbook publishing it is especially desirable to demonstrate that the criteria we advocate are not merely permissible from a civil liberties point of view; the criteria are mandatory from a civil rights point of view, under the Fourteenth Amendment to our Constitution. The Fourteenth mandates: "No state shall . . . deny to any person within its jurisdiction the equal protection of the laws."

Children at school are *compelled* to read textbooks, and the texts are paid for by the taxpayers' dollars. Despite the private enterprise and private profit involved, the whole textbook purchase operation is basically an action taken by "the State," since every public school is a state or government agency. Moreover, because all young people are force-fed a textbook diet for at least 12 of their formative years, the values, perspectives and information contained in the books mold minds and shape our future society.

One consequence is that many people, especially those who refuse to recognize that the U.S.A. has never really been a land of "freedom and justice for all," see textbooks as a way to stop the clock and preserve historical inequalities. Clearly, their efforts to exert leverage on publishers are inimical to a public interest shaped by a Constitution designed to achieve a secular, egalitarian society. Recognition of that very Constitution also suggests that "the State," and the publishers selected to fulfill its educational obligations, are accountable to students, to parents, to educators and to taxpayers.

Of course, the ideal way for publishers to discharge their accountability is by self-regulation. But it is important to understand and to stress that such self-regulation is not to be thought of as a pure matter of choice. There is no "option" to evade a Constitutional mandate. It is for that reason the Council wishes to present some issues related to the Fourteenth Amendment for publishers' consideration.

Books That Perpetuate Injustice

The Council has been a constant critic of both trade and textbook publishers for nearly 15 years. As our name suggests, we emerged from the Civil Rights Movement of the 1960s. Ours has been one voice among many pointing out that the all-white, middle-class world of children's books failed to reflect the realities of present or past U.S. life. Ours has been one voice among many analyzing the prevalence in trade books and textbooks of stereotypes, distortions and omissions about the lives and perspectives of women, of blacks, of Chicanos and of other racial minority peoples. We have also been one among many organizations, and among many educational researchers, whose studies have documented the pervasiveness of age and handicap bias, in addition to race and sex bias, in children's reading materials. Yet, as critics, we have also hailed some positive signs of change, as publishers recently began to make their books more multicultural and less sexist.

Given the concerns of this issue of *Publishers Weekly*, we are focusing this article on school textbooks that have had the result (and perhaps the purpose) of rationalizing and perpetuating interracial injustice. While there has been change, we feel the changes made in textbooks are insufficient.

Let's examine statistics about the makeup of the student body in U.S. schools. Females, of course, comprise slightly over 50% of the students. But language arts, math and science texts assuredly do not offer them anything like 50% of the positive role models or the page space offered to males. Nor do history texts do justice—in fact they do serious injustice—to the role of women in our economic and cultural growth and development as a nation. Research shows that biased textbooks harm the self-image of girls. We believe this textbook treatment is related to the reality that working women earn 58% of the amount earned by working men.

About one of every five students is a member of a racial minority group. If present population trends continue, that figure is expected to reach one of every four students in the very near future. While there is greater visibility of darker-skinned people in the newer textbooks, the proportion of characters and perspectives does not begin to approach their proportions in our student population. As with women, the importance of minorities in U.S. cultural and economic growth is undervalued and underrepresented. We believe there is a relationship between those facts and the fact that median income of minority families is only 59% that of white families.

One of every 10 students is, to some extent, disabled. They, too, are entitled to positive textbook images and have a right to see their special concerns reflected in school materials. Today, more than one of every five children comes from a single-parent household. Within a few years it will be one of every four. Why do textbooks continue to emphasize the nuclear family in which daddy works while mom and kids stay at home? Today, only one of every seven children is from such a family. Reality for about half of all students is that their mothers work (that percentage is rising). Reality for many students is that their families live below the poverty level. Yet inspection of current textbooks offers a totally misleading picture of the realities of U.S. life.

Once it is recognized that government and professional educators have obligations to all groups of children, textbook publishers should become more aware of their own legal—as well as moral—obligations. Publishers are very much aware that some states have antibias guidelines, or regulations, for textbook purchases. Publishers are also very much aware of their First Amendment rights. However, the *California Law Review* (v. 62, 1974), in an article by Carol Amyx titled "Sex Discrimination: The Textbook Case," states:

Publishers who wish to sell to schools or any other government agency have always had to publish what those government agencies wanted to buy in order to make the sale; this fact has never been considered a violation of the publishers' First Amendment

rights. Although publishers may publish what they choose, the government is not obligated to buy. . . . The schools, as government agencies, are obligated by the Constitution not to discriminate and it is, at most, doubtful that they would have some First Amendment rights to discriminate where books are concerned but not in other respects.

Since all the states compel students to attend school, and to use the textbooks they furnish, it follows that all states must see that those textbooks do not deny "equal protection." So, if publishers wish to sell their textbooks to public schools, the question is not: Is racist and sexist content protected by the First Amendment? The question becomes: Is racist and sexist content something that "the State" can sponsor by allowing it in books that are mandatory reading, paid for at public expense?

This leads to an examination of just what "equal protection" entails. At the very least it entails an obligation not to undermine the Constitutional guarantee by a textbook presentation that helps cause differential treatment of any group of persons. To call such presentations "racist" or "sexist" is but an abbreviated description of the process. Creation of negative racial, sexual or other stereotypes traditionally has produced discriminatory, that is, unequal treatment. The publishing industry has, in part, confessed to past exclusion or distortion of information by recent movement in the direction of change. That change may be analogous to "affirmative action," as that concept is used in other contexts. We feel, however, that the industry must go much further in the direction of inclusion, and in the correction of distortion, so that the result can fairly be called "remedial history"—an affirmative search for the correction of past injustices. If substantial elements of a racial and ethnic hostility are due to past sins of omission and distortion, the obligation to remedy this is not merely moral; it is essential to implementation of the Fourteenth Amendment and, hence, is Constitutional and patriotic.

The National Council of Teachers of English (NCTE) states: "It is essential that the materials schools provide foster in the student not only a self-image deeply rooted in a sense of personal dignity, but also the development of attitudes grounded in respect for, and understanding of the diversity of, American society."

Children's sex and race are unalterable conditions of their very being. Children must not be forced to read textbooks that demean their identity, negate their culture or stifle their potential. Children must not be forced to read texts that distort their history, ignore their heroes or omit their people's perspectives. They must not be excluded from the pages of their textbooks. Each and every group and sex must feel included. Such *inclusion* is the moral and legal responsibility of educational publishers.

Although this may sound simple, publishers face enormous pressures for continued exclusion by those people who want to pretend the U.S. is all-white, all-Christian, all middle-class, nuclear, suburban family. This depiction of society is supported by well-organized and well-funded fundamentalist and John Birch-type organizations.

It is important that educational publishers avoid confusing criticism and pressure for greater *inclusion* of ideas, peoples and perspectives, with pressure for *exclusion* of ideas, peoples and perspectives. The former asks for implementation of the obligation to offer equal protection under the law. The latter asks for censorship.

The definition of censorship we offer is adequate for present purposes. It is derived from an article by E. J. Gaines in "Organized Censors Rarely Rest" (1977) edited by Edward A. Jenkinson: "Censorship in its broadest terms is the attempt to prevent the movement and the sharing of information." When information about and perspectives of women, racial minorities, agnostics, or any other large group of Americans are omitted from textbooks, it may be due to ignorance or it may be due to deliberate self-censorship by publishers.

Often such self-censorship is imposed to placate the exclusionists. It is an attempt to avoid controversy and consequent loss of sales. Ironically, however, it usually fails to placate the exclusionists, whose ultimate goal is to strip textbooks of all ideas and perspectives other than their own and to keep children innocent of the realities of U.S. life and even of the very meaning of the U.S. Constitution.

Publishers can take a number of steps to counteract the censors, and to fulfill their Constitutional obligations, while still selling their books.

They can make certain, for example, that the editors and writers assigned to prepare a new textbook represent a variety of perspectives or are, at the very least, sensitive to a variety of perspectives. This most likely will involve awareness-training of publishers' in-house staffs. It will involve input from groups whose history has traditionally been omitted or distorted (not just the customary use of photos of minority consultants as window-dressing, but actually soliciting and presenting their perspectives). It will involve developing publishers' in-house guidelines to avoid bias, in addition to seeing that the guidelines are actually used. It will also involve the industry's publicly stating its recognition that the U.S. is a pluralistic society and, therefore, bias-free textbooks are an industry goal.

Admittedly, inclusiveness in textbooks is not easy to achieve and will add extra burdens to the publishing process. But continual bowing by publishers to censors will result in class action suits, under the Fourteenth Amendment, by parents and by minority and feminist groups. The position educational publishers can take is to stand proud and unafraid and say forthrightly: "Look. Different groups have different perspectives. We live in a pluralistic society and have a social responsibility to all children and all parents. We are trying our best to include your perspective—along with many others—so that children can learn to understand and function in a multiracial, multicultural society. We refuse to censor particular perspectives just because your group objects to them. Nor will we censor your perspective to please other groups. We are accountable to all taxpayers, to all children."

Such a forthright stand could unite publishers with most educators, with most parents, and with most major church groups. Such a stand may not altogether quiet the censors, but it would surely pull their fangs and greatly reduce their credibility.

THE WOULD-BE CENSORS OF THE LEFT[5]

The traditional nay-sayers have always rampaged on the fringes of publishing and library service against what should not go into books for children—the super-patriots, the religious proselytizers, the total abstainers from everything, be it chewing gum or sex. The children's book world has grown used to efforts at censorship from this direction and is more or less prepared to combat them.

We are not so well prepared for the growing number of yea-sayers—those pushing such worthy causes as permanent peace and social justice for all. These groups have not only adopted the removal tactics of the nay-sayers, they press on to insist that their ends can only be achieved through children's books written and evaluated according to their so-called guidelines.

Last spring when he was moderating a panel as president of the Children's Book Council, Jim Giblin pinpointed these growing sources of censorship with a phrase. He called them "the would-be censors of the Left."

This phrase exactly fits the activities and stated motives of the ten-year-old Council of Interracial Books for Children, Inc. (CIBC), well-funded by annual gouts of money let from the coffers of the Carnegie Foundation for Change. CIBC has steadily expanded its founding concerns about the representation of racial minorities in children's trade books. Textbooks were added as targets for criticism. Then, ethnic minorities became a cause for CIBC concern. Two years ago CIBC discovered the women's rights movement and took up anti-sexism. Latterly, CIBC has also descried evidences of material-

[5] Editorial by Lillian N. Gerhardt, editor. *School Library Journal.* 23:7. Ap. '76. Reprinted by permission.

ism, individualism, escapism, and conformism in children's reading matter. In order to continue to exist, CIBC must continue to peddle the notion that children's books of the past and the present teem with evil hidden messages that publishers were too careless to prevent and librarians too dumb to discern.

CIBC's latest vehicle for this notion is a paperback it hopes to sell for $7.95 setting forth its peculiar method for judging children's books along narrowly doctrinaire lines. *Human (and Anti-human) Values in Children's Books* is, according to its subtitle, a set of "new guidelines for parents, educators, and librarians." (Presumably, this group will punish through failure to purchase the work of any writers or publishers who fail to pay attention to CIBC's dicta.)

A close reading of the unsigned, 24p. introduction to a collection of about 250 book reviews prepared by applying CIBC's definitions of the values it designates as human, shows there is nothing new in censorship whether it comes from the Left or the Right. There is the same old call for the control of writing, publishing, and evaluating children's reading matter. There is the same old insistence that tomorrow can be a better world if only the children of today are forced to ingest through their books what CIBC considers good for them. There is the same old refusal to grant authors their intents. (Good intentions, says CIBC, are not enough.) If writers fail to promote anti-sexism, anti-racism, anti-materialism, anti-elitism, anti-escapism, and anti-ageism, their books can only be rated as "harmless" or worse—sexist, racist, etc. "by omission." If the books are in any way anti to the antis listed above, they are harmful and to be shunned. No books or library collections can survive a CIBC guided scrutiny.

Let's try the CIBC method on Beatrix Potter's *The Tale of Peter Rabbit.* Peter is shown as actively naughty and his sisters as placidly obedient. (On CIBC's checklist, tick off "sexist.") Mr. McGregor is old, crotchety, and violent (tick off "ageist"). The picture and story show a fussy concern over clothes and food (tick off "materialist"). Peter's disobedience gets him a dose of medicine and his good sisters a lovely supper (tick off "conformism"). Consider the fact that Mr. McGregor fails to catch Peter and Peter is thus allowed to evade the reality of being eaten (tick off "escapist"). Refuse to consider any of Potter's well-documented intentions in writing and illustrating the story. What did she know? She might have included a positive note about race and she didn't (tick off "racist by omission").

Can Peter Rabbit be saved from such would-be censors of the Left? Yes. All it takes is enough common sense among librarians to see that censorship looks, sounds, and smells the same whether its coming from the Left or the Right. As CIBC says, its good intentions aren't nearly enough. Its methods must be judged by the destructive results.

CENSORSHIP IN THE SCHOOLS[6]

The first public burning of a book in America took place in 1650, when Thomas Pynchon's *The Meritorious Price of Our Redemption* was set aflame in the Boston marketplace by the common executioner. In his book *The First Freedom*, Nat Hentoff recalls the reason given for that burning: "The author's religious ideas, declared the authorities, differed from the colony's established religion and so had to be obliterated."

The last public burning of a book in America (as of this writing) took place in 1977, when 40 copies of a textbook, *Values Clarification*, were burned in Warsaw, Indiana, by a group of senior citizens. The book (along with the high school course for which it was used) had to go, the group claimed, because it taught situation ethics, moral relativism, and secular humanism. They feared it would destroy home-taught values.

[6] Article entitled "Censorship in the Schools: Something Old and Something New," by Dorothy C. Massie, NEA Teacher Rights Committee. *Today's Education.* 69:30 GS-34 GS. N./D. '80. Reprinted by permission of the National Education Association.

If a message is to be found in these two sad stories, perhaps it is this: Over centuries, though times and life-styles change and wars transform the political geography of the globe, the fundamental issues that divide one person from another remain much the same.

In 1977, as in 1650 and throughout the intervening years, supporters of some established version of morality and truth have condemned ideas they considered offensive and prohibited their utterance.

Book burnings in the public marketplace are not common occurrences. In public school classrooms and libraries, however, First Amendment rights are tenuous at best and often in conflict with other perceived rights. There, books, various other teaching materials, and entire courses of study are at all times vulnerable to the pressures of censorship. Probably at no time have the pressures been more severe than they are just now.

From the American Library Association (ALA), the National Council of Teachers of English (NCTE), newspapers, and teachers in all parts of the country come reports of angry citizens groups organizing to protest what they describe as the anti-Christian, anti-American, anti-authority, antifamily, pornographic influence of certain books and other instructional materials in the schools.

Judith Krug, director of the ALA's Office for Intellectual Freedom, estimates that between 1975 and 1980, three times as many censorship attempts were reported as in the preceding decade. She believes the cases that make the news don't begin to tell the whole story of censorship in the country today. Three hundred censorship controversies may be reported in a given year. Krug suggests that there may be ten times as many instances of uncontested removal or restriction of library and classroom materials and an even quieter kind of censorship—avoidance of all materials that might be controversial.

Who are the censors? Anyone with enough authority is a potential censor. The list of those who can censor school materials is long.

School boards. In 1979, a high school principal in Matthews County, Virginia, told one of his history teachers to withdraw assignment of Huxley's *Brave New World.* When the teacher went ahead with the assignment, the school board notified him that his contract would not be renewed.

In January 1980, the North Jackson, Ohio, board of education ordered removal from the high school library shelves of seven books: *Catcher in the Rye, Go Ask Alice, Hooper, Manchild in the Promised Land, Slaughterhouse Five, To Sir with Love,* and *Up the Down Staircase.*

The Anaheim, California, school board has banned from the schools all of Shakespeare but *Hamlet* and *Romeo and Juliet* and all of Dickens except *Oliver Twist.*

School administrators. A high school principal in Knoxville, Tennessee, cancelled the school library's subscriptions to a county newspaper after it criticized the school's policy of taking a commission on the charges for student pictures. The principal said he felt it was his duty to censor any publication that was not in the best interests of the school.

In May 1980, elementary students in Portsmouth, Rhode Island, received coloring books (published by the U.S. Environmental Protection Agency) with pages torn out. Their principal had found objectionable the portions of the books that alluded to the dangers of overpopulation. The deleted pages warned that four billion people inhabit the earth and that overpopulation can lead to crowded neighborhoods, heavy traffic, and air and water pollution.

Teachers and librarians. A 1977 survey by the National Council of Teachers of English indicated that teachers accounted for nearly 7.5 percent and librarians for nearly 3 percent of censorship in public schools.

State education agencies. In 1976, the Texas State Textbook Commission banned five common dictionaries that contain allegedly obscene definitions—for example, a definition of *bed* as a verb. The banning was prompted by complaints presented by Norma Gabler, who, with her husband, regularly submits bills of particulars on objectionable portions of textbooks being considered for adoption. From their home in

Longview, Texas, the Gablers operate Education Research Analysts, a tax-exempt organization that assists local censorship efforts. For a modest, tax-deductible contribution, they will send a file of textbook reviews that point out questionable items.

Textbook publishers. In 1974, violent book protest confrontations drew national attention to Kanawha County, West Virginia. The controversy heralded the current wave of censorship in the schools. In response, textbook publishers began to delete some of the materials that they were just beginning to include in the texts—materials that portrayed, for the first time, the racial and cultural diversity of the nation and the perspectives and contributions of minorities and women.

In a recent *Sixty Minutes* appearance, several textbook publishers acknowledged that they have revised some of their publications to ensure that they will pass the Gablers' scrutiny.

State legislatures. In 1975 the Oregon legislature adopted a textbook selection guidelines law which included the following language: "No textbook shall be used which speaks slightingly of the founders of the republic or of those who preserved the union or which undervalues their work." Similar legislation has been introduced but not passed in several other states, including Indiana and Pennsylvania.

The U.S. Congress (potentially). In September 1979, Sen. Paul Laxalt (R.-Nev.) introduced S. 1808, the Family Protection Act. Equal Rights Amendment opponent Phyllis Schlafly hailed the bill as marking "the dawn of a new era in federal legislation . . . toward more family responsibility and less federal control and spending." The proposed legislation has an ironic twist: Right-wing forces traditionally oppose federal aid to public education and its alleged consequence—federal control. S. 1808, however, provides the incentive of federal money to induce public schools to comply with the provisions. If S. 1808 were to become law, any local or state agency that did not comply with its provisions would lose funds under all applicable federal programs.

Education issues comprise the major portion of the bill.
Notably, it prohibits—
—Teaching of any course of instruction "seeking to inculcate values or modes of behavior which contradict the
demonstrated belief and values of the community."
—Use of any educational materials that would "tend to
denigrate, diminish, or deny the role differences between the
sexes as it [sic] has been historically understood in the United
States."
The bill also supports school prayer and private education
and attacks equal opportunity for young women in athletics,
agency shop for teachers, and the nondiscrimination requirement for federal aid recipients.
Who's pressuring for censorship?
An irate citizen storms into the educator's office, demanding
that a "subversive" textbook be censored. An equally angry visitor
insists that "money is being spent foolishly." A group descends
upon the superintendent to plead for a "return" to the three R's. A
minister lambastes the schools from his pulpit, while a politician
builds his criticism into his platform. Patriotic organizations bemoan the lack of fundamental Americanism, and college professors
decry the lack of fundamental learning.
Not only is American education under fire; the practice of criticizing our schools is well on its way to becoming a national pas-
time. For some, it is already a favorite armchair sport. For others,
it has become a full-time career.

That account might have been written yesterday, but it
wasn't. It is, in fact, the opening paragraph of a book published 18 years ago, *The Axe-Grinders* by Mary Anne Raywid.
Its analysis of the organized patterns of right-wing extremist
criticism of the schools is as timely today as it was in 1962.
This is not to say that all criticism of the schools is organized, right-wing in origin, or unjustified. It would be absurd
to claim that mistakes are never made in the selection of instructional materials or the shaping of educational programs
and methods. Reasonable, constructive criticism is necessary
to ensure that schools remain accountable to the people and
to help them do a better job.
Not all attempts at censorship, furthermore, come from

right-wing extremists. Efforts by minorities and women to remove such books as *Little Black Sambo* or *Mary Poppins* from
school libraries are efforts to censor. On the other hand, those
same groups often try to persuade schools and textbook publishers to provide books that treat women and minorities
fairly and that include their contributions to and viewpoints
on history. Such efforts seem to be just the opposite of censorship; they seek fairness and honesty, not exclusion.

At present, in fact, the schools are the target of criticism
and pressure from many segments of the population. In his
1976 book, *Values in Education,* Max Lerner analyzes this dilemma:

> Curiously, the people in the society expect the school to act as
> the final fortress, remaining firm even as the cracks are opening up
> in the society around it. The fact is that the family, the churches,
> the neighborhood, the community, the party system, the class and
> ethnic systems, the legal and sexual codes, the value system, have
> all been subjected to an intensive battering. So have the schools.
> Yet with a real confusion about what the schools can and can't do,
> many people expect them to assume the burdens which the other
> institutions have faltered in bearing.

Such times are the most hospitable to the demagoguery of
the radical right. Confused people often look for simple answers. Frustrated and angry people look for something or
someone to blame. People suffering the trauma of rapid, un-
settling change tend to look nostalgically to the past.

When the civil rights movement gathered momentum in
the early 1960s, many Americans were confused and fearful
for a variety of reasons. The right-wing extremists were ready
then with simple answers, easy culprits, and "good old days"
solutions.

At the peak of the civil rights movement in the later 1960s
and during the antiwar and student rights movements of the
late 1960s and early 1970s, the voices of the right were muf-
fled.

Over the past five years, however, those voices have returned in full force. They offer the schools as a scapegoat for
much of what is wrong with our society, offer the "good old

days" solution of censorship for what is wrong with the schools.

The targets of the censors today are similar to those of two decades ago. Prominent on their hit lists are materials by or about minorities and women; about the problems of poverty; or about cultures that differ markedly from that of white, middle-class Americans.

Sex education remains a major concern of the censors. *The Family Issues Voting Index,* a rating of Congress published by the Christian Voters' Victory Fund, complains that—

We know that love and sex should be taught in the home, accompanied by Biblical values and genuine compassionate guidance. But we allowed our schools to become smut factories, our textbooks sexbooks.

Teachers themselves are a central target of censors who call their competence and good faith into question. The censors allege that instead of teaching Johnny to read, teachers are clarifying his values; instead of teaching students to respect flag, God, and family, they are indoctrinating them into a "religion" called *secular humanism.*

Any teaching that encourages children to value human beings, their different cultures, beliefs, ways of life; any teaching of how human cultures developed on the earth or, indeed, of how life developed on the earth is considered the teaching of secular humanism. Some fundamentalist and right-wing groups maintain that secular humanism is a religion so they can argue that curricular areas they dislike are unconstitutional. The First Amendment mandate that our country have no officially supported religion prohibits the propagation of religion in public schools.

The censors of the radical right have many other concerns: not only what they want out of the schools, but what they want in—for example, prayer, the teaching of the creationist theory of how life developed on earth if the theory of evolution is taught, and the teaching of unquestioning loyalty to the free enterprise system and to the values of the Judeo-Christian tradition.

In general, the right-wing critics of education are moving in the same directions they have moved in the past. But in 1980, they are moving with new confidence.

The renewed vitality of right-wing censors today comes from the company they keep. Some of their associates are such men as Paul Weyrich, Richard Viguerie, and Howard Phillips, leaders of the ultra-right political apparatus headquartered in Washington, D.C., that is known as the New Right. Others are electronic preacher/politicians such as the Rev. Jerry Falwell, a Baptist minister from Lynchburg, Virginia, who has broadcast from coast to coast the message that "we must bring immoral public education to its knees." Falwell heads Moral Majority, a coalition dedicated to

mobilizing the grass roots of America . . . lobbying intensively in Congress . . . helping the moral majority of America fight obscene school textbooks. . . . and recruiting and training moral American men and women for political office.

Rev. Falwell's *Old Time Gospel Hour* finances his project with the $1 million a week it reportedly produces from his television congregations.

The censorship battles that teachers are confronting in school systems around the country are no isolated academic concern. Censorship activity is no longer the work of a few fanatics but an important tool in the political power plays of the radical right.

Such people as Mel and Norma Gabler, the textbook critics of Longview, Texas—even such men as the Reverend Jerry Falwell—are not at the center of New Right organization and influence. But theirs are the issues that give life to this movement. Through them the New Right hopes to translate its own political and economic agenda into the nation's political and economic agenda.

The ethics of the New Right's use of family issues to engage the attention and support of the American people is dubious. Certainly such use obstructs rational public discussion of important matters that require reasoned examination and debate.

Teachers and their organizations need to confront some serious issues in public education:

—Tax support of the schools

—The balancing of student rights, parent rights, and professional rights in the selection of instructional materials and development of educational programs

—How far First Amendment protections extend into the public school classroom, the school library, the public library.

Teachers and school administrators need to listen, too, to the legitimate concerns and criticisms of parents—conservatives, moderates, and liberals. The sound and fury raised by the extremist school critics stifles reasonable debate and threatens to place teachers in the position of retreat and self-defense.

Teachers and their advocates must recognize demagoguery for what it is and refuse to let it cut them off from attending to the real needs of parents and students.

EDITOR'S INTRODUCTION

When thousands of pupils boycotted the Kanawha County, West Virginia, public schools for a full school year in 1974–1975, national attention was drawn to a continuing and growing problem concerning parents, teachers and librarians, school boards and administrators, and students. Questions arose: What is to be taught in the schools of America and who decides? In Kanawha County, objections were to "vulgar language," "criticisms of Christianity," "emphasizing the violent and depressing aspects of life," and recently, questions of race and sex education, and "scientific creationism" versus evolution. The articles in this Section deal with school censorship at all levels of the educational establishment.

"The grand crisis of education: how to prevent the masses from learning what is fit only for their leaders," is how Walter Karp put it in his review of Frances FitzGerald's prize-winning *America Revised* in *Harper's*. He indicates that the first place in the schools where censorship can occur is in textbooks. He claims that throughout history those in power tended to depart from fact, and adapt historical concepts in textbooks to political needs at the time. English Professor Kenneth Donelson, in an article in *Top of the News*, cites censors on the teaching and library level; those who "prefer the old, the classic, the noncontroversial," and "never do anything remotely suspect or controversial or censorable," at the risk of violating students' rights.

As far as teacher censoring and having to contend with censoring is concerned, the Wisconsin Department of Public Instruction plan entitled "Dealing With Censorship" presents some simple, direct advice on how teachers and librarians can handle the censor and states "the more involvement reflected in selection, the less likely the chance that schools will find it necessary to mount a defense of materials." In a well-organized study published in *Contemporary Education*,

Carolyn Atkins and John Carline, educators at West Virginia University, examine court censorship cases and school district written policies (like the Wisconsin plan) concerning selection and restriction of materials in public schools.

In the fifth article in the Section, from *Phi Delta Kappan*, Professor Franklin Parker investigates all sides and all arguments in the bitter censorship battle of Kanawha County. Although it was about textbooks, the confrontation really involved the school board versus community control over education. The problem of textbook removal is also the subject of Pham Thien Hung, a Ph.D. candidate, in a Freedom of Information Center Report. He provides statistics on the large number of censorship cases involving the community and schools, but assures us that it "will abate in the long run."

The final article in the Section is an analysis of the derivation of school board authority. Martha L. Black explains, in the *Journal of Urban Law*, the term *in loco parentis* and its relationship to student's rights and she discusses the resulting court rulings pertaining to both.

TEXTBOOK AMERICA[1]

Writing American history is a harmless occupation, but teaching it to American schoolchildren is a political act with far-reaching consequences. The reason for this is clear. You cannot recount the past without making fundamental political judgments, and you cannot deliver those judgments in a classroom without impressing them deeply on the minds of future citizens. Children know a great deal about many things, but about public affairs they know virtually nothing. Most of us carry to our graves scarcely altered the political lessons we imbibed half-consciously from long-forgotten his-

[1] Article by Walter Karp, contributing editor. *Harper's.* 260:80–8. My. '80. Copyright © 1980 by Harper's Magazine. All rights reserved. Reprinted by special permission.

tory textbooks. Professors of American history erect Gothic cathedrals of erudition on political axioms acquired from their fifth-grade "social studies" readers. To teach American history to a great mass of American schoolchildren is to exercise genuine political power. Yet of all forms of political power, the power to teach history to children is the only one Americans have handed over without a struggle to a remote and unaccountable few, commonly known as the educational establishment. *America Revised*, by Frances FitzGerald, is an attempt to describe what the educational establishment has done with that power through the years.

FitzGerald's main achievement is the scutwork. She has pored through the pages of hundreds of musty American history textbooks, something nobody, I believe, has ever done before. She describes their contents, delineates their overall "philosophy," and shows how they changed from generation to generation. About what it all signifies, however, she has only confused and contradictory notions. She never really understands that her subject is the education—and miseducation—of a self-governing people. Still, FitzGerald's material is invaluable; when cast into a political history of which Fitz-Gerald seems blissfully ignorant, it reveals a great deal about the way we are currently ruled.

The history begins just before the turn of the century, when the first school managers powerful enough to impose their conception of history on a large number of children introduced the first American history text to the public schools. Until then what little history American schoolchildren learned they had direct from their schoolmarms by way of a sort of oral tradition. What they learned, however, they learned so well that historian Mark Sullivan blamed nineteenth-century schoolmarms for delaying our entry into the first world war. The only history they taught, Sullivan complained in his six-volume chronicle *Our Times*, was the American Revolution, and the way they taught it had made it impossible for most Americans to believe that England was fighting for "democracy against autocracy" in the trenches of France. The schoolmarms' American Revolution is readily reconstructed. On one side stood the tattered sons of liberty, whose forebears had come to an unknown continent in search of religious freedom. On the other side stood a tyrannical king and his arrogant Redcoats, foredoomed in their pride to a stunning defeat. What better way than this to inculcate love of liberty and hatred of tyranny in the future citizens of a free republic?

Since American educators always claimed they were providing "training for citizenship," the first history textbooks might have been expected to fortify the oral tradition of the schoolmarms. In fact, they did exactly the opposite. According to FitzGerald, the first history text taught children that the colonists had come to America for "commercial motives" and not for religious freedom at all. With that premise laid down, FitzGerald writes, the texts "looked on the American Revolution as a matter of practical politics more than anything else." Instead of the sons of liberty, the pioneer texts offered the sons of the dollar; instead of a revolt against arbitrary power, squalid maneuvering for economic advantage. The obvious lesson of these texts is that Americans who profess to fight against tyranny are probably hypocrites trying to make money, an excellent lesson if you happen to favor tyranny. Such was the "citizenship training" offered by the pioneer textbooks. Most American schoolchildren never read them, however, since they were used exclusively in a few big-city school systems "to Americanize" (as the phrase went) the children of immigrants. The first exercise of the power to teach history was an attempt to corrupt the utterly defenseless. It was also a harbinger of what was to come.

"Americanizing" native Americans was a far more delicate problem, and educational leaders were long reluctant to try it in any systematic way. The problem became inescapable, however, in the early years of the twentieth century, when, for the first time, Americans in large numbers began attending public secondary schools. This new turn of events, so far from being a source of pedagogical satisfaction, threw educators into a panic and set off the greatest crisis in the history of American education. The crisis was this: the public secondary schools, which had catered chiefly to the well-to-do and successful, adhered to a conditional liberal-arts curriculum of history, language, and literature—the "arts that liberate," as Montaigne has called them. With the children of ordinary people attending high school, American educators found themselves face to face with the specter that had haunted Europe for a century: the danger of educating people *beyond their station*, or, as the National Education Association preferred to put it, leading them "away from the pursuits for which they are adapted." The danger was largely political. By teaching the liberal arts to commoners, the new secondary schools might well become the spawning ground for popular tribunes, politically ambitious gutter snipes, and similar dangerous malcontents. As J. E. Russell, head of Columbia University Teachers College, put it in 1905: "How can we justify our practice in schooling the masses in precisely the same manner as we do those who are to be their leaders?"

Something had to be done quickly or democracy might one day break out. Educational leaders quickly worked out a solution. Let the secondary schools teach the children of workers what was fit only for workers. As Woodrow Wilson, president of Princeton, sternly advised the Federation of High School Teachers: "We want one class of persons to have a liberal education and we want another class of persons, a very much larger class of necessity in every society, to forgo the privilege of a liberal education and fit themselves to perform specific difficult manual tasks." Since there was no way to stop "the masses" from entering high school, the only way to meet the crisis, in short, was to prevent them from learning anything liberating when they got there. Instead, the educational leaders said, the new secondary schools should offer vocational training in particular and something called industrial education in general. This, the influential Douglas Commission said in 1905, was a "new idea" in education, and in truth it was. Until ordinary Americans began attending secondary school, no secondary school in the civilized world had ever seen fit to teach its students a trade. FitzGerald attributes this vulgar innovation to the supposed fact that lofty university presidents like Wilson and Russell had *lost* their influence over public education—a perfect example of thoughtless snobbery.

The "new idea" must have been somewhat perplexing to schoolmarms of the old-fashioned sort. The public schools were supposed to train citizens, yet here were the country's leading educators—"we"—insisting they regard their pupils not as future citizens but as future working hinds, whom Charles W. Eliot, president of Harvard, urged teachers to "sort" by their "evident or probable destinies." If the schoolmarms were troubled, however, a stalwart band of educational reformers stood ready to reassure them that training Americans for their industrial "destiny" was the heart and soul of "democratic" education. By far the most important of the reassurers was John Dewey.

Neither the subtle reasoning nor the ardent idealism of the famed educator mattered much in the history of American education. What proved important were a few of his salient principles. Suitably adapted, they have supplied educational leaders with the lasting framework for a pedagogical system designed to prevent "the masses" from ever learning in a classroom what a free people ought to know. For that purpose, Dewey's most important contribution was his conviction that democracy has little to do with politics and government. Democracy, according to Dewey, was "primarily a mode of associated living," which for most Americans chiefly meant working together in factories. Having stripped democracy of its political character, Dewey and his colleagues, who prided themselves on their "realism," went on to redefine it as "industrial cooperation." With this new, "realistic" definition, they effected a permanent pedagogical revolution. For one thing, it enabled the Deweyites (and more interested parties) to sever the venerable ties that bound the common schools to the needs and requirements of popular government. The schools were to be adapted instead, Dewey wrote in 1897, "to the circumstances, needs, and opportunities of industrial civilization." Instead of the American Republic, the

American economy would call the tune. The new "realistic" definition of democracy even stripped public education of its *theoretical* republican objective, which was, as Jefferson had said, to teach future citizens "how to judge for themselves what will secure or endanger their freedom." Such knowledge was unlikely to enhance, and might well impair, "industrial cooperation." The new object of "democratic" education, Dewey said, was to teach every child "to perceive the essential interdependence of an industrial society." Thus instructed, the future citizen (i.e., factory worker) would develop what Dewey called "a socialized disposition."

With economic "interdependence" as its subject and a "socialized" worker as its goal the new "democratic" curriculum had little place for history. For *political* history, which recounts the diverse deeds of men, there was to be no place at all. Jefferson had urged the schools to teach children political history so that Americans might "know ambition under all its shapes and [be] prompt to exert their natural powers to defeat its purposes." From the political past they would learn to detect the would-be despot wearing the cloak of the popular tribune and the oligarchy masquerading as the enlightened and the elect. How could free men protect their liberties if they never learned from political history that liberty, in fact, has ambitious enemies? To Dewey, on the other hand, political history was "undemocratic" (and FitzGerald wholeheartedly agrees with him) precisely because it deals with the deeds and intentions of ambitious men. The doings of the high and mighty, in Dewey's "realistic" view, were no business of American schoolchildren, who were to share in the public life of America by leading "a socialized life" in the American work force. Instead of political history they were to be given "social studies," which would teach them, among other industrial matters, about the modern division of labor ("how milk is brought to the city") and, in the loftier grades, about the "evolution" of American industry. Given such instruction, Jane Addams noted in her 1902 work *Democracy and Social Ethics,* American children would not only develop a cooperative disposition, but they would find their adult toil "much more exhilarating," realizing, as they did, the useful slot they were filling on the national industrial "team."

Stripping Deweyite "realism" of its idealistic trappings proved but the work of a moment to the educational leaders, who knew a good thing when they saw one. In 1911, a committee of the National Education Association, the largest and most influential of the teachers' organizations, urged the nation's high schools to drop history altogether, on the Deweyesque grounds that it failed to promote the "social efficiency" of the ill-bred. Social studies, history's fledging rival, would be better able, said the committee quite correctly, to "accommodate youngsters to existing conditions." That was not what Dewey had in mind, but it was latent in his "cooperative" precepts, and the educational leaders were not the only ones to realize it. Revealingly enough, the first public-school system organized on Deweyesque lines was established in 1907 in Gary, Indiana, a one-year-old company town founded by, and largely in thrall to, the U.S. Steel Corporation. J. P. Morgan knew a good thing when he saw one too. So did the United States Congress. Under President Wilson's leadership, it began funding "vocational education" in the public schools, the first serious federal attempt to shape the content of public education.

To the purblind Deweyites political history was elitist; to the powerful few it was politically dangerous—then and always. "Throughout history," as FitzGerald rightly notes (though, alas, only in a passing remark), "the managers of states have with remarkable consistency defined good citizenship as a rather small degree of knowledge of, and participation in, public affairs." To replace political history with Deweyite social studies was the perfect means of meeting the educational requirements of the powerful. In social studies, American youngsters would learn that America was chiefly an industrial system and not a republic at all, that a "good citizen" is a worker who gets up when the alarm clock rings and speeds to his job on time. In social studies, too, they would learn that the "real" history of America is the "development" of American industry—history without politics in it, which teaches the most corrupt of political lessons, that politics does not matter. Pedagogical wit could scarcely devise a better instrument for ensuring "a rather small degree of knowledge of, and participation in, public affairs." To replace political history with social studies has been the abiding goal of America's educational leaders since ordinary Americans began attending high school. Interestingly enough, it took them more than half a century to register a complete triumph.

FitzGerald does not try to explain why American parents, teachers, and local school boards resisted, circa 1911, what Americans since 1965 have accepted without demur. The general explanation, perhaps, is that corrupting a venerable republic is not the work of a day.

For one thing, the "new idea" of industrial education was a new idea seven decades ago. At the time, millions of Americans believed strongly that America was a democracy corrupted by industrial capitalism, alias "the money power." That America was nothing more than industrial capitalism—the essential axiom of social studies and Deweyism—had never crossed their minds. Indeed, it was still a fairly new idea even to advanced intellectuals. Americans were still a political people who thought in political terms. Samuel Gompers, the British-bred trade unionist, used to complain bitterly about the political proclivities of America's trade-union members. Instead of "bargaining at the workplace," as all good workers should, they insisted on contesting elections, backing insurgent candidates, and behaving for all the world as if they were citizens. Not surprisingly, Gompers was an ardent champion of "industrial education." Because Americans thought in political terms, they cared greatly about "the money power" but little about the division of labor. As for history, the only idea they had of it was political. In a history book you read about armies, wars, generals, rulers, heroes, and villains—George Washington on the one hand, George III on the other. What social studies was designed to root out of the popular mind had yet to be rooted out when the NEA urged the high schools to replace history with social studies.

The old habits of thought would no doubt have proved a

flimsy barrier had the educational leaders enjoyed in 1911 the power to impose their will on America's decentralized public education. Today, a quite small number of educators have virtually unchecked sway over the curriculum of America's public schools, which have become, as one educator put it in 1962, "a monolith under oligarchic control." The "textbook philosophy" (FitzGerald's phrase) the educational oligarchy propounds is the "philosophy" the textbook publishers dispense—one that the large majority of school districts will buy, and pass on to the overwhelming majority of students. In 1911 the educational elite had no such sweeping power. Local control of the common schools, though waning, had not yet become a sham. To a degree, it could still meet the purpose for which it was originally intended: preventing the "managers of states" from teaching a republic's children that "good citizenship" consists in "a rather small degree of knowledge of, and participation in, public affairs." The usurpation of local control in the years after World War I was to be an essential element in the corrupting of a venerable republic.

Events on the national political stage proved a still more formidable barrier to the designs of the educational leaders, and almost derailed them completely. When "industrial education" was first concocted, Americans had seemed a thoroughly defeated people. A handful of finance capitalists controlled the economic arteries; a disciplined Republican party held national politics in thrall. A powerful few seemed to reign supreme in virtually every career and profession. America, as Henry Cabot Lodge said at the time, had at last become "an aristocratic republic." Then, quite suddenly, middle-class Americans awoke from their slumber and discovered that they were as powerless as everybody else. To the shock and dismay of Lodge—who thought it the end of civilization as he knew it—middle-class Americans, a complacent bourgeoisie for decades, began pouring into the public arena, determined to overthrow "the machine," to curb monopoly and bring the "money power" to heel. Just when the leading educators were urging the schools to look on America as an "industrial society," middle-class Americans—who did the teaching, served on the school boards, and voted in the school board elections—had suddenly remembered that America was a republic, and an endangered one at that.

Traditional modes of thought, the absence of an educational oligarchy, and the middle-class political revolt combined to produce a surprising result. Although the new "industrial" pedagogy made rapid headway, America's schools, despite the united urging of big businessmen, trade unions, and leading politicians, refused to let go of history. Instead they fortified the curriculum with the only American history texts ever used that were not intended to corrupt future citizens. These texts flourished in the years between 1910 and 1930, which FitzGerald terms the "Hundred Flowers" era of American history texts. Written by trained historians, representing diverse points of view, the new texts, born of the Progressive revolt, were intensely political and remarkably free of cant. Their virtues are well worth noting, because eliminating those virtues was to be the immediate task of the educational establishment, which had to put off for another generation the extinction of political history.

The most popular textbook of the period was *American History,* by David Saville Muzzey, first published in 1911. It was the antithesis of "industrial education" in every respect, since the grand lesson of Muzzey's text was that politics matters greatly, and matters to every citizen. Muzzey's readers learned, first and foremost, that the actions of people made American history and that the high and the mighty, in fact, have power—a liberating truth in itself. Moreover, the powerful bore constant watching, for villainy was not unknown in high places. In Muzzey's history President Polk, for one, was a bastard who instigated an unjust war with Mexico in order to grab some territory. Readers of Muzzey learned that democracy in America, too, bore watching. Indeed, Muzzey's history of America is largely the history of the vicissitudes of democracy. A Yankee Republican of the old school, Muzzey seems to have viewed all modern life as one giant menace to liberty and self-government. The major problem of the age, he warned young readers, was "the corruption of the government by the money power." American democracy needed defending, and it had nothing to do with industrial cooperation.

Muzzey's most successful rival was Willis Mason West, whose textbook *American History and Government,* published in 1913, seems to have been a rejoinder to Muzzey's. Whereas the latter thought democracy in America had gone from a Golden Age to the dogs, West, more a man of the Left, commenced his history with the bold assertion that "democracy has as yet been tried only imperfectly among us." Politically divergent though they were, the two leading texts agreed on the main point. American history was essentially political history, and the dramatic theme of that history, the impulse of political life and the catalyst of action, was the struggle over democracy itself.

While texts such as these were circulating (often in watered-down revisions), the educational leaders seem to have bided their time until they were powerful enough to eliminate from the curriculum history lessons so inconducive to "social efficiency" and so unlikely to "accommodate youngsters to existing conditions." All through the post-Versailles years the nascent educational establishment, backed by state legislators, strengthened its hold on the public schools and on the schools that train public-school teachers. During those years the number of local school districts was cut from 120,-000 to less than half that number. State educational commissions were established to reduce still further the formal autonomy of the remaining districts. By a dozen different devices—licensing laws, state guidelines, and so on—control of the curriculum passed completely out of the hands of citizens and into the grip of an increasingly tight-knit, ingrown professional oligarchy. All it needed to emasculate the lingering "Hundred Flowers" tradition was a sharp change in the political atmosphere. With the outbreak of World War II the oligarchy struck at once, and the tradition, FitzGerald says, came "abruptly" to an end. For the next twenty-five years every new textbook used in the schools was written on the assumption that its readers were potential subversives.

In the new textbooks, which soon swept the country, political history became a hollow and meaningless form. Politics was reduced to acts of government, and villainy in high places vanished from the past. All American wars were now righteous and all American Presidents virtuous men who did, FitzGerald writes, "as well as could be expected given difficult circumstances." Imperialism, a term freely applied in the earlier texts to America's seizure of the Philippines, was now reserved exclusively for overseas ne'er-do-wells. Jingo nationalism, refreshingly absent in the "Hundred Flowers" era, pulsated through every page of the new propaganda texts. "There is a fascination with patriotic symbols," FitzGerald reports, "the flag, Independence Hall, the Statue of Liberty." Readers were adjured to accept, admire, and adore virtually everything about America except its republican institutions. In the new propaganda texts—and this is the telltale of their calculated corruptness—democracy ceased to be the theme and catalyst of American history; it excited no strife, inspired no banners, and suffered no defeats. Instead it became the fixed and unchanging attribute of the United States, like the spots on a leopard—"a Platonic form abstracted from history," as FitzGerald well puts it. Severed from history, democracy ceased to be menaced by anything except foreign enemies and their domestic agents, whose activities in the neighborhood, one textbook advised, should be promptly reported by "young people" to the FBI, "in line with American traditions."

Even as a "Platonic form," however, democracy was too dangerous to describe at length. From the new textbooks readers learned that democracy meant the right to vote and nothing more, a definition that does not distinguish America's republican institutions from the totalitarian politics of the Soviet Union. Even reduced to a nullity, democracy, to the educational establishment, was still too dangerous to praise too highly. The fear that citizenship might break out haunts the pages of the propaganda textbooks. Instead of lauding democracy, the textbooks found subtle ways to denigrate it. One

of the major texts of the era, FitzGerald says, "concludes with
an essay extolling the virtues of freedom not for its own sake
but merely as the greatest asset in the world struggle." A
more common technique of denigration was the textbooks'
insistence that what was truly great about America was its
enormous gross national product. The textbooks, FitzGerald
says, were "far more enthusiastic" about the GNP than about
the Bill of Rights. Without eliminating political history entirely, the textbooks, which devoted considerable space to
"industrialization," were hearkening back to the corrupt
basic tenet of Deweyism—that America was not a republican
polity but, far more important, an industrial system. Times
had changed, however. Whereas "cooperation" had been the
dubious deity of the original industrial pedagogy, the new
deity enshrined in the propaganda texts was productivity
pure and simple. One prominent junior-high-school history
text argued, for example, that slavery was not all that bad because it alleviated America's chronic shortage of labor.
Whereas Lincoln had said that if slavery were not evil then
nothing was evil, this modern school text, still in use ten years
ago, taught children that nothing is evil if it enhances production—the common principle of the capitalist, the commissar,
and the tyrant.

Such were the corrupt history textbooks the educational
oligarchy inflicted on a republic's children, from the bombing
of Pearl Harbor to the bombing of North Vietnam. Around
1965 that textbook era, too, came to an end with what Fitz-
Gerald calls "the most dramatic rewriting of history ever to
take place" in America. The cause of this eludes her, but it
was quite obviously the civil-rights movement that provided
the main spur for revision. At a stroke it exposed the sham of
the propaganda textbooks. American democracy could hardly
remain a "Platonic form abstracted from history" while
Americans were out in the streets and on the hustings fighting
for political liberty. Moreover, insurgent blacks demanded a
place in the history texts, which had ignored their very existence for decades. Thanks to the civil-rights movement the
time was peculiarly ripe for restoring to American classrooms

a deeper and more exacting political history than even Muzzey and West had provided. Here was yet another educational crisis, almost comparable to the construction of high schools at the turn of the century. Educational reformers hit on a solution at once. If the corrupt political-history texts were doomed, what American schoolchildren should get in their stead was no political history at all.

One group of reformers, known as "The New Social Studies Movement," urged the educational establishment to teach sociology instead of history. Whereas the established social studies made do with crude notions such as the division of labor, the New Social Studies would teach budding scholars how to use such refined social-science concepts as "role," "status," and "culture." This, the reformers said, would sharpen their "cognitive skills," as it had so manifestly done for professors of sociology. The American past could remain in the curriculum, but only as a "laboratory for testing social science concepts," to quote a New Social Studies manifesto. Grinding American history into sociological mush readily recommended itself to the educational bureaucrats in the Kennedy Administration, which supported the endeavor with the customary avalanche of grants.

A second group of reformers urged the school managers to offer textbooks that were "relevant" to the immediate problems of "disadvantaged" minorities. What these disadvantaged needed, their self-appointed spokesmen said, were history texts that enhanced their ethnic and racial "pride." Since no political history of America could possibly make anyone proud of being scorned, proscribed, betrayed, or enslaved, the new ethnicity, too, won rapid and pious approval. Through a judicious blend of "social-science concepts" and sops to ethnic pride, the educational establishment has found another way to secure "a rather small degree of knowledge of, or participation in, public affairs." It is not really new, however. It is simply the old industrial education dressed up in a new disguise.

As in the old industrial pedagogy, the first principle of the contemporary textbooks is that America is not a republican commonwealth. It is merely a society like a dozen others, including outright tyrannies and totalitarian regimes. That, of course, is fundamental to any system of corrupt education in America, as educational leaders had realized more than half a century before. Over the years, however, industrialism had lost its savor. The new America of the textbooks is not an industrial society anymore. It is now, FitzGerald says, a "multiracial, multicultural society" composed of distinct ethnic groups and races, each with its own history, achievements, and heroes—César Chavez for Mexican-Americans, for example. This new textbook America, with its "multiple perspectives," FitzGerald regards as an intellectual advance over the "outdated" view of America as a nation-state. On the other hand, she notes, taking both sides of every issue from sheer inability to decide what is important and what is mere cant, this new textbook America is indistinguishable from Yugoslavia, or, for that matter, the Ottoman Empire. America's future citizens, previously taught to regard themselves as workers, are now taught to regard themselves as ethnic tribesmen—"We're family"—who must learn to live harmoniously with other tribes cohabiting on the North American continent and especially with American Indians, who, being the most tribal, are the most admired figures in the contemporary history texts. Millions of young Americans, for example, know more about Ishi, the last "wild Indian"—he was captured in 1911—than they do about the Founding Fathers. A number of contemporary history texts begin with glowing accounts of the Aztecs and the Mayans in line with the basic textbook principle that America is a lot of tribes living in North America. "Poor Columbus," FitzGerald writes. "He is a minor character now, a walk-on in the middle of American history." So, too, is the American republic.

Like the old social studies of "industrial development," the new history texts offer a past shorn of politics and virtually devoid of people. The educational leaders have at long last triumphed over the very idea of political history. In the new textbooks no man and no deed is responsible for anything. History, in the social-science "laboratory" of the textbooks, is now the product, FitzGerald says, of "impersonal institutions and faceless social forces," which she regards as more "democratic" than political history—exactly what it is not and can never be. On the other hand, she is dismayed to discover that "there is no known case of anyone's creating a problem for anyone else" in this wonderland of abstractions. It is impossible for anyone to do so. In the new sociologized history texts, no human being has ever enjoyed sufficient power to do anything for good or ill. Famous men, in this "democratic history," are loci of impotence with illustrious names attached. Watergate, in the latest texts, is something that *happened* to Richard Nixon, and history in general is a slew of forces, pressures, and disasters inflicted by fate on the high and the mighty, who appear as hapless men of goodwill. "There are," FitzGerald says, "no human agencies left."

To erase every trace of human action, the textbooks perform prodigies of verbal mendacity. In one typical textbook, FitzGerald says, the authors attribute the "problems" facing post-Reconstruction America to "the era of Reconstruction," as if an "era" can possibly cause anything. In the no-action history of the textbooks, abstractions do everything because humans are forbidden to do anything. At all costs the readers must never be allowed to suspect that people are capable of making a difference. Like the Stone Age tribes they are asked to admire, our children are now taught to regard the American past as an incomprehensible destiny as empty of human purpose as the landscape of the moon.

With the extinction of political history the educational oligarchy has finally resolved the grand crisis of twentieth-century education: how to prevent the masses from learning what is fit only for their leaders. From the new textbooks, the children of the American republic will never gain knowledge of, or the slightest incentive to participate in, public affairs. Nor will they ever learn from their sociologized texts how to detect "ambition under all its shapes." What the new textbooks teach on every page and with every passive verb is that, for all practical purposes, there is no such human activity as public affairs and no such human motive as political ambition. How can there be when "faceless social forces" make our history and the high and the mighty appear only as the victims of fate? No reader of these degraded texts will ever learn from them how to "judge for themselves what will secure or endanger their freedom." The new textbooks have snuffed out the very idea of human freedom, for that freedom at bottom is precisely the human capacity for action that political history records and that the textbooks are at such pains to conceal. In the "multiracial, multicultural" America of the textbooks every citizen is a tribesman and every tribesman the hapless subject of powers and dominions he does not even know exist. Such is "good citizenship" in the corrupted common schools of contemporary America.

The educational establishment, FitzGerald concludes, has deprived Americans of their "birthright," a personal loss she sincerely laments, but the judgment scarcely covers the ground. What the *political* history of the textbooks reveals is that a powerful few, gaining control of public education, have been depriving the American republic of citizens, and popular government of a people to defend it. And the American history textbook, so innocent-seeming and inconsequential, has been their well-chosen instrument.

TEACHERS AND LIBRARIANS AS CENSORS[2]

I've been an English teacher since I left the University of Iowa twenty-seven years ago clutching a master's degree in English and an Iowa Teaching Certificate and wending my way to a small western Iowa town to teach ninth- and tenth- and eleventh- and twelfth-grade English classes plus one speech class. Given the period, I wasn't surprised to learn

---

[2] From article entitled "The Enemies Within: Teachers and Librarians as Censors," by Kenneth Donelson, professor of English, Arizona State University. *Top of the News.* 35:233–6. Spring '79. Reprinted by permission of the American Library Association. Copyright © 1979 by the American Library Association.

from the superintendent that I was doomed or destined to other duties, among them supervising a study hall, advising the school newspaper staff, preparing kids for speech tournaments, directing the junior and senior class plays, and running the small school library. (Later, I was to be line coach in football and freshman basketball coach, the only assignments for which I received additional pay. The superintendent was genuinely surprised and irritated to find out that I did not want to drive a schoolbus, since other teachers often supplemented their meager salaries that way.) I was young, doubtless unprepared for the reality of teaching, but even at that, the enormity of my job (or jobs) at times annoyed or frightened or bewildered or intrigued or disturbed me.

I should have been more disturbed and far more prepared than I was, for in that first year I came under attack from the censors for books I used in my classes, for books I ordered for the library, for plays I considered for the senior class production, and for some readings I okayed for both humorous and dramatic interpretations in speech tournaments. My knowledge of censorship was entirely academic, a reverence for Milton's *Areopagitica* and a graduate paper on the 1737 Licensing Act. About censorship in schools I knew nothing, but I was a fast learner, and some conversations with other English and speech teachers and librarians and as much reading as I could find in various professional journals alerted me to a problem and a way of life of which I had been totally unaware.

What I read and heard from others all those aeons ago annoyed and frightened and bewildered and intrigued and disturbed me. I heard about administrators and parents and school boards who feared controversy and who clearly didn't want their children educated but indoctrinated. That surprised me, though it does not surprise me now. But I was shocked and dismayed to discover that many teachers and librarians for any number of reasons or rationales or rationalizations did not consider education the duty of the school. Whatever their motivations, they favored restrictions and censorship and indoctrination. With them around, the rest of us sometimes worried more about enemies within than without.

Of course, outside pressure groups still abound under names like Parents for God, Home, and Country; Churches United for Decency; Save Our Children; Concerned Citizens and Taxpayers for Decent School Books; and Parents of New York—Unite. Some administrators can still be counted on to say things such as "We don't wish to have any controversial books in the bookstore or the library." Some students would like to censor books to save other students from their baser natures. And we will always have with us people like Mel and Norma Gabler, who help us move steadily onward and into the nineteenth century.

These people—the parents, the administrators, and the students—I can survive, just as education can survive them. What I cannot accept are those enemies within, English teachers and librarians who for one reason or another or for one approach or another ally themselves with the censors outside the schools. I have thirteen types I could do without. Education could do without them. Students could do without them.

First, some teachers/librarians wave the banner of "high standards" and mouth words like, "We have to set some *standards* for these kids" or "Students should be allowed to read only the very best." They impose on young people, not the freedom to read, but a duty to read only that which these teachers/librarians think good. They prefer the old, the classic, the noncontroversial, and become the natural allies of censors in getting rid of suspect or controversial or modern materials. Censors like restrictive teachers/librarians.

Second, some teachers/librarians say, "We have no right to teach or stock or recommend anything anybody might object to. If we can't abide by the standards of the community, we ought to get another job." I'd agree that we probably ought to remind ourselves periodically that the teacher/librarian as town censor is a far older notion than that of the teacher/librarian as educator and fighter of censorship. But

English teachers have supposedly allied themselves against censorship since the publication of the first edition of NCTE's "The Students' Right to Read" in 1962; and whatever the feeling of early members of the American Library Association, 1939 supposedly marked its turning point, for in that year ALA adopted the first version of the Library Bill of Rights. Teachers/librarians who see themselves as guardians of the status quo of the community and who look upon people who do not share that belief as radicals set back the cause of education. They do not so much ally themselves with censors; they are censors.

Third, some teachers/librarians can say with a straight face, "Young people are so sweet and innocent. Why do teachers want to corrupt them with literature that is filthy and indecent? After all, filth is filth, and a dirty word is a dirty word no matter who uses it or how it is used." These people are so ignorant of reality and literature and kids that they have no business being in the schools. They too are censors.

Fourth, some teachers/librarians have no self-image, viewing themselves as educational doormats waiting patiently for administrators or parents to walk over them, giving in at any time to any pressure, no matter how slight. They may once have been hurt in a censorship battle and lost heart, or they may play the role because they know no better. They may bore kids to death, the only crime for which I still favor capital punishment, but they never do anything remotely suspect or controversial or censorable. Censors like to walk on them.

Fifth, some teachers/librarians say, "If we don't talk about censorship or even think about it, it won't happen." Presumably, the belief of these ostrichlike people is that to name something is to cause something. These people will rarely talk about past censorship incidents because they are fearful, and, being fearful and being unwilling to communicate to other teachers, they almost certainly insure the likelihood of other teachers being totally unprepared to face similar incidents. They inadvertently help the censors.

Sixth, some teachers/librarians refuse to accept the possibility that censorship can strike them. They refuse to prepare selection policies or ways of handling censors since that "would irritate the people around here." The censor could ask for no better help than an unsuspecting and unprepared teacher/librarian.

Seventh, some teachers/librarians lack the guts or drive or ingenuity to work toward establishing clear guidelines for selection and a policy to handle censorship. These teachers/librarians are unprofessional or lazy or both, and they do not consult ALA or NCTE materials that might help them. The censor would be happy to have many more of these teachers/librarians.

Eighth, some teachers/librarians do establish guidelines for selection of materials and a policy to handle censorship, but they do not involve the administration in the policy-making decisions. Lacking the administrators' involvement or awareness, they may not get their support; they certainly don't deserve support. Or they may get administrative support, *but* they then fail to bring their work before the school or library board for formal and necessary approval. Or they do not remind the board yearly about the policies, particularly for new members after the board election. I have known several schools to have good policies about which the boards knew nothing and could not support out of ignorance. The censors like teachers/librarians who irritate administrators and board members.

Ninth, some teachers/librarians fear censors so much they place offending books on closed or reserved shelves, even hiding them, thus making books inaccessible while not precisely banning them. The card files may indicate that these books are still available, while students will be told that they are "lost" or "stolen" or "in the bindery" or something of that nature. One public librarian said she'd withdrawn a book under attack and added, "I've put it in a special place and haven't told anyone about it. Isn't that a good way to handle it?" The censor would think that was an excellent way.

Tenth, some teachers/librarians handle the problem by ripping out offending pages or marking over offending passages or "diapering" offending illustrations (that last really happened with Sendak's *In the Night Kitchen*). These people aid censors by doing their work for them.

Eleventh, some teachers/librarians question whether controversial or widely censored books need be available in the libraries or the classrooms since kids can find them in bookstores anyway, as one person told me recently and sneeringly, *"If* they really *care* for *that* sort of thing." Budgets and selection policies may be involved here, but the teacher/librarian who bans books from the school solely or primarily because they're available elsewhere is guilty of class censorship, since only kids who can afford the book will find it readily available.

Twelfth, some teachers/librarians are so passionately dedicated to intellectual freedom and so opposed to censorship that they jump into any battle without determining the facts, a noble way to make asses of themselves. One rule of thumb in any censorship incident is to find out what happened before defending anyone or attacking anyone else; otherwise we may harm our cause and our book. That would please any censor.

Finally and sadly, some teachers/librarians see themselves as agents of social change and use reevaluation of books as a way of censoring evils. They are usually liberals who hate racism and sexism and attempt to eliminate these evils by eliminating books they see as racist or sexist. Dedicated they are, and I fear them, since they are censors of the left, and their form of censorship, for good and noble reasons, clearly differs in motivation but not at all in outcome from the more conventional and conservative censors. I object to this last group more than any other because they are thinking people who censor, people who ought to be freeing children but instead are restricting them. Once the door is open to anyone to censor, then it cannot be closed because one kind of censorship is said to be good and another is said to be bad. All censors would argue that they censor for good and moral reasons.

The freedom to read allows our students and us to consider and question and wonder about the truths proposed by writers, past and present. Reading encourages our students and us to challenge anything in our search for our own truth or truths. In our search through books, we may find some truths and conditions and situations and people that are distressing or unpleasant—which says little about books but much about the nature and state of humanity. Students live with mortals, not angels, and books tell about our relationships with one another. Students have the right to pursue ideas and truths wherever those ideas and truths take them. To restrict the students' right to know is to censor, and *that* teachers/librarians must oppose. Not to oppose censorship and those teachers/librarians who practice or support it is to be derelict in our duty to ourselves, to our society, and, most of all, to our students.

DEALING WITH SCHOOL CENSORSHIP[3]

Introduction

Education of students requires that materials be selected for use in instruction. The task of selecting appropriate media center materials is not an easy one. Even the most carefully and thoughtfully chosen material in a print or audiovisual format can be subject to question.

This document focuses primarily on censorship as it relates to media center materials. Its purpose is to identify the procedures that should be followed in the development of appropriate standards of selection, to identify procedures for handling complaints that may arise, and to provide a list of appropriate agencies which can offer assistance in dealing with censorship in Wisconsin schools. Although similar suggestions are available from many sources, especially national ones, a need exists for a document with suggestions from a Wisconsin viewpoint.

[3] From publication entitled *Suggestions for Dealing with Censorship of Media Center Materials in Schools: a Wisconsin Plan,* by the Wisconsin Department of Public Instruction, Division for Library Services. Rev. Ja. '81. p 1–5. Reprinted by permission.

Materials Selection Policy

The Department of Public Instruction urges every Wisconsin school district to have an official board approved policy for the selection of materials used in the instruction of its students. Such a policy expresses the philosophy of the school district and indicates the role of selection in furthering the aims of the philosophy. It includes the following major areas:

    I.   Statement of policy
         A.   Objectives of selection
         B.   Responsibility for selection
    II. Statement of selection procedures
         A.   Criteria for selection
         B.   Procedures for selection
    III. Procedures for reconsideration of challenged materials

The Bureau of Instructional Media Programs recommends that "Policies and Procedures for Selection of Instructional Materials, 1976," published by American Association of School Librarians, be used as a guide in the development of or review of a materials selection policy.

Another recommended guide available for the development or revision of selection policies is "Selection of Instructional Materials: A Model Policy and Rules," 1980, developed by a committee of the Iowa Department of Public Instruction and published by the Iowa Department of Public Instruction.

A decision should be made at the outset as to whether the policy will cover all instructional materials or only those purchased by or housed in the instructional media center. Wherever possible, one policy for the selection of instructional materials including IMC and classroom materials should be adopted. While active participation by persons including teachers, administrators, students and media specialists in the development of a selection policy is always expected, a materials selection policy which includes classroom instructional materials such as textbooks and supplementary readers must be developed through a broad base of participation by teachers, such as subject area representation on the planning committee.

The bureau suggests that the materials selection policy:

a. be developed by media specialists, administrative staff, and teaching staff with input from the community;
b. be approved by the school board;
c. be reviewed for currency every three years. The school board should review and approve any recommended changes.
d. provide the basis for in-service training for teaching and administrative staffs in the area of material selection and utilization;
e. be the actual basis for selection of instructional and recreational materials, including materials reflecting the cultural diversity and pluralistic nature of American society. The selection process should actively involve media specialists, teachers, and students.
f. reflect the needs of all students, including those with exceptional education needs.

It is also suggested that a note be made of the anticipated need served through purchase of the material such as the curricular area to which it relates or recreational use.

Policy for Reconsideration of Materials

Every selection policy should include a section relating to procedures to follow in reconsidering materials which are questioned.

It is suggested that the reconsideration policy for materials:

a. be developed cooperatively with media specialists, teaching personnel, administrative staff with input from the community;
b. be reviewed carefully before presentation to the school board—a dry-run through the policy is advisable;
c. be reviewed and approved by the school board as part of the materials selection policy and, as such, be reviewed every three years;
d. be presented in in-service training sessions to teachers and administrators, with invitations to school board members and interested community members to attend.

An example of a citizen's request for reconsideration is found in "The Students' Right to Read," published by the

National Council of Teachers of English in 1972. In addition, "Policies and Procedures for Selection of Instructional Materials," published by the American Association of School Librarians, includes a checklist for the school media advisory committee with the responsibility of reviewing the material in question.

Public Information

One of the keys to meeting the challenge of the prospective censor is to maintain an ongoing public information program within the environs of the school, parent community, and community at large. This is an endeavor that must not be taken lightly. The more involvement reflected in selection, the less likely the chance that schools will find it necessary to mount a defense of materials.

It is recommended that:

a. media specialists, teachers, and administrators promote the media program, not only within the school, but also to parents and the general community on a regular basis. In order to accomplish this task successfully, a media program of which the school and community can be proud should be developed. Remember: the trust and respect of the community is earned, not given.

b. media specialists personally meet and become acquainted with the editor or education editor of the local newspaper. This may be accomplished by a personal visit or phone call, initially, followed by appropriate news releases or other contacts. Remember to also make contact with the local radio and/or television station, as well.

c. the materials selection process be shared with parents and other interested parties. Don't make the process a mysterious secret. Aside from articles in newspapers and general school communications, consider a program for parents, students, and others that would define the process and answer questions.

d. teachers be involved extensively in the selection process. Teacher support is as important as that of the community.

e. the school principal be involved in determining appropriate selection and reconsideration policies, and once these are

adopted by the school board, that he/she keep them in easy
reach.

f. the media specialist periodically review the approved selection and reconsideration process with administrators, teachers, and school board members.

Challenged Materials

Regardless of how carefully material is selected, some
members of the community may express concern or dissatisfaction about the appropriateness of selected materials. It is
important that the approved steps in the reconsideration
process be followed. If concern is expressed or an inquiry is
made to a school board member, administrator, or teacher,
that person should be sure to direct the complainant to the
appropriate professional person, and *not* attempt to assume
sole responsibility for reconsideration. The steps are set up to
be followed in sequence when they are needed. Not following
the steps can result in unnecessary confusion or delay.

When a concern is expressed, it is recommended that:

a. the person expressing concern be treated with respect. Remember that such a person has the *right* to request that material be reviewed. Do not take the inquiry personally.

b. material which is questioned should remain in normal use
until a final decision has been made based on the approved
reconsideration policy.

c. school personnel behave in an objective manner. Always follow the predetermined reconsideration policy.

d. the school administration be informed of the initial question
immediately, and be kept informed of any further developments that may occur. Use this as an opportunity to reac-
quaint the administrator with the written and approved policy.

e. accurate information from the school perspective be provided through proper school channels (such as the public relations officer or district administrator) if the inquiry reaches
the press.

f. it be remembered that while a parent has the right to judge
whether material is acceptable for his/her child, "no parent
or group of citizens has the legal right to abridge the rights of

other parents and teachers or children to have access to the information which is part of the educational program."
g. complaints originating within the school (from teachers, students, administrators, media specialists, and others) be governed by the school's written and approved policy for selection and reconsideration of materials.

READING MATERIALS IN THE PUBLIC SCHOOLS[4]

Introduction

Historically, there have been many conflicting opinions and much violent action regarding the selection and restriction of reading materials in the public schools. The significance of the problem becomes apparent when the following questions are considered: Does the First Amendment to the Constitution of the United States guarantee to public school students the freedom to read any material? Does an attempt by parents or others to restrict reading materials which they deem objectionable constitute a violation of the First Amendment? What role, if any, should the public play in the selection and restriction of public school reading materials? Finally, if interested citizens do object to specific public school reading material, what procedure should educators follow to resolve the conflict?

The purpose of this investigation was to examine relevant court rulings and current public school district written policies pertaining to the selection and restriction of reading materials. Specifically, the study was designed to gather and present information related to the two critical areas of (1) selection and restriction of such materials, and (2) written policies relevant to such selection and restrictions. First, briefs of

[4] From article entitled "Reading Materials in the Public Schools: Selection and Controversy," by Carolyn Peluso Atkins, assistant professor, department of speech pathology and audiology, and John L. Carline, associate dean, College of Human Resources and Education, West Virginia University. *Contemporary Education.* 51:182–5. Summer '80. Reprinted with the permission of the authors and Indiana State University.

leading cases were presented which define the law in regard
to the selection and restriction of reading materials in the
public schools. Secondly, written policies are given that represent current practices in public schools.

Upon examination of cases handled by state and federal
appellate courts, thirteen appeared to be relevant to the
issues of concern in this investigation. Thus the thirteen cases
from both the state and federal courts involving the selection
and restriction of reading materials in the public schools were
analyzed and briefed. These cases were divided into four
groups based upon similar issues: (1) cases involving evolution
and the freedom of religion; (2) cases seeking to have reading
materials used in the public schools; (3) cases seeking to prevent the use of materials in the public schools; (4) cases involving dismissal of teachers for use of certain reading materials. For the sake of brevity, abstracts of the cases will not be
presented in this article. However, it can be concluded that
controversies involving the selection of reading materials in
the public schools appear to be increasing. This is evidenced
by the fact that eight of the thirteen cases which have
reached the appellate court level have occurred in the 1970s.

While recognizing the responsibility of the courts to safe-
guard First Amendment freedoms of religion and expression,
the courts have invariably confirmed the authority of the legislative branch of government to control the public schools.
Therefore, the courts are reluctant to intercede in disputes
arising in the school system and will do so only to protect
basic constitutional rights. (*Scopes vs. State of Tennessee*,
1927; *Epperson et al. vs. Arkansas*, 1968). In those cases
where a procedure was established and followed, the courts
have refused to question the decisions reached, unless there
has been a clear showing of arbitrary and capricious actions
on the part of those conducting the proceedings (*Minarcini
vs. Strongsville City School District*, 1974). The court actions
indicate the importance of school systems' having an established written policy or procedure related to the selection
and restriction of reading materials (*Grosser vs. Woollett,
1974; Parker vs. Board of Education of Prince George's*

County, MD, 1965). Such policies must be available and well-known to all persons involved and interested in the selection and/or restriction of reading material (*Parducci vs. Rutland, 1970*). Without an established policy or procedure, the risk of having selection and/or restriction decisions overturned is increased. The risk is not necessarily because the decisions arrived at were erroneous, but because the parties involved were denied due process of law in the decision-making proceedings. Administrators or school boards must insure opportunities for the concerned parties to be heard and must have justification for their actions (*Parducci vs. Rutland, 1970*).

Population

The population for the survey of current written policies consisted of 989 public school districts within the states of Rhode Island, Indiana, South Dakota, Idaho, West Virginia, Kentucky, and Florida. Each state was randomly chosen from one of the seven geographical areas designated by the National Reporter System. The selection of the regional system provided a diversity of district population thereby allowing policy surveyed to range from large urban systems to small rural systems.

The school districts were categorized by size based upon 1973–1974 pupil enrollments in grades K–12. The following three classifications were selected: small schools (0–4,999 pupils); medium schools (5,000–19,999 pupils); large schools (20,000 or more pupils).

Procedure

The questionnaire concerning written public school policies on the selection and restriction of reading materials was sent to all superintendents in the large districts and a 10% random sample of superintendents in the medium and small districts. Justification for this procedure was that previous research has indicated that large districts are more likely to have written policy than small or medium sized districts. The instrument concentrated on three major areas of concern: first, the selection and adoption of reading materials in the public schools; second, the restriction of the reading materials in the public schools; finally, the resolution of conflict in censorship situations.

Analysis and Results

A total of 129 public school districts were surveyed to determine whether written policies concerning the selection and restriction of reading materials in the public schools were currently in effect. An examination of the findings provided by the 101 districts responding prompted the following conclusions. Less than half (49.5%) of those 101 districts responding had any written policies in any category. The large and medium sized districts (over 5,000 student population) were more likely to have written policies concerning the selection and restriction of reading materials in public schools than the small districts (less than 5,000 student population). More written policies existed in the elementary schools than in the secondary schools. Copies of the written policies received from the public school districts responding were vague, and there were no clear-cut guidelines which specifically defined the procedures to be followed in the selection and restriction of reading materials.

Regarding input into the selection and adoption of textbooks, all districts named teachers as the most involved, with administrators, the school board, and parents following in that respective order. Likewise, all districts named educators at the university level as least involved in the selection process. Next to the university educators, students were the least likely to be involved. Therefore, it is concluded that on a continuum of one to seven with one being the most involved and seven being the least involved, the following groups of people have input into public school textbook selection and adoption process: 1—teachers; 2—administrators; 3—school board; 4—parents; 5—textbook company representatives; 6—students; and 7—educators at the university level.

In all of the districts responding, there were more likely to be written policies regarding restriction of reading materials in the elementary schools than in the secondary schools. However, medium sized districts (5,000–19,999 student population) were the least likely to have written policies regarding the restriction of reading materials. Regarding input into the restriction process, the large districts were more likely to have written policies involving administrators and teachers while the small districts were more likely to involve parents and teachers.

Large districts were more likely to have written policies regarding the resolution of conflict in censorship than small or medium sized districts. Seven of the districts sending copies of resolution of conflict policies used the form provided by the National Council of Teachers of English entitled "Citizen's Request for Reconsideration of a Book" or a briefer facsimile.

Conclusions and Implications

A. THE LAW

The following represents a synopsis of the United States Supreme Court rulings examined in this study:

1. The legislative branch has authority to control public schools.
2. The courts are reluctant to intercede in school system disputes and will do so only to protect basic constitutional rights.
3. The courts have avoided raising questions in cases where clear, published procedures were established in a school district.
4. The courts have acted in cases where there is clear, arbitrary, capricious action on the part of the school system.
5. The courts have shown concern for due process of law in the proceedings.
6. There must be opportunities for those offended to be heard.

7. School systems must have justification for their decisions and
   actions.

B. WRITTEN POLICIES

As evidenced by the findings, court cases involving the selection and restriction of reading materials in the public
schools have been on the increase in recent years. Therefore,
school boards run a great risk of being involved in litigation
regarding this matter. In order to anticipate such problems
and their possible ramifications, sound written policies regarding the selection and restriction of reading materials
need to be developed at both the elementary and secondary
levels. Such policies are essential for the administrator who is
called upon to resolve conflicts in censorship situations.

Teachers who use potentially controversial reading materials in their classrooms should have written rationales prepared before actually using a book or article. Such rationales
should lend evidence and support to the use of the material in
the event of a controversy.

Inservice days focusing on the selection and restriction of
certain textbooks and other reading materials would be helpful not only for teachers but also for parents. This would en-
able all persons involved to more fully comprehend all procedures of selection and use. Effective public school curriculum
planning, therefore, should include more active community
involvement. Good faith involvement would identify and
eliminate minor problems before they escalate to major proportions.

Educators at the university level should also play an increasing role in the volatile area of censorship of reading materials in the public schools. Through their general education
and teacher preparation programs, university faculty can address the problem and better prepare future teachers to deal
with the critical issues.

THE BATTLE OF THE BOOKS: KANAWHA COUNTY[5]

NEA Inquiry

Public resentment of school authorities had been spurred by school consolidation, schedule changes, and sex education (Mrs. Moore was elected on an anti sex-education platform), said President Roscoe Keeney, Kanawha County Association of Classroom Teachers. He asked for a National Education Association (NEA) inquiry on October 14. The ten-member inquiry panel, representing the NEA, Association for Supervision and Curriculum Development, National Council for the Social Studies, American Library Association, and the National Council of Churches, took evidence December 9–11 in Charleston.

"If the climate between the board, the superintendent, and the public had been healthy and open, this would not have happened or it would have been short-lived," Keeney said. A citizens' school advisory committee had "ceased to function before the current textbook controversy. Whether by design or accident, I don't know."

The panel asked Underwood how such a controversy might be avoided in the future. He had no ready answer:

We're still in the middle of this dispute. We have not had the . . . time to sit down and try to assess this situation. . . . It might take a decade before we can understand what happened.

Text selection committee members complained at having to defend the books "over catcalls and threats" during public meetings. One teacher said the controversy "cannot be solved by emotion," pointing to the heckling then being done by protest leader the Reverend Ezra Graley.

Methodist Bishop Frederick D. Wertz called the text cri-

[5] From Chapter II, "Why It Happened," and Chapter III, "Lessons," of *The Battle of the Books: Kanawha County,* by Franklin Parker, professor of education, West Virginia University. p 20–34. Phi Delta Kappan Foundation, '75. Reprinted by permission of the Phi Delta Kappan Educational Federation.

sis a "trumpet for powerless people. . . . In the years ahead, it would be a mistake to exclude parents from the textbook selection process. The law does not provide that they must take part, but neither does it prohibit their participation."

Agreeing with the bishop, *Mail* editor Jack D. Maurice said that "the school must . . . assure parents that not only are their judgments sought but seriously entertained." He added, "If this does not help to close the gap, maybe we should consider the decentralization of the school system. We may have just gotten too big." Referring to parents, he said, "The issue is who shall control the education of their children? . . . Many believe no one has really paid any attention to the nature of their grievance." (Maurice won a 1975 Pulitzer prize for his editorials on the controversy.)

Antitext Baptist minister Henry Thaxton of the Christian American Parents said his organization would "work as long as is necessary . . . to see that the decision to reinstall the books in the schools is overturned." The controversy, he said, was "the key to exposing the entire system of arrogance and pseudo-intellectualism—an attitude that would otherwise be difficult to expose."

A pro-text English professor at West Virginia State College said that West Virginia has been "used" in an attempt to destroy intellectual freedom. "West Virginia is a place to recognize students have rights, too." Students have a right to intellectual freedom, which includes their right to have materials which are interesting, relevant, and stimulating, she said.

State School Superintendent Daniel B. Taylor, who questioned NEA's decision to hold the hearings under conditions then prevailing, wrote in his statement, "Both sides may . . . use these hearings as a forum to prove the correctness of their positions, to reargue the appropriateness of the books and to refight the battles of the past months." Dr. Taylor agreed that, "In addition to the professional educator, whose role is indispensable, there is room for lay citizen assistance in textbook adoption."

PTA Council President L. W. Seaman called the school

board's failure to listen to opposing views a major factor in the controversy. The battle was not between the affluent and the nonaffluent, he said, pointing to people in the affluent section where he lived who also opposed the books. He proposed separate schools for those who want their children to use the books and other schools for those opposed to the books.

School board president Kinsolving gave as reasons for the controversy a lack of parental input and a lack of policy guidelines on text selection.

Book protester David M. Staton said, "Thousands . . . in this valley are tired of experiments and want to go back to basic education . . . reading, writing, and arithmetic," with some chemistry and physics at higher levels.

Teacher morale had suffered, said school principals, who found "unmanageable and unreasonable" the scheduling of classes in libraries where the school board had placed the disputed books for use by students having their parents' permission. One principal complained that although the school year was half over, language arts instruction had hardly begun. Another complained that most elementary schools had not yet had books returned to their libraries from storage.

A principal said, "I believe the good Christian people of Kanawha County have been used by far right groups for propaganda purposes. They have used the emotional turmoil of the issue as a cover to recruit."

A specialist on right-wing groups agreed. He told the NEA panel that the organizations sending representatives to Kanawha County had the same ideology as the John Birch Society.

NEA FINDINGS

The NEA findings, released February 6, 1975, said that the controversy would not have been so prolonged and intense "had it not been infiltrated by representatives of highly sophisticated, well-organized right-wing extremist groups."

The 87-page report listed the John Birch Society, Citizens for Decency Through Law, the Heritage Foundation, the National Parents League, and the Ku Klux Klan.

The report cautiously approved the school board's plan for alternative schools; that is, having some elementary schools focus on the three Rs without using the controversial books. "The separation of students for these purposes might increase factionalism," it warned, pointing out that alternative schools "would tend to isolate further the mountain people of the county."

The NEA panel also recommended that:

—Principals and school staffs in rural areas mount an aggressive human relations effort;

—The school board meet in different parts of the county for residents to ask questions and express views;

—A public information program be started through the media.

On text selection, the report said, "Parents should be consulted and . . . involved in the selection process . . . as advisors and not as censors." The panel asked that no state legislation be passed that would limit teachers' rights and responsibilities to select educational materials.

The report listed these cultural differences that prompted the controversy:

—A community long divided along class lines, with differing urban and rural life styles, religious beliefs, and cultural values;

—A school system that, in its liberal educational philosophy and "apparent domination by the higher status groups within the city," had grown remote from and alien to its conservative rural communities;

—"A failure on the part of the board and central administration to communicate effectively with their rural constituency;

—"The board had failed to anticipate an adverse reaction to the texts, failed to prepare in advance for the possibility of a protest, and failed to respond promptly and effectively to the first challenge against the books."

The report found that the protest was in part "a reaction to the black presence in America." To counteract racism, it was essential that

Public education . . . treat students honestly—to inform them honestly of the history of this nation and other nations and to provide them with a vast diversity of literature, classical and contemporary, according to their level of maturity, in order that they may understand and appreciate the many cultures, races and ethnic groups that comprise our society.

MRS. MOORE OBJECTS

Mrs. Moore, who declined to attend the NEA hearings, said on December 5, "The NEA is here to decide if there is a well-financed conspiracy to take over the schools. I can save them the trouble." She charged the NEA with conspiring to take control of schools away from parents. She went on, "When they can put $4 million into electing their own candidates to Congress, you better believe it is well-financed." She asked, "Who gave the NEA the right to come into Kanawha County to judge the mentality and intelligence of Kanawha County parents, especially with regard to moral and spiritual values?"

Mrs. Moore responded on February 7, 1975, to the NEA findings. On teachers and school administrators taking mandatory human relations courses, she said, "Human relations courses, the kind they're talking about teaching, are secular humanistic approaches to education. . . . I think it's time we got off this ethnic kick," she continued, "It's ridiculous to point to children and tell them they're from a particular ethnic group. They're Americans and that's all that matters."

On the report's charge that objections to black writings indicated a reaction to the black presence in America, she said: "Multi-ethnic, multicultural textbooks had nothing to do with it [the protest]. We've had that kind of content in books for years," she said. "We've never had any problem like that and trying to create one is scraping the bottom of the barrel."

On outside extremists she said, "Whatever role any right-

wing group has played has been small. . . . What brought this
national attention," she explained, "was when several thousand coal miners walked off their jobs." Only after the boy-
cott was under way, she said, did John Birch Society representatives show up and much later the Ku Klux Klan came.

The battle of the books is a battle for man's destiny. The
control of schools is a legally shared responsibility that gives
all the people a chance to help shape that destiny.

What of tomorrow? Hopefully, Kanawha County's winter of discontent is past. And with spring has come growth,
change, and wisdom. It is time again for peace in the valley.

Analysis in the Press

Insights into the controversy came from Charleston Epis-
copal minister James Lewis, admired for his moderate views.
"This county is experiencing a religious crusade as fierce as
any out of the Middle Ages," he said. "Our children are being
sacrificed because of the fanatical zeal of our fundamentalist
brothers who claim to be hearing the deep, resonant voice of
God." Elsewhere he wrote that the antitext people were confused and angry about everything from marijuana to Watergate. Feeling helpless and left out, they were looking for a
scapegoat, eager to exorcise all that is evil and foul, cleanse or
burn all that is strange and foreign. "In this religious war," he
wrote, "spiced with overtones of race and class, the books are
an accessible target."

One writer grouped together book banners, those opposed
to sex education and sensitivity training, basic education and
reading phonics advocates, disciplinarians, and antibusers as
part of a comprehensive assault on the public schools. They
want to recapture schools from a secular humanism, offensive
to their beliefs, he wrote. He saw "a kinship with the community control advocates of the late 1960s in New York and elsewhere who wanted to rescue their schools and their curriculum from the imposed values of the white majority." The
book banners are winning, he concluded. A vacillating school
board has favored citizen selection which "may exclude all

but the most bland and noncontroversial materials."

NEA Executive Secretary Terry Herndon preferred to see the school as an agent of change. "In most places, the traditional values have included racism, sexism, white-male dominance, Protestantism," he wrote. "Some of these values should not be preserved. . . . A good school system," he concluded, "will expose children to both traditional and alternative values and let the children decide."

Writing from the mountaineer point of view, a Kanawha County librarian referred to the dominance among the contested books of those with special appeal for ghetto blacks and other minority groups. "Are the deep-felt religious needs of Appalachians of less importance?" She quoted a mountaineer woman, "I have every right to say that my children not be taught disrespect to law officers, parents and most of all to God." The librarian agreed and wrote, "As minors, children do not have the right to intellectual or academic freedom *if* their parents veto it." The librarian also chided some intellectuals for polarizing the issue by lending their prestige to the books without reading them or understanding the community. She pointed out that the eastern part of Kanawha County is served inadequately by bookmobiles and that "the only book many of these people use is the Bible."

Another sympathetic writer, a news editor and Davis Creek resident, held that working parents had grounds for complaint. The books, whose values were not theirs, played up urban intellectual alienations and university protest angers of the 1960s. Some "selections were unpatriotic, sacriligious and pro-minorities," and would disrupt and change their children. The Kanawha County people, he wrote, did just what New York City black people did in the 1960s by grabbing control of their schools from unsympathetic professional educators. On religion, he wrote, "It's not that they want religion in the schools as much as that they don't want antireligion to replace it." On racism he wrote, "It wasn't so much that people couldn't stomach militant black writers, as that they couldn't abide them alone." The bad books, he felt, were a substitute for bad conditions: inflation, drugs, abortion, permissiveness, pornography, TV violence, biased media, death of God, antiwar protests, black militants, communist subversion, Watergate. "The books had a little of everything that a lot of people didn't like: people felt they could do something about the books."

A recently resigned Kanawha County school official gave as one reason for the controversy some protesters' own bad school experiences. At school the mountaineers were sometimes ridiculed, forced to drop out, and denied other avenues to gain needed skills. "Even today," he wrote, "25 percent of the students . . . drop out before graduation. Now the adult public is striking out, because of current and past frustrations." He concluded, "Local schools get blamed and attacked for developments over which they have no control."

Another former county school leader recalled local objection in the 1950s during Senator Joseph McCarthy's anticommunist drive to a civics book containing a picture of Joseph Stalin. The objectors then, he said, were the educated and affluent in the suburbs whose equivalents are now text supporters. When an investigating commmittee learned that the civics book's author was a Republican on the far right with no desire to communize youth, they dropped the matter. He did not think "the current textbooks were worth the divisiveness, the uproar, the violence," and suggested that the school board get back closer to the people.

A New York *Times* writer familiar with Appalachian problems listed these reasons for the textbook controversy: antagonism to such disrupting changes as short skirts, long hair, civil rights, nudity, dirty movies, and racism. To these he added: have vs. have-not class tensions, prudery, contempt for school authority that had lost touch with its constituents, corporate exploitation, and absentee-owner colonialism.

Superintendent Underwood (succeeded by John F. Santrock on February 1, 1975) said, "I think a confrontation had to happen" over textbooks or a multitude of things. "The stage was set . . . five years ago with sex education," he said, "and it has grown deeper. It goes back to the differences in educational philosophy. . . . This county is extremely diverse," he went on, "and sooner or later the groups had to meet in a confrontation."

The best explanation for changes in textbooks in recent years was given by a publishing company editor. "Until the late 1950s," he wrote, "schoolbooks were homogenized and largely without individual voice and point of view. Suddenly," he pointed out, "the television generation grew up, and with the 1960s came Vietnam, the generation gap, race consciousness, women's liberation, student activism and many other issues. . . . Individualism and sensitivity to diversity were in," he continued. "The industry hustled to catch up, 'recycling' old series and creating new ones."

He explained, "There are now two sets of pressure groups—the old one on the Right and the new one on the Left. Textbook publishers are struggling to catch up with the second without leaving the first too far behind. . . . Where is the parent in all of this?" he asked. "Theoretically, parents, through their school teachers, administrations and boards of education, have ultimate control of textbook content. Yet their complaint that the ordinary taxpayer has had no real voice is justified," he believed. "Now, however, parents are gaining influence at the local level, both by law and by sheer vocal power. Lay screening committees are springing up."

The publishing executive went on, "Such committees often reveal that the argument is less with the publisher than with opposing elements within the community. The offending textbook," he wrote, "becomes merely a catalyst that reveals deep community divisions. In Kanawha County, for instance," he explained, "one advocate of the offending literature series holds a doctorate from Yale, while the leading opponent is the wife of a self-ordained Church of Christ minister."

RACISM

Racism was charged but denied as central to the textbook dispute. Mrs. Alice Moore, speaking of the textbooks' racial content, said: "I know that state law says our books must reflect multiracial, multi-ethnic, and multicultural viewpoints, but that's no excuse for teaching or even legitimizing non-standard English." She continued, "They imply that if you're black you have no chance for success in this country—that the only solution is to go get your gun and join the revolution."

A thread of racial feeling runs throughout the year's happenings. Court testimony given in mid-October charged a white demonstrator as shouting over a bullhorn at a black teacher, "You black nigger." White women protesters at a rally also shouted their objection to the textbooks' black material.

The Charleston NAACP president declared that race was involved in the controversy. He told of signs painted on rocks on the outskirts of Kanawha County saying, "Get the Negro literature out of the schools." White protesters had told him that "references to people like Eldridge Cleaver are a disgrace and they don't want people reading about accomplishments of this kind of person. . . . In the eastern end of the county," he said, "it has been freely stated to us that there is heavy opposition to blacks being represented [in textbooks] and the quotes of blacks being used." NAACP, he asserted, would seek legal means to require the school board "to employ more black administrators, teaching and support personnel" and to require all teachers to take courses in human relations.

A black woman wrote in a letter headlined "Prejudices Surfacing" in the *Mail* that one white person told her, "I should be against the textbooks because they degrade blacks. After I wouldn't sign a petition against the books, another person said hatefully, 'I don't want my kids speaking that filthy ghetto talk your people use.'" She wrote that when she crossed a picket line to take her sister to school, "the word 'nigger' rang out from the mouth of one of these so-called Christians."

The possibility for an ugly racial incident occurred when 100 whites, some armed, assembled Sunday night, November 10, 1974, after an antitext rally. A rumor had swept Campbells Creek, spread by word of mouth and by citizens' band radios, that carloads of blacks were heading there "supposedly to raise hell." Police patrolled the area, called the rumor unfounded, and dispersed the whites gathered for possible confrontation.

In January 1975 Ku Klux Klan leaders came to Charleston. A Charleston NAACP representative said that the KKK needed members and was trying to use the textbook issue to set up a beachhead in West Virginia. One KKK visitor from Ohio, a minister dressed in KKK's red theological garb, warned an antitext crowd about intermarriage and "niggers that rape our daughters, flood our jails and burn our cities." Derogatory remarks were also made about Jews. At an NAACP news conference, the KKK was scored as trying to "interject the poison of racial bigotry and hatred among the people of Kanawha County to such a magnitude that has not been seen in years."

Klan leaders offered legal aid to the Reverend Marvin Horan, an antitext leader. Indicted with others on January 17, 1975, for plotting the bombing of Midway Elementary School, he was found guilty and sentenced on May 19, 1975. His sentencing marked a probable end of the bitter textbook controversy that had rocked Kanawha County. But scars remain.

PLACARD SLOGANS

Feelings generated by the controversy were expressed in these representative signs carried at rallies and on picket lines.

Pro-textbook: —No Books No School
—Books In! People In!
—We Have the Right to an Education With the Books

Antitextbook: —I Belong to God
—Please Take Out Those Books
I do not want my mind
Corupted [sic]

—I HAVE A BIBLE
I DON'T NEED THOSE
DIRTY BOOKS
—No Peaceful Coexistence with Satanic
Communism
—Trash is for Burning
—Wish We Had More People Like Sweet
Alice [Alice Moore]
—NEA, Con Artist for Control
—Jesus Yes, Textbooks Nyet
—Even Hillbillies Have Constitutional Rights

Lessons

What lessons can be drawn from Kanawha County to
avoid or resolve similar controversies?

It remains true that the American people ultimately control education, that the U.S. Constitution reserves to the
states and local communities control of schools. But with
schools forced to be agents of social change, more community
groups now attempt to use the schools for their own ends.

American education has always reflected national social,
economic, and political movements. School and society have
always been interrelated, one serving, affecting, and being affected by the other. But the 1954 U.S. Supreme Court school
desegregation decision made schools instruments of national
social policy. Along with school desegregation has come a
drive to recognize cultural diversity. Ethnic pride has modified the melting pot theory. A new determination has grown
to preserve minority values and perspectives. Consequently,
administering local school systems has become more difficult.

When all or most of the people are not involved, as happened in Kanawha County, educational professionals tend to
monopolize school control. If reaction sets in, as it did in
Kanawha County, quiescent people become vocal. Benign
issues like textbook selection become explosive. Confrontation occurs. Then, hasty decisions must be made, and policies
that appease one group antagonize another. To do nothing is
also dangerous. School leaders, suddenly and vigorously chal-

lenged, grope to find ways to contain and manage conflict, to negotiate and win compromise.

School leaders need legal sophistication, not only to help them through the maze of federal and state rulings, but because power groups use the courts to force their own ends.

How can school leaders anticipate and prepare for contingencies, as they perhaps could not do in Kanawha County? They need to be informed of the interests of all segments of the community. Such awareness can provide precious lead time. A school leader obviously benefits from an early warning system. It pays to have antennae to detect distant rumblings before they build feelings. He needs contacts throughout the community whom he can call or who will call him about important developments. Such a network, an informal "school board," can usefully extend the school leader's own eyes and ears. He is in contact with such major community groups as business and commercial interests, women's and church groups, but perhaps not with minority groups and movements. These may be elusive or restrictive. But if such groups are identifiable, the school leader's perspicacity in making contact with them will stand him in good stead.

Similarly, exposure of the school leader's views and concerns and regular exchange of ideas and issues through any medium, organization, or platform, is helpful. He can try to anticipate and formulate contingency plans, try to construct guidelines covering such possibilities as riots, boycotts, demonstrations, fire bombings, explosions. These guidelines can be discussed and might even be improved through conferences with law enforcement, media, and other community leaders. One would hope that, by having and sharing guidelines on possible catastrophes, the media, for example, would be prepared to report but not sensationalize, would analyze in depth, and would help citizens achieve mature understanding, as indeed the Kanawha County media tried to do.

School board members, who formerly represented major community concerns, now often represent special interest groups. A school leader's challenge is to work with such board members, try to broaden their horizons as they try to broaden his, to acquaint them with educational problems, as they try to acquaint him with their group's special interests. The school leader's job, now more than ever before, is to work out compromise among group interests and school interests. As much as he administers the school system, he now also works to "orchestrate" special pressure groups, to harmonize them with the schools' best interests.

As for citizen involvement in textbook selection, heart of the Kanawha County controversy, bills have been introduced to amend the West Virginia state law to assure such involvement. In Kanawha County, where citizen input had been removed, its reinstatement under heavy fire led to a swing of the pendulum toward dangerous citizen censorship. A fair balance is necessary between citizen input and the professional direction of teachers who work closest with the books. Student input is also desirable at upper school levels since they learn from the experience and also can perhaps explain more effectively to parents what the books and the schools intend to accomplish. The role of the school board members and of the superintendent and his staff is crucial in having soundly rationalized textbook selection guidelines, in examining the books, and in monitoring the entire selection procedure to assure that good judgment and careful selection preclude the impulse for censorship.

Kanawha County provides insight into our time—that people feel helpless, voiceless, and afraid of rapid change. They are put off balance by the concentrated troubles of our times. Kanawha County parents struck back at the schools through textbooks in the same way the English Luddites sabotaged the spinning jenny and French peasants once threw wooden shoes to disrupt textile machinery. As the Bible is accepted as the perfect guide, so having McGuffey and similar safe textbooks was comforting and secure.

People see the school as a last bastion of community control and the textbook as its ultimate symbol. The angry ones cannot burn Washington, but they can attack what is theirs, their own schools. Textbooks, which in every age mirror the morality, social relations, and political consensus of the time, reflect these same things now. But the status quo in America is not peace and plenty but wrenching change and the frustration of unfinished challenges.

PARENTS PROTEST TEXTBOOKS[6]

Around the 4th of July each year—as school children across the nation are celebrating Independence Day with fireworks and colorful parades down Main streets—school boards must begin the difficult task of selecting textbooks for the coming year.

And, ironically enough, while the children are celebrating the day commemorating the true spirit of the American Revolution—freedom from foreign domination (independence) and freedom from internal repression (freedom of expression)—some of these selfsame freedoms are being challenged in their academic world.

The controversy centers on the school board and its authority to choose texts for the children, as opposed to parents and militant groups who protest some of the board's choices. The controversy evolves into a whirlpool of arguments vis-à-vis "freedom" and "responsibility" that has merit on both sides.

School boards embroiled in these controversies are finding today that their task of maintaining academic freedom while protecting children is becoming increasingly complicated and challenging, involving liberal ideas and traditional, conservative values. And, besides organized pressures from citizen groups, the school board is having to deal more and more with vocal parents and, added to this group, students who de-

[6] From report by Pham Thien Hung, Ph.D. candidate, school of journalism, University of Missouri at Columbia. *Freedom of Information Center Report No. 401.* Mr. '79. Reprinted by permission.

mand their right to read "offensive" books—even as some board members seek to remove them (sometimes as a personal protest against the books' contents).

This report analyzes this trend during the period beginning with the bicentennial anniversary of America to the present. [As originally printed, this report included a table listing 66 censorship incidents reported in the United States, between Jan. 1, 1976 and Nov. 1, 1978, involving about 205 textbooks and five magazines.]

For purposes of definition, an action will be considered bona fide censorship when a high school/elementary school textbook is actually, physically banned from classroom use (curriculum or reading list) and/or removed from the school library. The term "textbook" will refer to any book used for educational purposes in the classroom or in the school library.

Mary Woodworth, a University of Wisconsin-Madison library school professor, estimates that for every case of censorship reported in the media, 25 go unreported. Various reasons are advanced for this. For instance, a resolution or compromise on some point may be reached before the incident becomes worthy of publication—or weighty enough to attract the attention of the local news media.

And, as Bruce Shuman points out, librarians frequently perform a prior screening of all seemingly controversial materials before purchase and thus avoid any polemics that might arise—especially for libraries in small towns and rural areas.

A decision to banish a textbook can be challenged by either a librarian or a teacher—supported in many instances by his or her union or association. Protest against removal of a book may also come from students or their parents. In a few cases, the school board's decision was contested in court—such as in Chelsea, Mass. But court verdicts usually take months, even years.

Overview

Analysis of the cases by state indicates that of the 32 states presented, Maryland leads the list with seven cases of textbook removal. The city of Rockville, Md., alone accounts for three incidents. In Howard County, Md., a Media Review Committee recommended removing 29 textbooks on drugs and sex education from the school system, one of the biggest withdrawals in the history of textbook censorship.

Illinois and New Jersey follow Maryland in the number of incidents of textbook censorship, each with four cases. California, Indiana, Iowa, Michigan and Pennsylvania follow with three cases each.

New York and North Carolina are next with two cases each. Of these, New York was involved not only with the removal of the largest number of books (69 in Levittown, L.I.), but also with the removal of prestigious, award-winning authors.

In Tar Heel, N.C., Hemingway's *A Farewell to Arms, For Whom the Bell Tolls* and *To Have and To Have Not* were banned.

In Levittown, the school board censored *Laughing Boy* by Oliver La Farge and *The Fixer* by Bernard Malamud.

Brighton, Mich., is second to none in its attempt to prevent sex education from invading its school system. It eliminated all books dealing with this subject— . . .

Such an innocent-looking and apparently neutral book as the *American Heritage Dictionary* brought down the wrath of three school districts—in Anchorage, Alaska; Cedar, Ind.; and Eldon, Mo.—for its sexual definitions.

But leading the list of book "culprits" is *Go Ask Alice*. This book was written as the diary of an anonymous young woman who took drugs and eventually died from an overdose. It is banned in five locations: Warsaw, Ind.; Trenton, N.J.; Levittown and Lyons, N.Y.; and Eagle Pass, Texas.

Other textbooks that appear on more than one prohibition list include:

Flowers for Algernon—Plant City, Fla.; Emporium, Pa.
A Hero Ain't Nothin' But a Sandwich—Levittown, N.Y.; Chatham, Ga.
Our Bodies, Ourselves—Ludlow, Mass.; Morgantown, W. Va.
Slaughterhouse-Five—Goshen, Ind.; Levittown, N.Y.

In the Night Kitchen—Springfield, Mo.; Northridge, Ill.
Naomi in the Middle—Brockport, N.J.; Rockville, Md.

Authors

Interestingly enough, the authors of the three most banned books are either anonymous—*Go Ask Alice*—or collective—*Our Bodies, Ourselves* and the *American Heritage Dictionary*.

Authors who were singled out in particular for criticism included (Des Moines Register, 1-20-76) J. D. Salinger, *Catcher in the Rye*; John Steinbeck, *The Grapes of Wrath*; Ken Kesey, *One Flew Over the Cuckoo's Nest*; Alexander Solzhenitsyn, *One Day in the Life of Ivan Denisovich*; Kurt Vonnegut, *Slaughterhouse-Five*; and Piri Thomas, *Down These Mean Streets*.

Geographical Interpretation

Shuman in his study "A Geography of Censorship" finds 10 states having a high incidence of censorship cases (seven or more cases in the period of two years). Breaking these down by regions, he finds in the Eastern Region, Maryland, New York and New Jersey; in the Northcentral Region, Michigan, Iowa, Illinois, Ohio and Wisconsin; in the Southern Region, Texas; and in the Western Region, California.

Strangely enough, while stereotypically the Southern states are considered the most conservative and intolerant, they account for only 20 percent of the censorship incidents, despite having 31 percent of the U.S. population.

Shuman generalizes from his findings that high-incidence states are likely to be populous, Eastern, urbanized and industrial. He also suggests that school libraries in large cities statistically have the greatest chance of being censored. On this point, one may speculate that the makeup of the people in these metropolitan areas has something to do with this extensive censorship. These residents, though geographically close, represent a variety of different cultures, political ideologies, religious inclinations and ways of life—hence they have different value systems.

The similarity between Shuman's findings and those [. . . found] seems to indicate that there is a correlation between those states and a high degree of textbook censorship. Or to say this another way: According to Shuman's findings, regional characteristics seem to be associated with book censorship.

The Dissection of Pressure

Regional pressure arising from society's mores, though pervasive, is not easy to pin down. By contrast, individual and group pressures exerted on school boards and teachers are more apparent. A quick look . . . discloses that unlike previous periods when pressure on textbook selection and use came from organized citizen groups, during the past two-and-a-half years, pressure has come predominantly from parents, resulting in 39 out of a total of 66 cases of textbook removal—or 59 percent.

Another unlikely, yet important, source of pressure originates with school board members and school officials themselves. This emerging group accounts for 13 cases of censorship, or 20 percent.

Organized citizen groups and unknown/unspecified pressure sources are responsible for six and eight cases of banning, respectively. Among the organized citizen groups— Citizens Advocating Responsible Education, the Maryland Chapter of the National Organization for Women and the Florida Action Committee for Education—each successfully urged the removal of two books.

A religious denomination and an Indian tribe each compelled the removal of one textbook.

Parental protests, on the other hand, during this period were still unorganized (except for one parent organization in New York—Parents of New York-United), although on the whole they were very vocal. For the most part, however, parental efforts seemed to be isolated, scattered and unstructured.

This trend is in diametric contrast to earlier decades, as reported by Fred Thompson and Max Marshall in Freedom of Information Center reports 194, 195, and 199. Previously, the effort to remove and censor textbooks was carried out actively by organized citizen groups and/or pressure groups such as the Citizens for Decent Literature and the National Organization for Decent Literature. However, in the period under study for this report, these organizations seemed to be dormant. None of the censorship cases [... cited] was brought about by any of these once very active national groups.

Successful cases of censorship by such organizations as NOW, FACE and CARE were predominantly local achievements, not nationally coordinated efforts as in the previous period. Nor was the Indian protest of a Vermont history book a continuous effort to suppress textbooks in general, but only an isolated incident. The Indian protest was (Kansas City Times, 5-27-76) similar to the actions of the parents of black pupils who attempted, out of pride and sensitivity, to censor Mark Twain's *Huckleberry Finn* in New Trier East High School, Illinois.

A new and growing concern of anti-censorship groups (the "right-to-read" activists) today is the direct involvement of school board members or school officials in protesting textbooks themselves. Their actions are responsible for about one-fifth of all the cases. As protestors, not only do they exert pressure on themselves, but as decision-makers they expurgate books from reading lists or library shelves. Their rationale is to "improve the education" offered by the school, according to one board member, William Chapel of Warsaw, Ind. Many feel, however, that a protesting board member who serves as both plaintiff and judge can neither do justice to a textbook nor serve education better, as claimed. Instead, many fear the school board member may destroy the present system of education, as charged by Edward Jenkinson, an Indiana University English professor and chairman of the Censorship Committee of the National Council of Teachers of English. According to this committee, the subversive acts of power-usurping board members present an unprecedented threat to freedom of choice of textbooks—and an ever-present headache for the right-to-read advocates.

Systematized Censorship

The professed reasons for which a textbook is censored are as varied as the censors' backgrounds. According to Ernest Lefever, personal taste and values, as well as religious beliefs and political philosophy, are often more controlling than any set of objective criteria.

Two important influences are presently at work: (1) a pervasive mood of conservatism throughout the country, and (2) a demand for a return to the basics in teaching language, literature and mathematics.

The main themes of the censorship criteria are neither new nor original, even though most of them have been "systematized," thanks—or no thanks—to Norma and Mel Gabler of Longview, Texas, who help protesting parents to be more effective in their endeavors. James Hefley also proceeds in the same direction with supportive literature.

The protesters' arguments, however, are not usually as articulate or persuasive as the right-to-read proponents whose arguments center, for the most part, on the First Amendment of the Constitution (freedom of expression) or John Milton's hypostasis of the free marketplace of ideas.

The numerous reasons for textbook censorship, as [... concluded], are generally defensive, repetitious, unpredictable and vague. The recurrent themes can be classified as follows:

1) Profanity, blasphemy and un-Christian thoughts.
2) Indecency: mostly related to sexual language, nude pictures, explicit sex descriptions and discussion of human sexuality.
3) Drug use (encouragement).
4) Radical liberalism.
5) Bias: sexist or racist ideas in language, racial stereotypes and derogatory descriptions of races.

6) Undermining the family, society, human relationships and traditional values through sex education, descriptions of extramarital affairs and expressions of un-American ideas.
7) No educational value, objectionable content, "trash" and "rotten literature."
8) Secular humanism and value revisionism.

These criteria seem to touch on all the principal facets of social life and morality. Parents of today do not seem to be willing to relinquish all responsibility for their children and allow the school—teachers, librarians and school boards—to be the only molders of their children's minds.

"Instant" Censorship

The Gablers in Texas go a step further by declaring that textbooks can cause irreparable damage to children. They are convinced that crime, violence, venereal disease and abortion rates will continue to increase until textbooks are changed. They even go so far as to assert that since textbooks shape the nation, they can be an influential factor in determining how citizens vote, and by extension, what the nation will become and where it will go. Because of this view, the Gablers call for protestations against hundreds of textbooks and, if necessary, expurgation.

At the same time, they understand that censorship is time-consuming and hard work and that most parents do not have the time to read textbooks and complete complaint forms as insisted on by school administrators, teachers and librarians, and without which they will not make a decision.

The Texans, therefore, have devised a system of organizing thousands of textbook reviews, which they distribute through their Educational Research Analysts organization. These reviews assist the would-be censors (they call themselves book analysts) in overcoming the drudgery of censoring the contents of the books. For a small contribution, the would-be censor can receive reviews from the Gablers' nonprofit organization in Longview. These reviews point out questionable content and help parents to complete the complaint forms rather easily and painlessly.

The Gablers' reviews also help the would-be censors sound rather professional. According to Edward Jenkinson, one parent in a small Iowa town, using a Gabler review, gave a two-hour speech criticizing a textbook and sounded like an expert.

The Gablers do not do all the reviews themselves but appeal to concerned parents all over the country to produce them, following a prepared outline that lists categories of objectionable content. Jenkinson cites a number of typical objections that appear in the reviews:

a) Passage is judged objectionable if it directs an attack on the Bible or Christianity, America, morality or traditional values.
b) Negative thinking exists—such as prejudice, skepticism, violence, "isms" such as communism or humanism, invasion of privacy, etc.

It seems likely that anything can be classified as objectionable—by either one reviewer or another.

Jenkinson cites the instance of a Gabler review that points out objectionable entries in Webster's *New World Dictionary of the American Language.* Most of the objections involved slang terms, but nine words (bed, fag, horny, hot, knock, queer, rubber, shack and slut) that appeared to be sex oriented apparently were the deciding factor in rejecting this dictionary. While it seems irrational to discredit a 1,000-page dictionary based on nine words out of 157,000 entries, nonetheless, a hostile review, coupled with a few letters of objection, knocked this world-famous dictionary off the state of Texas' purchase list.

Jenkinson notes that the Gablers' reviews have made an impact on schools throughout the country and the use of their materials and reviews is on the rise. More and more school teachers and administrators are finding that much of what the textbook protesters are saying invariably comes from that little town in Texas where the Gablers reside. Jenkinson also contends that the Gablers' apparently successful campaign against textbooks has led them to expand their efforts to other school materials as well.

Jenkinson warns that the Gablers and their dedicated followers have put public education "on trial," or worse, and could destroy the present system of education through the "game of instant censorship." He feels their efforts should not be taken lightly nor discounted as a passing phase in the battle of textbook censorship.

Appraising Censors

Other opponents to textbook censorship join Jenkinson in perceiving the danger of this trend, and they are earnestly and methodically working to refute censors' efforts and the protesters' drive to ban texts—at times with strong emotions.

In a speech before the National Science Teachers Association, Gerard Piel, publisher of *Scientific American*, warned of the militant activities of textbook censors. These "vigilantes," Piel charged, have carried their vociferous protests into the classroom—into proceedings before school boards and state education authorities—into the courts—and into the streets. Last spring, the censors managed to carry their "agitation" to the floor of Congress and, Piel warned, these "troubled" people may have succeeded in bringing to a halt the science "curriculum reform" movement.

Piel pointed out that unsuccessful amendments, introduced by Reps. John B. Conlan of Arizona and Robert E. Bauman of Maryland, would have given Congress a veto power over the content of curriculum and research projects sponsored by the National Science Foundation. As it was, implementation funds for National Science Foundation projects for that fiscal year were canceled. Piel angrily pointed out that the "evil" aspect of these cuts was that they were the result of a few congressmen who wanted to censor only one course of study. Piel also cautioned that the textbook vigilantes' activities could unintentionally invite the federal government's meddling in public education—the very thing they most wish to avoid.

At the National Council of Teachers of English annual meeting last year in New York, Jenkinson warned that contemporary censors of school material are going after these materials "with a vengeance." According to Jenkinson, they come from all walks of life. His Committee to Study Censorship has come across 40 national or state vigilante groups that exist primarily to censor textbooks and other school materials, focusing on about a dozen targets, including: books on drugs, ghettos and conflict with parents (or containing negative statements about parents); character dialogue not spoken in standard English; and works by "questionable" authors such as Langston Hughes, Ogden Nash, Joan Baez, Malcolm X and homosexuals. "Trash" textbooks are listed as *Catcher in the Rye, Soul on Ice* and *Black Boy*. Other taboos include secular humanism (or courses involving value clarification) and self-understanding (social and ethnic heritages or cultural aspects of family life).

Who Are the Censors?

While the term "censor" is a technical one, to the lay public it frequently carries a negative connotation, and anyone who happens to protest a book or disagree with the appropriateness of its contents is labeled "censor." This is the other side of the coin in the quest for a middle ground in choosing textbooks. As the education director of the Heritage Foundation in Washington has pointed out:

The word censorship is a red flag being waved by those who would prefer to exclude parents completely from the selection of their children's books. The issue is not censorship, but whether parents have the right to some input into the selection of books that their children read and that they are paying for with their tax money.

Protesting parents have often been pictured by book proponents as reactionary, repressive, troublemaking, fundamentalist, or stupid and uneducated individuals. Critics have failed to distinguish two kinds of textbook protesters:

1) *The organized citizen group*—such as Parents of New York-United, the Daughters of the American Revolution or

other permanent citizen organizations that have long-range planning and a fixed goal of protesting or censoring textbooks that do not fit their standards.

2) *The individual parent or one-shot protester*—such as an individual who considers a book offensive and protests its use to a teacher, school official or school board member. [Research reveals] that most parent protesters belong in this category.

To label a one-shot textbook protester a "censor," "book burner" or "violator of the First Amendment" may not serve any useful purpose for the right-to-read supporters—other than name-calling. Many of the protesters think of themselves as little people having no ambition to undermine or change the public school system. They simply want to protect their children from being exposed to ideas or influences contrary to their religious beliefs or traditional values, morals or way of life. They demand that schools take due precautions in selecting textbooks and be more responsible in using them in teaching.

Reasons for the Censorship Rise

According to Jenkinson, social unrest is to blame for much of the rise in censorship during recent years. The school has become the scapegoat of concerned parents and vigilante groups who lash out in their frustration against change that they do not understand. According to Jenkinson, the public school system is the most visible and most accessible level of government and frequently becomes their target.

Other authorities explain textbook protestation in terms of a general tendency in America to return to conservatism— a reaction to the liberal or radical 1960s with its war protests, drug culture and sexual liberation.

On the other hand, Barbara Luebke says that book protest is an attempt by parents to demand accountability from the public education system.

Book condemnation has also been interpreted by others as

a way to release the anger and tension accumulated from the difficulties of daily life, from a sense of powerlessness against big government and big business, and from feelings of alienation in today's society because of changes one doesn't understand and can't control.

A Viable Compromise

Whatever the reasons behind the individual textbook censorship syndrome, educators and school officials in some places are trying to temper their relationships with these protestors with understanding and compromise instead of brushing aside all their complaints as bigotry or repression.

In Wisconsin, the state superintendent of schools has conceded that a parent has a right to judge whether a textbook or other material is acceptable to his or her child. On the other hand, she has said that "no parent or group of citizens has the legal right to abridge the rights of other parents, teachers or children to have access to the information which is part of the educational program."

This is a step further, and a more liberal position, than that of Ken Donelson, an English professor at Arizona State University who has proposed a more defensive position for English teachers.

A report prepared by the Bureau of Instructional Media Programs of the Wisconsin Department of Public Instruction and the Cooperative Children's Book Center advises local school districts that parents have "the right to request" that a textbook selection be reviewed. The report also recommends that a "reconsideration procedure" be set up to deal with any problems that arise. According to library science professor Mary Woodworth, "reconsideration" means establishing a process whereby any individual may challenge and ask for a reconsideration of the removal of any book from the library shelves or curriculum. Woodworth holds this process is necessary because, "One of the problems is that librarians forget that they're not God—that they can make a mistake in a selection." One might add that this also applies to school boards and other school officials in their dealings with protesting parents.

The National Education Association suggests that parents should be consulted and involved as advisers in the book selection process.

This idea is shared by Assemblywoman Rosemary Gunning of Queens, N.Y., a vocal yet pragmatic defender of rights of parents:

I think if you take a fair representation of parents you'll always find enough common sense to make an appropriate selection of books. It is total conceit to assume that the judgment of "professional educators" is superior. I'm sure that many of us who have friends in the academic world would agree that they are not always the smartest or the most sensible of people.

Right-to-Read Successes

In spite of high-sounding complaints of protesters and the alarming tones of educators and school officials, the right-to-read supporters have scored quite a few successes against the would-be censors in this period under consideration.

In addition, the courts have frequently ruled in favor of the right-to-read proponents. The U.S. District Court in Boston, Mass., held recently that a school board could either buy or not buy a book, but that once the book was on display, it was illegal for the board to remove it, as this act could be construed to be an effort at mind control and would violate the First Amendment.

Pro-book organizations such as the special committee on access established by the New York Librarians Association and, in Chelsea, Mass., the Right to Read Defense Committee have been an effective brake to censors' advances.

Future Trends

On the other hand, ethnic groups (blacks, Indians, etc.), other minorities and social groups (for example, NOW) will continue exerting pressure on textbook publishers and others in an effort to change their public image in a favorable direction, as well as to remedy past grievances and inequalities. It is estimated that texts reflecting racial bias and social injustice will account for most of the removals in this category in the future.

Strong pressure will still continue to come from various vigilante citizen groups, the self-righteous, the tyrannical right or left, the true believers (such as the Gablers and their followers), and the "professional" protesters (especially those who have too much free time and don't know what to do with it).

But individual cases of textbook protests, so regnant in this period, will abate in the long run, it is felt. Not only will library materials become too varied and complicated for the single parent to evaluate and protest effectively, but also the right-to-read people are becoming better organized in refuting their claims—as borne out in the Chelsea case. (A combination of effort/pressure from the NEA, the ALA and their liberal supporters is an awesome force to be reckoned with.) Better organization by these groups will bring about more contributions and, for that matter, better legal advice when the censorship case goes to court. The courts, on the other hand, will hand down more and more rulings that standardize the handling of disputed textbooks—mostly in favor of the pro-textbook forces, it is felt.

Above all, there seems to be a new attitude of accommodation or even coordination among educators, school officials, even publishers, and protesters. Guidelines and procedures are being set up to handle protesting incidents more effectively, and less painfully, on both sides. Step by step, book proponents have come to grips with a delicate situation and have ceased to eschew textbook protest cases as a dangerous antecedent, endangering their occupation and their children's intellectual life. Publishers, in particular, are also making modifications in the content of textbooks to live up to the new trend. Houghton-Mifflin, for instance, has issued anti-stereotype guidelines to achieve 20 percent minority representation and a 50/50 male-female balance in all of its educational publications.

Finally, if literature is—as it is said to be—a reflection of society, and if the general milieu of society now is as conservative as some say, then one would expect the textbooks of the future to be less controversial.

Given also the assumption that people's general educational level is steadily increasing, it is expected that in the future it will be easier for the public to absorb and cope with controversial topics and to be more receptive to others' views. . . .

THE STUDENT'S RIGHT TO KNOW[7]

"That they [Boards of Education] are educating the young for citizenship is reason for scrupulous protection of the individual, if we are not to strangle the free mind at its source and teach youth to discount important principles of our government as mere platitudes."

A library exists as a resource for a free exchange of ideas and is open to works of controversial authors, dissenting points of view, and differing literary tastes. When a school board bans books from a public school library, First Amendment principles are violated and constitutional guarantees rendered meaningless. A student's right to know, as set forth in this comment, is predicated on the First Amendment and severely limits the circumstances under which a school board may remove books from a public school library.

The First Amendment guarantees that government cannot interfere with the free exchange of ideas without a showing of a serious threat to national security. This protection has

[7] From article entitled "School Library Censorship: First Amendment Guarantees and the Student's Right to Know," by Martha L. Black, staff attorney/writ clerk, Federal District Court, Eastern District, Michigan. *University of Detroit Journal of Urban Law*. 57:523–45. Spring '80. Reprinted by permission of the journal and the author.

traditionally been extended to freedom of speech or expression. Protection of First Amendment freedoms of expression for students in public schools is judicially mandated. Judicial recognition of "reciprocal rights"—freedom of speech and the "right to know"—has developed distinctly. As an essential counterpart of their right to freedom of expression, students may properly assert a claim of access to controversial literature and freedom from school board censorship based on social or political taste.

An analysis of the development of public education and of the two theories that have supported judicial deference to the decisions and actions of school authorities is necessary to understand the relevant factors affecting judicial recognition of student claims. The *in loco parentis* doctrine and the "indoctrination theory" are the traditional bases for judicial deference toward school officials' authority. The "indoctrination theory" remains a significant factor in decisions that have rejected the student claims. A review of parents' status, their relation to schools and their control over their children's education follows an analysis of the complexities of traditional authority of schools over the education of young people. It is in this context that the development of students' rights may be more clearly understood. A close look at the judicial development of the "right to know" is essential in determining whether it exists as a constitutionally protected right. If a right to know does exist, it should apply to public school students. Included in this analysis is the special relation between the "right to know," the school, and the development of children. The "right to know" takes on particular importance in a country of self-governing people educating their children as effective and compassionate members of society.

The importance of the elements of this theme makes the school setting a uniquely appropriate place to protect the "right to know" because students may not realistically have alternative time, ability, or motivation for access to a wide range of literature. The case development in this area is recent and conflicting. The Sixth Circuit has recognized a stu-

dent's claim for access to controversial literature which has
been censored or removed by a school board, while the Second Circuit has rejected a similar claim.

This comment will trace some of these elements which
form an explanation of the current status of students claiming
the "right to know." If a right to know exists for adults, and
case law indicates that it does, a student's right to know is on
the threshold of judicial recognition.

The Traditional Bases for School Officials' Authority

In *Tinker vs. Des Moines Independent Community School
District,* the Supreme Court recognized a student's First
Amendment freedom of expression and established a relatively narrow standard for restriction of this freedom by
school authorities. This decision has opened the door to students asserting claims under the Constitution, and particularly, the First Amendment. The recognition of a student's
"right to know," however, has been slower to emerge.

One reason for this slower development is the traditional
reluctance of courts to intervene in educational matters. The
historical judicial view is that the very purpose of secondary
education precludes the school from being a First Amendment forum. Under this view, schools exist *in loco parentis,*
and their primary function is to "indoctrinate" children into
the mores of society. The *in loco parentis* doctrine has lost
much of its force as a justification for judicial deference to
school officials' authority in educational matters. The indoctrination theory continues to have judicial respect as a justification for broad authority resting with elected school officials
in the educational system. Under the indoctrination theory,
students are expected to assimilate accepted attitudes and
learn basic skills and a prescribed body of knowledge.

The *in loco parentis* doctrine originated in the English
common law with the view that parents delegated their authority over children to the teacher. A similar view developed
in the United States. In early American life the education of

the child was the parent's responsibility. The home was a self sufficient unit in economics, health, education, moral training, and other areas. Schools were established as voluntary options for families willing to delegate their authority over educating their children to "teachers." By the nineteenth century, however, the judiciary erected the doctrine of *in loco parentis,* which gave school teachers broad authority in areas of punishment for student misconduct and regulation for the protection of the morals, welfare, and safety of students. The teacher's authority existed in the absence of specific parental approval or "delegation." The teaching and socializing functions of voluntary education were established in a mandatory education system to further the goals of literacy, economic self-sufficiency, and sufficient self awareness to adopt societal norms. Even after schooling was no longer a parental option, judicial application of the *in loco parentis* doctrine continued.

Providing schools for children became the responsibility of the states. State control over an educational system typically originates in state constitutional provisions for the encouragement of education and in compulsory attendance laws. Statutes provide the basic framework for the system and then delegate the power to formulate and effectuate educational policy to various state and local school boards. School board responsibilities include the determination of courses, the certification of teachers, the selection of textbooks and library materials, and the establishment of disciplinary procedure for student misconduct. These matters are inherent in the organization and operation of any school system.

School authorities have traditionally used corporal punishment to control student misconduct. However, the theory that a school board's authority over discipline and control is based on the *in loco parentis* doctrine is diminishing as the artificiality of the rationale becomes apparent. Parents themselves are challenging school disciplinary practices in court. Courts have become concerned that *in loco parentis* empowers school officials to interfere in students' private lives. In

Johnson vs. Horace Mann Mutual Insurance Co., a case involving the paddling and whipping of a high school student by his physical education teacher, a Louisiana judge stated:

It might have been said, in days when schooling was a voluntary matter, that there was an implied delegation of such authority from the parent to the school and teacher selected by the parent. Such a voluntary education system, like the system of apprenticeship . . . has long since disappeared. Parents no longer have the power to choose either the public school or the teacher. . . . Without such power to choose, it can hardly be said that parents intend to delegate the authority to administer corporal punishment by the mere act of sending their child to school.

Although the Supreme Court has held that the cruel and unusual punishment clause of the eighth amendment does not apply to disciplinary corporal punishment in public schools, lower courts and school authorities have rejected *in loco parentis* as a justification for corporal punishment and have limited the use of corporal punishment in public schools.

This same reasoning applies to other rules and regulations justified by the *in loco parentis* doctrine. Officials in the Ohio Department of Education have recognized this limitation on their authority:

To stand *in loco parentis,* one must assume the *full* duties, responsibilities and obligations of a parent toward a minor. School teachers and administrators obviously do not support the children in their care, nor do they provide most of the tangible and intangible necessities and securities that the child finds in his home. In fact, school authorities stand *in loco parentis* only to the degree that they may act somewhat like a parent does only some of the time for the purpose of maintaining order in the educational system.

Student Challenges to School Authority

The opportunity to challenge school authority on the basis of students' constitutional rights came in the late sixties. In 1969, perhaps owing to the fervor of the times, the Supreme Court announced the broadest affirmative statement yet on students' rights to freedom of expression and their status as citizens under the First Amendment. This marked a pronounced change in judicial attitude toward the educational system. In *Tinker vs. Des Moines Independent Community School District,* five students and their parents brought suit after the students were suspended for wearing black armbands in school. The armbands were worn as silent protest against the war in Vietnam. The *Tinker* opinion significantly qualified the indoctrination theory of education and established a burden upon school officials to justify their actions when challenged on First Amendment grounds. The Court held that school officials could not prevent students from wearing armbands in political protest of the war without a showing that the forbidden conduct would materially and substantially interfere with school operations. The *Tinker* decision has been seen as a de facto rejection of the "reasonable educational basis" standard for reviewing school board action in favor of a test requiring a "clear and present danger" to legitimate educational activities.

Freedom of expression has been a closely guarded right and the "clear and present danger" standard, first enunciated in *Schenck vs. United States,* and later refined in *Brandenburg vs. Ohio,* requires expression tantamount to action that would present a clear and present danger to the protection of the country before governmental restraints on such speech will be upheld. The Court's extension of this right to students acknowledged a corresponding interest of the state in an orderly educational system, but left no question that students had acquired rights under the First Amendment. "It can hardly be argued that either students or teachers shed their constitutional rights to freedom of speech or expression at the schoolhouse gate."

The question whether a student can assert a corresponding freedom to read without interference by school authorities is more complex and includes elements stemming from a different judicial tradition and development. *Tinker* dealt only with the freedom of expression and, even in this area, did not entirely resolve the "uncertain interplay between the schools, the courts and the Constitution." However, certain aspects of the Court's decision in *Tinker* support a constitutional freedom to read. The difference in the Court's opinion in *Tinker* from earlier deference paid to educational decisions by school authorities was signaled by the Court's discussion of the function of public education, the First Amendment interests of students, and the nature of school premises.

The *in loco parentis* doctrine cannot, therefore, be the sole basis for defining parent-school relationships merely because the schools perform one function in the parents' stead. In the absence of *in loco parentis*, school authority can have only one source—legislative authorization. The standard for that authority is simply the legitimacy of its goal and the rationality of the employed means: "regulation of conduct [of students] by school authorities must bear a reasonable basis to the ordinary conduct of the school curriculum or to carrying out the responsibility of the school."

The "indoctrination theory" is also a justification for the authority recognized in local school boards to determine the structure and purposes of a public education system. The theory maintains that local school officials must be given broad discretion in shaping young minds to accomplish the goals of socialization and academic achievement. The idea that the function of schools is indoctrinating youth for these purposes is accepted as a valid one in our culture. One reason is that schools have become centralized into systems within the political structure of our communities. People are raising and educating their children in these communities. They also elect the officials who have the power to establish and make changes affecting the educational system.

The fact that parents elect local school officials is reflected in the judicial tendency to uphold school boards' actions whenever the courts have found a reasonable educational basis for those actions. The implicit assumption is that the educational value and significance of the school day experience is to be determined by school authorities.

Parental Challenges to School Authority

The current development of the traditional choice of parents regarding how their child is reared and educated may now, ironically, infringe upon the rights of parents to control the upbringing of their children traditionally recognized at common law. Parents may differ with school authorities on what values are important and on the means used by schools to guide their child's development. When parents have felt that the schools were restraining parental interests, they have sought judicial protection of their own beliefs and the individuality of the child. These cases established the presumptive authority and discretion found in the decisions of school officials. It is instructive to examine this precedent, for it contains the seeds for the recognition of students' rights. In these parental challenges, the students' rights were seen as dependent upon the parents' right to control the upbringing of their child founded in the First and Fourteenth Amendments. Thus, in *Meyer vs. Nebraska* and *Pierce vs. Society of Sisters*, protection of the student's right to escape a standardized education was accomplished coincidentally by the judicial recognition of parental preference. This protection still erects limits on the state, and provides the potential for the student challenges to come.

In *Meyer* and *Pierce*, the Supreme Court established that a state legislature cannot override the constitutional rights of parents to provide their own children with alternative schools or curriculum offerings, nor can it exercise its power to protect the welfare of young people by attempting to standardize all children. This principle was reasserted in *Wisconsin vs. Yoder*, which upheld the right of Amish parents to educate their children at home after the eighth grade. In *Meyer* and *Pierce*, the Court decided on substantive due process grounds that the school board's actions violated the basic liberties guaranteed by the Fourteenth Amendment. In *Yoder*, the attack on the curriculum was based on First Amendment prohibition of an establishment of religion and its mandate of free exercise of religion.

The traditional authority of schools over all aspects of a student's educational experience has been successfully challenged by parents asserting specific constitutional rights. However, challenges to the broader goals of education have largely left intact school discretion that stems from and closely approximates a blindly applied *in loco parentis* doctrine.

The cases involving parental challenges of general curriculum, courses, or books provide an illustration. Claims have been based on the rights of free exercise, parental nurture, privacy, and other theories maintaining the parental right to socialize children according to the parents' own values. The courts have responded by holding that the personal attitudes and values of individual parents "must not be allowed to stifle the free interchange of ideas in public school needed to achieve the goals of the educational system." In this area, courts have regularly deferred to the school board's judgment.

In *Davis vs. Page* apostolic Lutheran parents charged that their children's exposure to audio visual equipment interfered with the free exercise of religion and the parental right to control education. They based their claim on the free exercise and nurture rights dignified in *Yoder*. The court found, however, that the interests of the school board outweighed the infringement on the parents' interest and that "to hold otherwise would frustrate the state's objective of exposing children to a broad educational spectrum . . . where . . . general knowledge is the right of all and not the privilege of a few." The parents' claims were viewed as objections to values taught in school and this seemed to affect the court's view of the parent's claim. The court was reluctant to become involved in school curriculum and educational philosophy, believing the proper forum for these parental objections to be a public school board meeting. Herein lies one difference from the *in loco parentis* approach taken by courts finding broad discretionary authority in school officials. The court's deference to school officials judgment in the face of parental claims to make curriculum choices questions the legitimacy of parental control itself. In so doing, these courts are nourishing the seeds for recognition of those student rights not raised in *Meyer* and *Yoder*. However, this implicit and explicit concern for students is still preoccupied with the discharge of state responsibility, rather than the individual dignity of each student. The fact that some courts have not gone further is partly explained by the reluctance of courts to become involved in educational philosophy, academic values, and the political realities of the educational system.

The Court relied on *West Virginia Board of Education vs. Barnett* to support students' interests under the First Amendment:

> [t]he Fourteenth Amendment, as now applied to the States, protects the citizen against the State itself and all of its creatures—Boards of Education not excepted. These have, of course, important, delicate, and highly discretionary functions, but none that they may not perform within the limits of the Bill of Rights. That they are educating the young for citizenship is reason for scrupulous protection of Constitutional freedoms of the individual, if we are not to strangle the free mind at its source and teach youth to discount important principles of our government as mere platitudes.

Tinker also, in emphasizing "personal intercommunication among the students" as not only an "inevitable part of the process of attending school" but also an "important part of the educational process," indicated that, without disruption, students may "inform, stimulate and provoke their fellow students with controversial ideas," regardless of the formal school curriculum or the authority of schools to control school premises. In effect, *Tinker* gives students a right of access to other students in the convenient forum of the public school.

The rationale of the Court contains these crucial elements: it affirms rights for students under the First Amendment; it proposes the important notion of a right-of-access in a convenient forum; and for First Amendment protections, the decision hurdles judicial reluctance to interfere with the finely tuned and complex discretion of the school board. Recognition of a student right to have literature, whether controversial or of "dubious" value to certain readers, made available once put on the shelves of a school library flows naturally from *Tinker.*

The Right to Receive Information—The Right to Know

Although some of the problems before the Court in *Tinker* are applicable to the question presented, there are elements unique to establishing a student's right to read. These must be addressed before turning to an analysis of the appropriate standard for courts' review of a school board's removing or banning books. The most important element is the recognition of a constitutional basis for anyone asserting the claim of a right to read. Without this basis, a court would lack authority to upset the decisions of the school authorities.

The emergent right to receive information forms the basis of the constitutional right to read. Commentators have viewed the right to receive information as logically compelled by the existence of a right to free expression, but its emergence as a distinct constitutional right is a relatively recent development. There is limited evidence that the framers of the First Amendment meant to protect both ends of the communication process. James Madison, chairman of the drafting committee for the amendment, made this prophetic statement about the relationship between information and responsible citizenship: "Knowledge will forever govern ignorance; and a people who mean to be their own Governors, must arm themselves with the power which knowledge gives. A popular government without popular information *or the means of acquiring it,* is but a prologue to a farce or tragedy, or perhaps both."

The earliest mention of a right to receive information was in the 1940s when the Supreme Court overruled statutes that regulated the distribution of literature. The first case to recognize an independent right to receive information was not decided until 1965. In *Lamont vs. Postmaster General,* the Supreme Court struck down a statute that required the Postmaster General to detain unsealed foreign mailings from communist countries and to deliver them only upon the addressee's request. The decision rested on the First Amendment right to "receive information and ideas." Almost ten years later, in *Procunier vs. Martinez*, the Court struck down censorship regulations for prisoners' mail. This decision was clearly directed to the addressee's right to receive information, since the Court did not consider what bearing the prisoners' rights might have had to the outcome of the case. Justice Powell emphasized that

[t]he First Amendment liberties of free citizens are implicated in censorship of prisoner mail. We therefore turn for guidance not to cases involving questions of "prisoner's rights" but to decisions of the courts dealing with the general problem of incidental restrictions of First Amendment liberties imposed in furtherance of legitimate governmental activities.

And cases like *Tinker* were accordingly "generally analogous to our present inquiry."

Just as prisoner status was of no significance in *Procunier*, student status should not affect the determination of First Amendment rights. The *Procunier* problem was also one of "access" to information and ideas, implicating First Amendment rights found to override any "legitimate governmental interests."

Other cases have refused the right to receive information when there was no personal contact between the communicator and the recipient. However, in the landmark case of *Virginia State Board of Pharmacy vs. Virginia Citizens Consumer Council, Inc.*, the Supreme Court upheld the rights of consumers to have access to prescription drug price information through advertising by pharmacists. The Court did not require the direct connection between the persons at either end of the communication, but found that "where a speaker exists, as is the case here, the protection afforded is to the communication, to its source and its recipients both." *Virginia Board of Pharmacy* does not generate a general right to read, but it establishes important factors significant to the question. When it is the communication of ideas that is protected, student readers have a greater chance of asserting their claim to many authors' works made available through the school library.

It is important to note that the Court in *Virginia Board of Pharmacy* also indicated that the possibility of gaining price information through the alternative of individual calls to pharmacies did not cure the burden created by the advertising ban. It may often be the case that literature once made available in a school library and removed by a school board could be available to students through alternative sources. However, the school setting is a uniquely appropriate place to protect the right to read with access through the school library. Students may not, realistically, have the time, ability, or motivation to gain access to alternative sources of a wide range of literature. Thus, the emphasis on access in *Virginia Board of Pharmacy* and the Court's refusal to accept a "cure" by alternative sources provide important support for the student claim.

Student Challenges of Book Removal by School Boards

The first case to address the issue of the removal of public school library books was *President's Council vs. Community School Board,* decided in 1972. The Second Circuit's opinion clearly illustrated the unsettled nature of judicial protection of students' rights and the status of the right to receive information. The court upheld a school board action revoking free library access by junior high school students to Piri Thomas' *Down These Mean Streets.* The court's opinion reflected the traditional deference to school board discretion and, in focusing on who should make these decisions, the court stated that such "intramural strife" between students and school authorities did not assume First Amendment proportions because the intrusion upon the plaintiffs' rights was not sharp or direct but "miniscule." The *President's Council* opinion exemplified the strict indoctrination theory of education and applied a pre-*Tinker* standard for justifying board action. The court refused to go beyond consideration of the students' right to freedom of expression, and ignored the possibility of a right to receive information: "[t]o suggest that the shelving or un-shelving of books presents a constitutional issue, particularly where there is no showing of a curtailment of freedom of speech or thought, is a proposition we cannot accept."

In 1976, the Sixth Circuit reached a contrary result when confronted with a similar question in *Minarcini vs. Strongsville City School District.* The Strongsville City Board of Education, under its discretionary power over textbook selection, rejected faculty recommendations and refused to approve the purchase of Joseph Heller's *Catch 22* and Kurt Vonnegut's *God Bless You Mr. Rosewater* for use in the high school curriculum. It also ordered two books, *Catch 22* and Vonnegut's *Cat's Cradle,* removed from the library, and issued resolutions disapproving of the three books. The sole explanation offered in the court record was provided by the School Board's minutes of a pertinent meeting. An excerpt from the minutes provides a clue to the Board's reasoning for the removal:

It is also recommended that *Cat's Cradle,* which was written by the same character (Vennegutter) [sic] who wrote, using the term loosely, *God Bless You Mr. Rosewater,* and which has been used as a textbook, although never legally adopted by the Board, be withdrawn immediately and all copies disposed of in accordance with statutory procedure.

The high school student plaintiffs brought a class action in federal district court claiming a violation of First and Fourteenth Amendment rights. The circuit court reversed the district court's decision that no constitutional rights had been violated. The Sixth Circuit held that the Board's exercise of curriculum and textbook control was not unconstitutional, and that the Board's decision in selecting textbooks was not arbitrary and capricious. However, in the absence of any explanation of the Board's action which would be neutral in First Amendment Terms, and in view of the evidence indicating that the School Board had removed the books from the library because it found them distasteful, the action of the Board in removing books from the library was unconstitutional.

The *Minarcini* court found that the district court had read

the *President's Council* decision as upholding an absolute
right on the part of the school board to remove from the library any books it regarded unfavorably, without concern for
the First Amendment. The Sixth Circuit panel would not accept such an unqualified reading of the Second Circuit opinion. The *Minarcini* court emphasized the significance of a
school library as a storehouse of knowledge and an important
privilege created by the state for the benefit of students. It
stated that the privilege is not subject to being withdrawn by
succeeding school boards whose members might desire to
"winnow the library for books the content of which occasioned their displeasure or disapproval." The opinion also
stressed the importance of the school library as an adjunct to
classroom discussion, and that the school board's action could
inhibit free discussion of these books in class. First Amendment protection of academic freedom would protect an
English teacher in saying that she found these books important and a student's right to find and read the book. In this
connection, the court found the removal of books from a
school library a more serious burden upon the freedom of
classroom discussion than the action found unconstitutional
in *Tinker.* This burden was not lessened by the availability of
the books elsewhere.

The *Minarcini* decision did not rest on the direct restraint
of speech. The court concerned itself with the student's right
to receive information and traced the development of the
right through cases like *Lamont, Procunier,* and *Kleindienst
vs. Mandel.* The court held that the language of *Virginia
Board of Pharmacy,* along with these cases, "serve[d] to
establish firmly both the First Amendment right to know
which is involved in our instant case and the standing of the
student plaintiffs to raise the issue."

In 1969 the Supreme Court, in *Tinker,* dealt with more de-
cisiveness and less difficulty in establishing students' rights to
freedom of expression than courts currently faced with establishing a student's right to read available material whose utterance is protected by the First Amendment. The *Minarcini*
court was the first to recognize the "right to know" as a "re-

ciprocal right" founded in the First Amendment. Before *Minarcini*, commentators had questioned the use of the term "right to know" in any constitutional context. The court's reliance on the right to receive information in a situation in which personal contacts between the communicator and recipient are lacking is said to make the decision vulnerable since the continued validity of the decision depends upon the breadth accorded to the Supreme Court's decision in *Virginia State Board of Pharmacy*.

In examining the decision made by the Strongsville School Board, the *Minarcini* court may have faced an easy case. The Board had not offered any reason for its ban; therefore, the lack of an educational rationale compelled the court's conclusion of arbitrariness. The court simply stated that the Board could not condition the privilege of library use on the social and political tastes of Board members, but must use criteria that are "neutral in First Amendment terms." The unknown future of the Court's construction of the right to know, and the lack of criteria for determining the scope of a school board's authority or the appropriate degree and manner of judicial intervention makes *Minarcini* an "exceptionally slender reed upon which to rest such an important principle."

Fundamentals That Compel the Existence of Student Right To Know

The import of *Minarcini* is strengthened by other factors fundamental to the existence of a constitutional right of students to receive information. The characteristics of a school library support the idea that this right may be constitutionally mandated.

In a library, there is no direct connection between the parties of a communication, namely the author of a book and a student. Both, however, have interests which are at least implicated by the First Amendment: the author in free circulation without governmental interference, and the student reader in the availability of a broad collection of books. *Vir-*

ginia Board of Pharmacy established that the communication of ideas is the protected element between speaker and recipient.

The state interests which courts consider compelling enough to justify incidental infringements on certain constitutional rights must be evaluated to determine the relative strength of those rights. Courts that have refused to recognize academic freedom in the high school classroom express two areas of concern and compelling state interest: the impressionability of youth and the judicial deference paid to school boards' discretion regarding educational policy and curriculum. Based on the premise that students are more impressionable than adults, school boards attempt to prevent teachers from indoctrinating students with their own idiosyncrasies, and to make judgments about the appropriateness of books in the school library. This authority stems from the board's interest in "youth's healthy development."

The first consideration, prevention of teacher indoctrination of students, loses its force in a school library context where the coercive aspects of a captive audience are not present. There is no required reading of particular books, and no penalties exist for reading one book over another, or for choosing not to enter the library. The professional responsibility librarians feel in carrying out book selection makes questionable the view the public school libraries contain harmful or morally inappropriate books for students:

It is the social responsibility of librarians to select library materials from all producers . . . to build balanced collections representing all points of view on controversial issues, regardless of their personal convictions or moral beliefs. Librarians regard it as an abuse of their position to exclude or remove books from libraries as expressions of facts, theories or opinions which present arguments against their personally cherished convictions.

Students are not required to read a book shelved in a school library. If the book is too mature or unappealing for any reason, it may be returned unread.

The second consideration, judicial deference to school board discretion, loses its force when First Amendment rights are at stake. The courts, as protectors of First Amendment rights, owe no deference to school boards' discretion over curriculum if this discretion is not constitutionally innocent.

Important fundamentals must also be considered in forming a view of the existence of a student right to know. "[F]aith in democracy is predicated on the belief that greater benefits accrue from freedom, instead of suppression . . . of thought." Education requires that each generation of students examine the prejudices and varying beliefs found in a community. "The resultant capacity to make informed, intelligent decisions strengthens the student's ability to reject attractive but shallow ideas in some later, less neutral, more emotional context." A compelling state interest for the protection of the moral welfare of students has been found on the basis of the impressionability of young people. This view is no longer universally adopted and is now subject to controversy. Ironically, censorship by a school board, the goal of which may have been "protection" of the minds of youth, may result in an adverse effect on students. If the students do not read the book they miss the value a book may have to offer. If they, on the other hand, defy the ban and read the book, they will probably find its content quite anticlimatic and not significantly different from other library books assigned in class. The unfortunate result would be that students may conclude that the First Amendment is not to be taken seriously. Equally damaging, students may assume that school officials consider students too immature or unintelligent to make rational decisions. "[P]olitical freedom is not merely a constitutional matter; [it is] . . . a state of mind, which can be either nurtured or blighted in school."

Given the right of students to receive information under the First Amendment, an effective method must be established for courts to promulgate rules for book removal challenges by students. When school officials have removed a book from the public school library, they have the burden of showing that the removal was constitutionally innocent. This was the approach of the *Minarcini* court, as it construed the available precedent. The *Tinker* standard requires school boards to

justify their actions when their removals and bannings involve
First Amendment interests. The *Minarcini* decision may have
established the existence of such constitutional student interests as the "right to know." The requirement of such a burden
on school boards would make judicial review more meaningful and help school authorities more carefully scrutinize their
own decisions. A ban imposed solely because of the author's
point of view is an unconstitutional abuse of the school
board's discretion.

Recently a New York district court considered a school
board's decision to remove eleven books from a high school
library on the suspicion that they were "anti-American, anti-
Christian, anti-Semetic [sic], and just plain filthy." The board,
shortly thereafter, placed a permanent ban on nine of the
books, on the basis that the purpose of education is the incul-
cation of community values and that the books failed to promote that purpose. Students and parents filed suit seeking a
declaratory judgment that the First Amendment does not
allow a school board, no matter how democratically chosen,
to exercise its discretion so as to impose an orthodoxy of belief
and taste upon the children of a whole community.

The district court was faced with the question of whether
removal of books from a school library was constitutionally
forbidden. The school board had majority support in the community for reasons that are contended to be consistent with a
traditionally accepted philosophy of education. The district
court was faced with the dilemma of achieving value inculca-
tion while preserving the free market place of ideas in a
school library. The court, following *President's Council*, did
not recognize preferred status for books placed on school library shelves.

School censorship is a counterpart to other First Amendment censorship and suffers from the same political pessi-
mism that has traditionally undercut the First Amendment.
Individual dignity, in the political and personal senses, is enhanced, not tyrannized, by complete access to First Amendment materials. The fallacy of school board censorship is not
mitigated, but is aggravated by the fact that the victims are

students rather than adults. Indeed, the right of freedom of thought belongs to the student. "[B]ooks alone will seldom change basic attitudes; rather, they tend to initiate a learning process by stimulating ideas held previously." Tension in the politics between local community control and the professionals within the educational system clearly exists. There is also pressure by parents asserting rights to participate in educational decision-making countered by degrees of responsiveness of the school administrators. However, in the context of a high school library, it is the students' right to know that should prevail.

IV. CENSORSHIP COURT DECISIONS

EDITOR'S INTRODUCTION

One would think that, once censorship cases were tried in the courts of the land, clear-cut, simple decisions would be forthcoming, to clarify the rights of all parties and the lines of authority in schools. We have an accumulation of somewhat differing·censorship decisions on the federal level that seem to vary from region to region (and some are unclear), which will be discussed in the articles in this Section. The legal picture is fragmentary and indecisive, leaving much to be considered by the states and local school boards. The first article, by lawyer William D. North, writing in *Newsletter on Intellectual Freedom,* describes the *Zykan vs. Warsaw* 1980 decision as "a model of judicial ambiguity." North thinks that as far as academic freedom rights are concerned, they belong more in the province of teachers and librarians than that of students. He warns that continual Court injunctions can lead to orthodoxy.

The right to know for students under the First Amendment was established by a series of Court decisions as described in the Black article preceding. In the second and third articles in this Section, we find, however, that rights of students under the First Amendment can be tempered by other considerations. In considering a number of Court decisions, Jeffrey H. Orleans, attorney and Special Assistant to the President of the University of North Carolina, sees no constitutional limits to the authority of school boards and administrators in educational decision-making. In his article in the *Journal of Law and Education,* he points out that the students' right to free speech can be in conflict with constitutional rights of other parties. Thus, he says that "a school board's choice of curricula, books, or methodology should therefore be justiciable only when alleged to violate

170

a specific constitutional or statutory right other than free speech."

In the next article, from the *New England Law Review*, attorney Alex P. Landy discusses the Chelsea case, which, he explains, involved a suit by students against the actions of their school board in Massachusetts. As far as the removal of books is concerned, the Court, in balancing rights, decreed that the First Amendment right to receive information applies only when it does not produce significant disruption in the educational process. In investigating other First Amendment decisions in the *NOLPE School Law Journal*, M. Chester Nolte, University of Denver professor emeritus, found that tempering and balancing occurred in other cases. As regards obscenity cases, the Courts ruled that First Amendment rights are predicated on contemporary community standards. Noting that in censorship cases rights can conflict, Nolte sees "two opposing and perhaps irreconcilable forces . . . these may relate to state responsibility for public education vs. a national constitutional standard; to the right to teach and the students' right to know; to the rights of society against the rights of the individual; and to adult rights against children's rights."

ZYKAN VS. WARSAW[1]

The decision rendered by the U.S. Court of Appeals for the Seventh Circuit on August 22, 1980 is remarkable only as an archetypical demonstration of the confusion which exists in the courts and among judges as to legal limits of secondary school censorship. The decision is a model of judicial ambiguity. Each of the important issues presented by the case is sententiously considered by the Court but left utterly unresolved

[1] From article entitled *"Zykan vs. Warsaw:* The Non-decision Decision," by William D. North, attorney and 1981–82 president, Freedom To Read Foundation. *Newsletter on Intellectual Freedom.* 29:119+. N. '80. Reprinted by permission of the American Library Association.

and unanswered. One looks in vain for any guidance or insight from the decision.

The case itself presented a truly unique opportunity for the court to clarify the appropriate limits of school board efforts to restrict the secondary school as a marketplace of ideas. Certainly no recent school censorship case has involved a wider range of censorship conduct and techniques, including, but not limited to, teacher dismissal, curricula revision, course cancellation, library purging, and even a classic public "burning of the books" abetted, if not actually sponsored, by the Warsaw School Board.

The *Warsaw* case was unique in yet another respect. The materials and curricula subject to censorship action by the school board were not alleged to be either obscene or pornographic and, of course, therefore unprotected by the First Amendment. Rather, the materials and curricula related primarily, if not exclusively, to perceptions of the political and social roles and relationships of women in American society.

Far from accepting the opportunities presented by the *Warsaw* case, the Court's decision appears to have been carefully drawn to provide every proponent of every perspective of the problem of secondary school censorship cause for both hope and discouragement, without suggesting the order of magnitude of either. This ambiguity is readily illustrated. Thus,

1. The Court rejects the School Board's contention that the case is moot but at the same time holds that the plaintiffs' complaint does not state a constitutional claim.

2. The Court recognizes a student's right to academic freedom but immediately suggests that such right, and even the need for it, exists primarily in "the rarified atmosphere of the college or university."

3. The Court recognizes that the discretion placed in school boards to control curricula and secondary education is not "unfettered by constitutional considerations," but proceeds to hold that any challenge to such discretion must

"cross a relatively high threshold" before it constitutes a cognizable constitutional claim.

4. The Court recognizes the repeated Supreme Court injunctions against conduct which would cast a "pall of orthodoxy" over the classroom, but then appears to view the function of the secondary school as the "nurturing of those fundamental social, political and moral values that will permit a student to take his place in the community."

While the *Warsaw* decision has little or no significance as a legal precedent, it is impossible to dismiss the decision as without lessons to teach.

The first lesson is that academic freedom rights are probably more effectively asserted by teachers and librarians than by students.

The second lesson is that a complaint of secondary school censorship must be carefully and precisely drawn to include those "magical legal and factual assertions and conclusions" which appear to be the *sine qua non* of staying in court.

The third lesson, and perhaps the hardest to accept, is that, somehow, the indoctrinative function of the secondary school has become the judicial rationale for Constitutionally protected "educational elitism." This rationale is clearly articulated by the Court in its assertion that academic freedom has limited "relevance" at the secondary school level and that those limits are defined in the following terms:

First, "the high school student's lack of the intellectual skills necessary for taking full advantage of the marketplace of ideas . . ." and

Second, the student's need for academic freedom "is bounded by the level of his or her intellectual development."

The theory that access to the marketplace of ideas is reserved to those who have the financial, physical or mental capacity to enter, in the words of the Court, "the rarified atmosphere of the college or university . . ." seems fundamentally at variance with the tradition of American education. But, perhaps of greatest concern, is the idea that the "need" for academic freedom is a function of intellectual development when most educators recognize academic freedom as indispensable to intellectual development.

It is possible to sympathize with the Court's reluctance to "second-guess" school board curricular decisions or to repudiate the indoctrinative function of secondary schools. But it is difficult to sympathize with the Court's refusal to recognize the minimal safeguards required to preserve secondary education from becoming primary brainwashing. Those safeguards should include, at least, two elements.

First, absolute insistence that the school board establish and observe a curricular and materials review procedure to assure broad and considered evaluation, and

Second, repudiation of those indoctrinative techniques which involve the suppression of "unacceptable values" as opposed to those techniques which involve the encouragement and nurturing of "acceptable values."

The academic and intellectual communities must take heed of the *Warsaw* decision even if they cannot take heart from it.

WHAT JOHNNY CAN'T READ[2]

The State by constitution is committed to the doctrine of education, committed to schools. It is committed to teaching and I assume when it is committed to teaching it is committed to teaching the truth—ought to be anyhow—plenty of people to do the other.

> Clarence Darrow in his opening
> statement on behalf of John Scopes
> July 10, 1925

Public opinion may prevent to public detriment the consolidation of school districts, the introduction of progressive methods,

[2] From article entitled "What Johnny Can't Read: 'First Amendment Rights' in the Classroom," by Jeffrey H. Orleans, special assistant to the President, University of North Carolina. *Journal of Law & Education.* 10:1–15. Ja. '81. Reprinted by permission.

wise investment in new school plants; it may force, also mistakenly, the disorganization of the curriculum by courses introduced to please "patriotic" or racial groups, a taboo on many subjects, including current politics, overemphasis on athletic victories, dismissals from religious preference or of married teachers, the elimination of physical education, shop courses, and domestic science. . . . Ignorant agitation, especially when focused by a slogan, can destroy years of construction. Yet we must remember that public opinion is the ultimate measure of public welfare and that if it cannot be guided the alternatives to yielding to it are revolution or tyranny.

> Nicholas Moseley,
> Superintendent of Schools
> Meriden, Conn., 1936

Prologue: on Textbooks

The decade just ended saw a wide variety of challenges to the inclusion or exclusion of texts and other curricular materials in public schools all over America. Whether political or legal in nature, these controversies usually were phrased as defenses of the "free speech" rights of students, teachers, or parents, particularly as to using material meant to supplement or offset school texts that had been ordained for classroom use by book commissions or school boards.

In that context, in my view, these challenges raise questions of politics and of governance rather than of constitutional liberties. They ask us to define the place for study and expression of diverse views and plural cultures and literature in school systems governed by centrist, majoritarian political processes.

Introducing "unauthorized" speech or print into the classroom subverts well established procedures, indeed originally reformist ones, for curricular control generally and textbook selection particularly. Thus dissenting teachers or librarians may be seen as opposing the exercise of legitimate political authority, as represented by the small groups of people to whom communities large and small delegate away the choice of what values and knowledge their children will experience.

That choice is often a volatile one. In the progressive eras of this century we sought to defuse it by depoliticizing it—devolving it on "citizen" school boards or "professional" pedagogues. But now deviations from the results they mandate invite offsetting interventions, and suddenly the presence in a classroom of a magazine available at the corner drugstore kindles a political bonfire. As is increasingly the case, in any area of American life, all parties then look to the courts.

The judiciary's response, not atypically, constitutionalizes a political problem. Litigants, courts, and commentators have sought to identify clear "First Amendment rights" of "free speech" for teachers or students—or parents or librarians or administrators or board members—as if all of them operated independently of each other and of "the government" in some public "marketplace of ideas." Instead, of course, all these groups are intimately entwined in a forum created, maintained, funded, staffed, and populated by public action and force, including the powers of taxation and (through truancy laws) criminal fines or imprisonment. In that situation, a search for relative First Amendment rights is a circular quest. The relationships are political and not constitutional; so must the solution be.

This essay's premise is that representative, delegated school governance by elected officials (or officers they appoint) intrinsically vests curricular control in those very officials. Because their offices are created so that the schools may be governed, they have authority to govern the schools—even especially—in the delicate and critical areas of deciding how and what the schools shall teach. Their authority is not restricted because they deal in speech and values. Rather, that authority was created precisely to remove the issues of speech and values from the central political maelstrom.

A school board's choices of curricula, books, or methodology should therefore be justiciable only when alleged to violate a specific constitutional or statutory right *other than* "free speech." As I suggest below, the most easily described and perhaps most important set of such challenges could be phrased as charges of discrimination cognizable under the

Fourteenth Amendment, for which there is precedent in statutory "bilingual" education requirements and analogy in a
line of "Confederate symbol" school desegregation cases.

This argument conflicts with the majority of the described
cases and with most of the commentary in this area. And its
result admittedly may appear a hard one at first glance,
seeming to leave students and teachers open to arbitrary and
narrow choices about texts or curricula that would appropriately be condemned as censorship if applied to the commercial sale of books, the production of plays, or the exhibi-
tion of movies or works of art. Yet it is important to
remember that clearly defined First Amendment protections
do exist for both students and teachers in many kinds of
school activities and in many classroom settings. And equally
importantly, the political and governance processes that in
my view are intended for the making of curricular choices in
public schools provide forums for challenging limits on what
may or should be taught, just as they provide the means for
establishing those limits in the first place. In other words,
what is proposed here is not censorship but government.

The stakes of curricular and textbook control are made
quite clear in a recent study of American history texts, and
their development, marketing and selection by Pulitzer prize-
winner Frances Fitzgerald. In *America Revised: History
Schoolbooks in the Twentieth Century*, she vividly illuminates
the shortcomings of what we read as children and of what our
children read now. Our vision of the United States is both
narrowed and fragmented by the texts we read, for each generation reads different books, and at any one time each age
group reads different books selected by a different generation.
Yet the books of any era seem to eschew criticism and controversy in favor of a bland and anonymous "American Social
Realism," in which chronology and narrative description substitute for analytical rigor.

At a deeper level, Fitzgerald writes troublingly of the
ways books unhealthily unify our personal visions (and our
children's) of ourselves and of each other. The books do not
speak to their young readers with nurturing voices. The chil-

dren they address are passive and put upon, given little to help them understand their social and economic world and even less to help welcome them into the adult community. The books are chosen "to instruct rather than explore," treating children as "subversives" who nonetheless have the gravest social "obligations," manipulating views and values from both "left" and "right."

One need not subscribe to the sweep or harshness of these judgments to acknowledge that the child in the classroom has no spokesman if teacher and parents combine to limit his view of the world. Children, after all, do not generally choose their own texts. Surely that has something to do with why they so strongly defend the books they do choose, or those their favorite teachers bring to them. Yet one need not be over thirty to suggest that the exercise of some adult discretion can genuinely help a child to shape independent judgment. And so we return to the question of who *is* to control what Johnny can read, seeking a better answer than the "free speech" analysis gives us.

Fitzgerald puts the question as well as it can be put. Early in the book she asserts that the competitive selling of texts is a form of market democracy that (textbook commissions notwithstanding) potentially guarantees some freedom from homogeneity and mediocrity. Yet she notes somewhat ruefully that such a system also subordinates independent thought to public whim, perhaps the classic regret of the democratic intellectual. And toward the end of the book she explicitly poses the case for public control, in responding to author and former teacher Jonathan Kozol's dismay when a middle class school rejects "his particular brand of effective action and social transformation":

From a left wing point of view [i.e., roughly, Kozol's], it was naive of Kozol to suppose that a school would not reflect the views of the community that paid for its services. *And if he was proposing that schools should not reflect community views, then he had to answer a number of questions about the role of democratic institutions which he in fact did not address.*

In sum, two important interests coexist uneasily in the classroom. The community, through the authority delegated to its proper agents, wants effective school administration that promotes the "right" values through the "right" curricular materials, however ambiguously the former are defined and however lacking the latter may be. Yet we also must recognize that children in the public school classroom are among the most vulnerable of political minorities, rarely able to act on their own behalf when subjected to unthinking authority. Are there, then, constitutionally justiciable circumstances in which children can legitimately protest the textbooks thrust on them in class, or their teachers assert the right to use others? And do such circumstances derive from values of "free speech," or from some more focused source?

"Free Speech" in the Classroom

The 1960s and 1970s witnessed a veritable pageant of attempts from all quarters to keep books *out of* school classrooms and libraries, or to take out some that already had made their way in, or to keep teachers from talking about particular subjects in particular ways. Simultaneously there were efforts to force particular books *onto* the shelves and *into* the classrooms, and to guarantee that faculty would indeed promote particular thoughts or theories. The country passed through the Cold War and Vietnam, civil rights ferment and a fundamentalist Christian revival, alternating waves of prosperity and want—all in the midst of the Baby Boom, the biggest generational conflict in our history. With plenty of insecurity and conflict to go around, the older generation divided over the wars the younger generation fought; over integrating the younger generation's schools; over the votes and beer and grass and language the younger generation wanted to cast and quaff and puff and flaunt.

Schools and colleges were the battlegrounds of these conflicts, from Prince Edward County to Dorchester, Berkeley to Columbia, Kent State to Jackson State. At the same time, a

newly active Supreme Court established rights of free speech
for teachers, for students, and (if only as to teaching Darwin)
sometimes for both of them. These decisions soon formed the
basis for numerous challenges to school boards' decisions as to
what properly should be taught or read in the public schools.

And these challenges raised perhaps unexpected fire-
storms of conflict. For our public schools are so symbolically
(and practically) powerful that they are seen as able to undo
all the teachings of home and church and scouting by doing
only what we ask of them—portraying values and thoughts
and transmitting knowledge. And so the struggles to control
the schools made them the stages for deeply felt, passionately
argued attempts to prevent obscenity (or encourage artistic
expression), protect classical religious values (or assure enlightened understanding of the teachings of natural science),
portray nonwhite America realistically (or avoid inflaming
racial conflicts).

The case law occasioned by these conflicts tries to balance
the authority of school boards with teachers' posited "First
Amendment rights" to determine what they teach and with
those of students to free exposure to ideas and values. I believe such balancing of school board "censorship" against
teacher or student "freedoms" can succeed neither practically nor conceptually.

Practically, "First Amendment" balancing will not work
because absent unlimited resources both of money and of
time, *some* limits necessarily must be set both on what can be
taught and on the medium of teaching. Someone must set
those limits. In accountable, representative government, they
are set by the citizenry's elected agents—in this case, the
school board—and not by the agents they appoint to execute
their decisions—the faculty. Selection of textbooks is no different in this sense from the highway commission's choice to
pave roads with asphalt rather than with concrete: the
teacher's obligation to use the one is no different from the
construction crew's obligation to use the other.

Conceptually, the First Amendment provides no standard
by which to judge school authorities' curricular decisions be-

cause no party can be identified to claim its protections. Teachers can be constrained in what they teach, as just suggested. Even if they purport to act on their students' behalf, that responsibility ultimately is the school board's. Then cannot parents champion what their children can learn? Yet parents, to come full circle a bit obviously, are the electors who delegate their power to the school board. A parent's right to have a child excused from exposure to an objectionable text or curricular element is effectively a personal retraction of that delegation, and representative government cannot tolerate that process with any regularity.

The case law's "First Amendment" analyses fail to break out of this circle. The decisions that do not find "free speech" rights, of course, have no need to. Those that do find such rights neither define them very well nor consider the legitimate interests of the governing agency alleged to be violating them (usually, a board circumscribing the interests of teacher or student).

These weaknesses are shown clearly in a recent and comprehensive attempt to define the "freedom of speech" theory. The article's premise is stated clearly, and indeed with an attempt to reconcile it with the principle of local school governance:

Schools should be a forum in which students are exposed to the diversity of views on which a democracy thrives. For schools to impose or encourage a single perspective on any issue would be inconsistent with our constitutional framework. . . . One of the most cherished tenets of education in this country is that responsibility for public schools lies primarily with local communities. The principle of state, and especially local, control is not only enshrined in American tradition but also has been recognized as an important, if not essential, component of federalism. . . . Nevertheless, close analysis reveals that the principle does not justify ideological censorship in the classroom.

The "close analysis" consists ultimately of the assertion "that, as a matter of constitutional [i.e., First Amendment] law, public school boards do not possess unrestricted authority to exclude material from the curriculum on the basis of ideological content." The assertion is supported by arguments that schoolchildren may not be indoctrinated by school boards, enjoy certain freedoms by virtue of the public school's status as a "limited public forum," and have a "constitutional right to receive information and ideas." The article then develops burdens of proof for plaintiffs and schoolboards litigating these issues, and does so both clearly and neutrally.

Yet in the final analysis, this approach simply substitutes the judge for the school board in making curricular choices. Students and teachers sometimes may have easier access to courts than to school boards, but ultimately they make the decision in neither forum. In any event, government by the judiciary should not be an appropriate result in a society dedicated to representative government, except upon a compelling showing of the need to protect a clear-cut right. And that protection still is not necessarily likely to occur when judicial relief is applied to a problem in which, as the article acknowledges, "potentially overwhelming problems of enforcement and administration remain." For by what standards shall the courts now choose the books?

The "free speech" rubric was used with particular superficiality, for example, in the most important recent federal attempt to address curricula. That debate, which is by no means concluded, asks whether Title IX of the Education Amendments of 1972 (20 U.S.C. 1681), which prohibits sex discrimination in federally-funded education programs, could constitutionally be applied by the Department of Health, Education, and Welfare to ban sexist or sex-stereotyping textbooks. H.E.W.'s proposed regulation sought comment on the issue, and an internal H.E.W. proposal called for school districts to have review procedures of their own. But in the final rules H.E.W. avoided the issue altogether.

The proposal had noted the possibility of coverage causing "grave constitutional problems concerning the right of free speech under the First Amendment to the Constitution"; the final rules also cited a lack of legislative intent. The truth appears to be that the Secretary of H.E.W. first failed to appreciate that some address of curricula was being considered, and then reacted with abrupt dismay when a college president alerted him to a draft regulation.

Title IX's potential address of curricula raises serious issues, and this essay argues that there *are* rights affecting curricula under the analogous race discrimination bans of Title VI of the Civil Rights Act of 1964. But H.E.W. never identified *what* or *whose* "rights of free speech" it felt were endangered, despite extensive public comment and argument that both students' and teachers' free speech (and other) rights would be injured if H.E.W. did *not* act. Rather, a Tenth Amendment problem of political (and structural) federalism—of rights to control curricula that the Secretary in effect wanted out of the federal domain and "reserved to the States respectively, or to the people"—was wrapped in a constitutional cover and dropped out of sight.

A current controversy resting on the First Amendment's religion clauses illuminates the limits of "free speech" analyses. At issue is the allegation that teaching the theory of evolution as proven fact rather than as scientific speculation, or without also teaching the creationist theory of life, violates the First Amendment rights to free exercise of religion by adherents to creationist beliefs. The free speech analysis again proves a hindrance rather than a help.

The situation admittedly has no clear resolution once the Supreme Court's opinion in *Epperson vs. Arkansas* is seen not to apply. *Epperson* teaches (with the ambiguity of four separate opinions) that curricular content should be a subject of political control so long as the curricular choice is not skewed for constitutionally proscribed religious reasons—a tautology, perhaps, but one that apparently had not occurred to the Supreme Court of Arkansas. Yet the adherent to creationism may not be charging a deliberate religious manipulation of the classroom presentation, but simply an adverse effect on his or her personal rights. Such an effect need not be intentional to violate the Free Exercise Clause if it could be avoided through appropriate means.

What could such measures be? As suggested above, representative government should not easily tolerate simply excusing creationist adherents from class, and in any event excusal would deprive students of instructional time which their parents' tax dollars have purchased. Either "neutralizing" evolution by the balance of creationist teachings, or excluding the teaching of evolution altogether, must rest on a non-religious character of the creationist objection which is far easier to posit than to maintain. Most germane to a "First Amendment" analysis, either of those curricular manipulations is said to conflict with teachers' "rights" to academic freedom and students' "rights" to be free of arbitrary curricular requirements.

Thus in the face of an alleged violation of a constitutional right *other than* "free speech"—here, free exercise of religion—the "free speech" analysis proves to be simply irrelevant. If a clear free exercise violation were shown it seems doubtful the appropriate remedy would be eschewed simply so as not to affect teachers' autonomy in choosing what to teach: that autonomy, after all, was infringed in the initial decision that evolution should be taught. The creationist objection does not fail to sustain the free exercise claim because a substantive challenge to curricular choices cannot be framed in the abstract. It fails only because the peculiar nature of the religion clause can sustain such a challenge only by seeming to establish favorable treatment for religions—an equally proscribed result.

The "free speech" analysis asserts the primacy of certain *results*—"the diversity of views on which a democracy thrives"—over the democratic *process* itself. Those results may be *important*—they are, in my view. But they are not necessarily more *legitimate* than the process of governance wherein elected officials supervise texts and curricula in the schools just as they do all the other functions of representative government. The issues raised in text and curricula disputes go to the heart of the role of American education. It is for just that reason that they ordinarily should be resolved in the traditional forums of educational politics and governance.

Race and Curricula

As suggested earlier, however, curricula disputes involving specific statutory or constitutional rights should be appropriate subjects of judicial review independent of any "free speech" analyses. The civil rights legislation of the 1960s engendered two lines of cases that support intervention in curricular settings, over "free speech" objections of both students and teachers, to secure other students' freedom from racial discrimination. Beyond the right not to suffer *personal* derogatory treatment by teachers, these decisions vindicate precisely the kinds of *group* interests at stake in the typical "censorship" cases discussed earlier, under standards that provide for appropriately limited judicial remedies.

MORE THAN ONE LANGUAGE, MORE THAN ONE CULTURE

The most sweeping affirmation of rights that might adversely affect "free speech" is the Supreme Court's 1974 opinion in *Lau vs. Nichols.* Title VI of the Civil Rights Act of 1964 (42 U.S.C. 2000d) commands that no person in a federally-funded education program suffer discrimination based on race, color, or national origin. Department of Health, Education, and Welfare guidelines implementing Title VI state that "Where inability to speak and understand the English language excludes national-origin minority group children from effective paticipation in the educational program offered by a school district, the district must take affirmative steps to rectify the language deficiency. . . . Through Justice Douglas, the Court in *Lau* upheld an interpretation of these guidelines requiring a remedy for non-English speaking Chinese students in San Francisco. Noting that "[n]o specific remedy is urged upon us," Douglas suggested that "Teaching English to the students of Chinese ancestry who do not speak the language is one choice. Giving instruction to this group in Chinese is another."

"Lau" cases are now so common that one easily overlooks the draconian effect of the Court's ruling on teachers' as-

serted "free speech" rights, effectively abrogating any "right" of teachers not to implement whatever remedy the San Francisco School Board chose. Thus even an atypically violent judicial attack upon *Lau*'s premises does not address faculty "free speech" rights, but rather asserts the political view that "whether the children of this nation are taught in one tongue and about primarily one culture or in many tongues and about many cultures cannot be determined by reference to the Constitution. . . . Such matters are for the people to decide."

As Fitzgerald notes, "there is a real dilemma in the very notion of the 'multiracial, multicultural history' " of the kind *Lau* is often taken to sanction. In its extreme view,

the message of the texts would be that Americans have no common history, common culture, and no common values, and that membership in a racial or cultural group constitutes the most fundamental experience of each individual. The message would be that the center cannot, and should not, hold.

The risk of the result informs the view that *Lau* holdings should occasion only special English instruction rather than "bicultural" curricula. Yet imposition of either type of remedy by a school board clearly overrides any asserted prerogatives of teachers to determine what to teach and how to teach it.

It should be noted here that this article does not address the question of whether Title VI guarantees such as those approved in *Lau* or suggested in the next section herein, or analogous ones that might arise under Title IX, can or should be enforced by administrative rule-making and procedures or, alternatively, only by private or federal law-suits seeking judicial relief. As recent new *Lau* proposals by the Department of Education suggest, the federal hand in the classroom may not be consistent with pluralistic, locally-controlled public education even when enforcing clear constitutional rights, if the enforcement touches on the central issue of curricular control. Rather, regardless of the method of their prosecution, my point is that proper challenges to such control in fact can be framed if the challenge does involve such a clearly articulated right.

WHISTLING DIXIE

In the early 1970s a separate line of decisions addressed the use of "Confederate symbols" in secondary schools seeking to eliminate the vestiges of official segregation. These uses included the playing of "Dixie" at school assemblies; the decision through student elections to use "Dixie," the "Rebel" mascot, and the "Stars and Bars" as school symbols; and individual wearing of Confederate flags and other symbolic clothing patches. Opponents of the practices alleged that they constituted "badges of servitude" upon black students that are condemned by the Thirteenth Amendment, and created or perpetuated school segregation in violation of the Fourteenth; proponents viewed them as representing expressions of First Amendment freedoms of expression.

Four courts of appeals divided on these issues. The Fifth Circuit banned use of the symbols both where school officials encouraged it and where they simply acknowledged the action as purported exercises of students' First Amendment rights. The Sixth Circuit approved limits on the use of symbols that were shown to provoke disruptions, citing the then relatively new standard of limited student speech set forth in *Tinker vs. Des Moines School District.* The Seventh Circuit affirmed a district court's findings that the choice of various symbols had been shown neither to bar black students from integrated use of a school facility nor to impinge on *their* rights to free expression. The Eighth Circuit approved suspension of black students for leaving an assembly at which "Dixie" was played, holding that they had been given the opportunity to avoid any "badge of servitude" by not attending at all.

These "Confederate symbol" cases all turned substantially on the disruptive effect of the symbols in question. But all also involved some version of a different inquiry: did use of the symbols violate black students' rights to be free of unconstitutional segregation? And all four courts of appeal overrode asserted "First Amendment" rights of the parties against whom they resolved that inquiry—while students or sponsoring school board authorities if the symbols were found offensive, black students if they were not.

Children who do not speak English certainly cannot comprehend teachers who do, and "whistling Dixie" had an intended message that was very clear to the black "Confederate symbol" litigants. Consensus as to what in a text is "racist" often is harder to achieve, but these analyses still may be applied to selection of curricular materials. A recent federal decision has used the legislative history of a textbook selection law, and statements of two members of five-person textbook commission majority, to find that rejection of a text on Mississippi history was motivated and influenced by racial issues ("to insure that textbook selection reflected the predominant racial attitudes of the day"). But the court also adopted limits to its remedy that recognize the themes on which this essay focused. Thus it declined plaintiffs' request to ban the use of the text that *had* been approved by the book commission, for "the court cannot now place the judicial seal of approval on the ideas found in one book and denigrate the ideas found in another."

A statutory proscription against educational racism presents an explicit, binding standard against which participants in educational governance can measure their decisions, and thus against which those decisions may be reviewed in a carefully limited manner. Invocation of that standard has led to substantial change within the established procedures of textbook selection. Individual questions of "racism" and "sexism" in texts, teaching presentations, and courses admittedly may be harder to define and resolve than those raised by the deliberate use of the Stars and Bars to make desegregation a hollow victory. But applying proscriptions against discrimination to curricular elements is consistent with both of the competing interests juxtaposed at the beginning of this essay.

When the community has banned discrimination, its interest is vindicated by testing whether the school board's actions implement that command. That testing is what we expect of any public agency subject to such a command, whether the mandate is a federal one or the act of a local school board. And the same testing vindicates the individual child's majestic constitutional right, not to read a particular book in the classroom, but to be personally free from the evil of invidious discrimination. Each episode of "free speech in the classroom" litigation, lacking any such polestar, continues unsuccessfully to seek the difference, in the words of Clarence Darrow that introduce this essay, between "the truth" and "the other."

THE CHELSEA CASE[3]

In recent years there has been a proliferation of suits by students asserting violations of their constitutional rights by local school boards. One area of the educational process that has been a source of current concern and controversy is the library. Most of the controversy surrounding school libraries has focused on the students' rights to access to literary material. The competing interests in these cases bring into conflict the traditionally broad supervisory powers of a school board and the students' right to read under the First Amendment.

In *Right to Read Defense Committee of Chelsea vs. School Committee of the City of Chelsea* the District Court for the District of Massachusetts was confronted with the issue of whether a school board could summarily remove material from a library shelf due to its allegedly offensive language and content. In an effort to avoid setting a precedent whereby future school boards would be at liberty to censor educational materials based solely on personal taste in violation of stu-

---

[3] Excerpted from article entitled *"Right to Read Defense Committee of Chelsea vs. School Committee of the City of Chelsea: the First Amendment Comes off the Shelf,"* by Alex P. Landy, attorney. *New England Law Review.* 14:288–316. © Fall '78. All rights reserved. Reprinted by permission.

dents' First Amendment rights, the court concluded that the school board's authority did not extend to such removal. Central to the court's resolution of this issue was the marketplace of ideas concept. This notion not only suggests the contours of students' rights in the schools but also prescribes the boundaries of the school board's authority.

It is the purpose of this comment to explore the issues raised and decided by the *Chelsea* case. A brief discussion of the factual background of the controversy is presented in Section I. Section II sets forth the development of the marketplace concept and its applicability to the issues in the case. Sections III and IV discuss the students' First Amendment right to read and the school board's authority as it conflicts with that right. A consideration of the standard of review employed by the *Chelsea* court is undertaken in Section V. The article concludes that *Chelsea* reinforces and expands the students' right to receive information in those cases where the material sought does not substantially harm or interfere with the educational process.

I. The Chelsea Controversy

A. *The Facts:* In March, 1976, a book entitled *Male and Female,* containing the poem *City,* was placed on a library shelf at Chelsea High School by the librarian Sonja Coleman. Coleman had become interested in the book through a reading program sponsored by Prentice Hall Publishing Company. The program offered one thousand paperback books assembled by professional librarians and teachers at an attractive cost. After complying with standard procurement procedures, Coleman purchased the books.

On May 19, 1977, Chelsea School Committee Chairman Quigley received a phone call from a parent whose daughter, a high school student, had borrowed the book containing *City* from the school library. The parent was concerned over the poem's offensive language. In response to the complaint, and without having read any other part of the anthology, Quigley concluded that *Male and Female* should be removed from the library shelf.

Quigley responded to the parent's outrage by scheduling an emergency meeting of the School Committee for May 23, 1977, to consider the removal of *Male and Female* as well as the procedure by which books were selected for the high school library. He also prepared an article that appeared in the morning edition of *The Chelsea Record* on May 20, 1977. Through this article, Superintendent McGee became aware of the controversy concerning the book. He obtained a copy of the poem on the afternoon of May 23, 1977, shortly before the emergency meeting. At that meeting, the Committee agreed to conduct a further inquiry into the matter.

Another special session was convened on May 26, 1977, to confer with the complaining parent and to receive a report by Superintendent McGee. McGee stated that in his opinion the poem, *City*, was the only objectionable part of the book, *Male and Female*. Further, McGee directed that the book be removed pending a final determination by the Committee. The options to be considered by the Committee were to excise the portion of the book containing *City* or to remove the entire anthology from the library.

On July 28, 1977, the Chelsea School Committee voted to ban *Male and Female* in its entirety from the library shelves. The Committee apparently based its decision to ban the book solely on the basis of the poem without reading any other section of the book. On August 3, 1977, a group of students, teachers and interested parties filed suit in the United States District Court for the District of Massachusetts charging a violation of their civil rights and seeking an order requiring that the anthology be returned intact to the library. Two weeks later, the Committee adopted two formal resolutions which were presented at a district court hearing the following day.

Following the contested hearing on plaintiff's request for a temporary restraining order, the court ordered the book placed back in the library and made available to students with written permission from parent or guardian. In addition, the Committee was enjoined from taking any action against either Coleman or those faculty members who were plaintiffs in the case. The parties then undertook several weeks of dis-

covery and after a six day bench trial the case was taken
under advisement by Judge Tauro on March 21, 1978.

   B. *Holding and Rationale:* The court in *Chelsea* held that
in light of the students' constitutionally protected right to
read, the School Board had exceeded its statutory authority
by removing the allegedly offensive poem from the library.
Thus, the court ordered that the book be returned to the
shelf. The court began its analysis with a consideration of the
conflict between the supervisory role of the school board, as
an arm of the state, in the education of its youth and the students' right to read under the First Amendment.

   The court sought to vindicate these competing interests
by employing a balancing test. The students' constitutionally
protected rights were balanced against the state's interest in
educating its youth. In applying the test, the court placed the
burden on the state to demonstrate that the removal of the
book was in the furtherance of a substantial interest, one comparable to school discipline. Relying on the concept of free
exchange of idea within the marketplace, the court concluded that, because there was no reasonable expectation of,
or actual harm to, any of the students, the school board had
not met its burden.

II. The Marketplace Concept

A. Origins of the Concept

   A fundamental element which the *Chelsea* court considered in resolving the conflict between students' rights and
school board authority was the marketplace of ideas concept.
The basic tenet of this theory is that students learn best
through exposure to a wide range of ideas. *Chelsea* adopted
this concept and found that the offensive character or language of *City* was not outside the range of ideas contemplated
by the marketplace model.

   The English Department at Chelsea High School offered
courses that dealt with ghetto life, homosexuality and sexual
experiences expressed in everyday street language similar to
that expressed in *City*. Therefore, because the poem was not

repugnant to the curriculum and course content of the school, the First Amendment was found to protect the students' right to read the poem.

The marketplace of ideas is both a legal concept and a foundational element upon which educational theory rests. A greater understanding of the legal formulation and ramifications of the concept can be attained by analyzing the development of the marketplace concept in the educational setting.

1. Educational Theory

For the past fifty years there has been a difference of opinion in the academic world over which of two polar educational models best prepare young people for the future. These two models are "essentialism" and the "open-classroom." The Essentialists insist that the purpose of school is to teach strong traditional values through instruction in the traditional subjects of reading, writing and arithmetic. The proponents of the open-classroom model contend that children should do their own learning with the teacher providing the child with materials of the appropriate level of complexity with which to experiment. This latter process has been seen as the forebearer to what has come to be known as the analytic model of education.

The 1960s witnessed a widespread acceptance of the open-classroom model. Regardless of any movement away from the popularity of the open-classroom in recent years, at least one authority insists that this concept is a permanent fixture in the educational setting. As will be discussed, the open-classroom doctrine as embodied in the marketplace of ideas concept remains vital to the adjudication of First Amendment claims in the school environment.

2. Legal Theory

The marketplace concept goes to the root of the First Amendment. Generally, the First Amendment preserves and protects the free flow of information to the public in a marketplace devoid of censorship and governmental suasion; it functions to insure that reasoned and informed political judg-

ments can be made by the citizenry. Ultimately, the free flow
of information, both good and bad, will produce decisions
based on truthful ideas, the best test of the truth of an idea
being its ability to prevail in the competition of the market.
Thus, the marketplace model has been viewed as deriving its
force by analogy to the free market system.

Central to students' right to read is the notion that the
classroom, the library and, in fact, the whole educational milieu rests upon the marketplace of ideas model. *Chelsea* recognized that the public school library is vital to the educational process. It is specifically dedicated to the broad
dissemination of ideas providing a sanctuary for students to
explore the unknown. As a forum of silent speech and a storehouse of ideas, the library is a repository for the First Amendment rights of students, teachers and librarians. Therefore,
Chelsea concluded that the library is a "mighty resource in
the marketplace of ideas."

B. Legal Development of the Marketplace Model

Much constitutional litigation with respect to the educational system has revolved around the concept of academic
freedom. While these cases have generally focused on a
teacher's right to teach by a particular method, they have resulted in a set of principles which are also applicable to a student's right to learn in a particular manner.

1. Academic Freedom

Under the marketplace model of education, students are
not insulated from controversial thoughts or language. This
analytic model was first applied to the classroom in the academic freedom cases. These cases indicate the nature of information to which students may claim access as well as the
limits of school board authority to deny such access.

The first circuit in *Keefe vs. Geanakos* considered a high
school teacher's suit to enjoin his discharge for the use of a
"dirty" word in the classroom. The court considered such
factors as: the appearance of the word in no less than five
books in the school library, its widespread use by radicals and

young protesters coast to coast and the educative usefulness of the article in question. Based on these facts the court concluded that the application of the word was proper. Through its holding, the court expressed its concern for the chilling effect of such rigorous censorship on the students' First Amendment rights as well as its fear for the students' future. In a sense, the court took a pragmatic approach in realizing that the word in question was available to the students both amid society at large and within the school library.

In *Parducci vs. Rutland,* a high school teacher selected and assigned Kurt Vonnegut's *Welcome to the Monkey House* in order to introduce the students to the short story as a form of western literature. After her dismissal by the school board for assigning a book that "condoned the killing of elderly and free sex," the plaintiff filed suit seeking her reinstatement as a teacher. In ordering the school board to return the plaintiff to her former position, the court stated that teachers are indisputably entitled to First Amendment protection. The court recognized the need to balance the right to teach, inquire and study against the state's interest in protecting young minds from any extreme form of propagandism in the classroom. An analysis was undertaken of the words and themes of the book, and the actual disruption resulting from its use. This inquiry yielded no showing of inappropriateness of the materials used by the teacher.

However, in *Mailloux vs. Kiley,* the suspension of a teacher was not reversed where the controversial teaching method used did not have the unilateral support of the teaching profession. The court reasoned that teachers' freedom is narrower in the high school environment than at the university level. Therefore, unless a teacher uses words or methods that are supported by a preponderance of the teaching profession, he or she may be suspended. Underlying this analysis is the notion that secondary schools are expected to convey to students the "best that is known and thought in the world."

A reconciliation of the holdings in *Keefe* and *Parducci* with the one reached in *Mailloux* can be traced to the educational models adopted by the different courts. In the former two it is the analytic and in the latter it is the prescriptive.

Both *Keefe* and *Parducci* stand for the proposition that a school board may not suppress the use of a teaching method in the classroom merely because it is potentially offensive or unnecessary. In recognizing the analytic model, these courts adhere to the philosophy that exposure to almost all words and ideas best serves the goals of the public school system. Conversely, courts applying the prescriptive model are preoccupied with the teaching method employed and the concomitant acceptance of that method by a consensus of the academic community. The indication is that a rigid standard will be applied in cases involving offensive language or themes used in the classroom.

The inconsistencies in this latter approach are readily apparent. The goal of the prescriptive model is to insure the transmission of certain basic and traditional values. The belief is that once students have learned these basic ideas, they will be prepared to cope in a larger world. However, students are confronted with a multitude of ideas outside the classroom. In the prescriptive classroom students are insulated from those ideas considered to be detrimental. Once outside the school environment students must evaluate the new ideas to which they are exposed without the guidance and protection that the classroom affords. It is precisely this problem that the marketplace approach seeks to resolve. The courts applying the marketplace approach focus on a number of factors in an effort to evaluate whether the student will be exposed to the same or similar controversial ideas beyond the educational setting. Where such exposure is found to exist, those courts which support the analytic model will protect the students' right to receive these ideas.

The Supreme Court has also held that students have constitutionally protected rights outside the classroom. Accordingly, the students' rights to free expression go beyond the structured exchange of ideas that take place between teacher and pupil within the classroom.

2. Outside Academic Freedom

In *Tinker vs. Des Moines Independent Community School District*, the Supreme Court enjoined local school authorities from enforcing a regulation prohibiting three students from wearing black armbands while on the school grounds. The court expanded and clarified long-standing constitutional doctrine when it declared that students possess First Amendment rights in the school environment. The regulation prohibiting student expression was held to be an unlawful attempt by the state to control the modes and means of student communication.

The *Tinker* court evaluated student activities in the school, including personal intercommunication. In recognizing the need to preserve and protect the students' ability to freely exchange ideas in the educational marketplace, the court held that students may express their opinions anywhere in school so long as they do so without disrupting the educative process.

3. *Chelsea* and Beyond

Chelsea stands for the proposition that the library is a "mighty resource in the marketplace of ideas." This reasoning is supported by a number of lower court decisions interpreting and expanding the principles of the marketplace approach as set forth in *Tinker*. However, the issues in *Chelsea* went further.

The court in *Chelsea* considered a poem that was legitimately offensive to a few students and parents, but not obscene. Thus, one of the threshold questions was whether the marketplace of ideas concept was broad enough to protect offensive material. The *Chelsea* court answered this in the affirmative. The court found that the language and theme of *City* expressing sexual experiences in street language did not conflict with the English Department curriculum at Chelsea High School. This approach was similar to that undertaken in *Parducci* and *Keefe*, and rendered similar results. The *Chelsea* court concluded that exposure is far less harmful than insulation and that such exposure should be as broad as possible.

Chelsea is a logical extension of the judicial attitude towards students' rights expressed in *Tinker*. In the absence of disruption to the educational process, access to legitimately offensive materials will be given First Amendment protection. However, it is not clear whether *Chelsea* represents the high water mark of the expansion of students' rights. Arguably, it is reasonable for a court adopting the marketplace approach to protect student access to those materials which are not disruptive because exposure is better than insulation. Nevertheless, *Chelsea* left unanswered the question whether students have a valid claim to materials which, while not offensive to them, are legitimately offensive to more than a few persons having an interest in the educational system.

At the point where challenged materials fall within the realm of ideas deserving constitutional protection, consideration must be given to the competing interests at stake—the students' right to read versus the school board's supervisory authority.

III. Constitutional Framework of the Right to Read

The right to listen, receive communications and read has been labeled the reverse side of the coin of the right to communicate. Freedom of speech presupposes a willing speaker. Where one exists, the protection afforded by the First Amendment encompasses the entire communication; otherwise, the right would be a hollow one. The goals of the marketplace presuppose this right to communicate and to share ideas with others. However, the application of the right to read to a given communication may inadvertently afford constitutional protection to the source of the information where such protection might not otherwise have existed.

A. CHELSEA AND THE RIGHT TO READ

The *Chelsea* court followed the reasoning of a sixth circuit decision which held that the students' right to know outweighed the state's interest in denying access to library materials. The significance of this decision was twofold. First, the opinion arrived at the right to read by analogy to the right to know in cases outside of the educational context. Secondly, the court stated that students' standing to assert this right was firmly established. However, since the right to read has not been recognized by the Supreme Court in the educational context, a brief consideration of the right to know cases will be undertaken in order to discern principles which are applicable to the circumstances of *Chelsea*.

B. THE "RIGHT TO KNOW" CASES

One of the earliest of the recent right to know cases is *Lamont vs. Postmaster General*. In that case, the Supreme Court considered the constitutionality of an act which permitted the Postmaster General to detain unsealed foreign mailings of "communist propaganda" and to deliver them only upon the addressee's request. The majority readily disposed of the case by declaring the act unconstitutional on the narrow ground that the act impermissibly burdened the addressee's rights by placing on him an affirmative obligation to make a request for his mail. In expounding upon the right which was implicit in the majority decision, Justice Brennan concluded that the right to receive publications is fundamental. He stated that without such a right there would no longer be an uninhibited marketplace but a barren one.

In *Red Lion Broadcasting vs. FCC*, broadcasters challenged the "fairness" and "personal attack" rules adopted by the Federal Communications Commission. The Supreme Court held that the rules and regulations were both statutorily authorized and constitutionally permissible. It pointed out that the case involved a mass medium and concluded that the rules in question protect the public's access to social, political, moral and other ideas. The right of the listeners rather than that of the broadcasters was paramount.

In *Stanley vs. Georgia*, law enforcement officers searched Stanley's home for evidence of illegal bookmaking activity. In the course of the search the police discovered several reels of film. After viewing the film, the officers seized them contending they were obscene. The Supreme Court reasoned that the First Amendment protects the right to receive information and ideas regardless of their social worth. As a consequence, a state's attempt to prevent individuals from receiving these ideas in their private homes amounts to an assertion by the state of a right to control the moral content of a person's thoughts. This, the court concluded, is wholly inconsistent with the First Amendment.

1. The Role of the Marketplace Concept in the Formulation of the Right to Read

The marketplace model mandates the free flow of information into a forum where ideas may compete for acceptance by the public. Ideas and information are essential in the formulation of social attitudes and political decisions. Although "speech" is expressly protected by the First Amendment, the constitution is silent as to the right to "listen." Conceptually, the marketplace concept, as expressed in *Lamont, Red Lion* and *Stanley,* lays the foundation for the expansion of "speech" to include the entire communication, *i.e.,* both the initial transmission and ultimate receipt. Thus, the theoretical gap between the protection afforded the speaker and that of the recipient is bridged.

The applicability of this principle to the right to read in the educational context follows logically. Clearly, the First Amendment protects learning. However, without the right of students to engage in the full spectrum of interpersonal communication—the giving as well as the receiving of information—the right of expression would be as empty as learning without access to learning materials. In finding that the wearing of armbands was "akin to pure speech," the *Tinker* court protected the students' right to express themselves. As an extension of this principle, the court safeguarded the rights of those students who did not wear armbands to observe these symbolic gestures and express themselves in return. While there is no specific judicial precedent for constitutional protection of the right to read, it is apparent that the students' right to receive information has generally been established.

2. *Chelsea* and Moral Development

Implicit in the *Chelsea* holding is the view that the school board's attempted removal of *Male and Female* was tantamount to controlling the moral contents of the students' minds. The Board alleged that the poem was offensive and concluded it was unfit for student consumption. While there is no dispute that schools are responsible for developing young minds, control of content based upon personal values is without justification. Not only does such control create the spectre of "sanitization," but it allows this manipulation to continue at the whim of each successive school board. As *Chelsea* rightfully concedes, the right to read minimizes such censorship. Nonetheless, students' rights must be viewed in conjunction with properly exercised school board authority.

IV. *School Board Authority*

A. LIBRARY ADMINISTRATION

Traditionally, school boards have derived their regulatory power over students from the common law doctrine of *in loco parentis*. This doctrine provides that a parent may delegate part of his parental authority to the schoolmaster. The schoolmaster possesses that degree of power necessary to carry out his assigned tasks. Contemporary judicial decisions have, however, tended to erode the authority envisaged in this concept. In light of the Supreme Court's declaration that students are persons under the constitution, a balance must be struck between the students' rights and the school board's authority consistent with the special characteristics of the school environment.

1. The Scope of Statutory Authority

In *Chelsea*, the school committee was charged pursuant to statute with the purchase, care and custody of library books. One case interpreting a similar statutory scheme concluded that school boards may remove books which have become obsolete or where limited shelf space required such removal. *Chelsea* broadened and refined this interpretation of the legislative intent. The court stated that the committee's authority to keep and care for books included the right to remove books because of obsolescence, improper selection, obscenity or shortage of money or shelf space. The court concluded, however, that none of these factors existed in the case. In the absence of these criteria, the court was left to determine the limits of the committee's authority under a statutory scheme which provided only for the purchase, care and custody of books but not for their removal.

B. Purchase and Removal of Library Materials

1. Creation of a Constitutionally Protected Interest

The *Chelsea* court intimated that, pursuant to the enabling statute, the school committee possessed nearly absolute discretion in selecting and purchasing books for the library. Despite the committee's absolute authority to select books, the court found that there were boundaries to its authority to remove them. The court reasoned that the committee was under no obligation to initially purchase *Male and Female;* however, once the book was purchased a constitutionally protected interest was triggered.

The distinction between purchase and removal was considered in two earlier cases in which the courts reached different conclusions. In *Presidents Council vs. Community School Board*, the Court of Appeals for the Second Circuit held that where the school board had the ultimate authority in the initial selection of books an equal authority existed for the removal of books. The court reasoned that if the book was improperly selected in the first instance, the board should have the unfettered authority to remove it.

This holding was refuted by the Court of Appeals for the Sixth Circuit in *Minarcini vs. Strongsville City School District.* The position taken by the Sixth Circuit Court was that the school board did not possess the same authority to select as it did to remove. The analysis focused upon the fact that the board was not compelled to provide a library or to choose any particular books; but once having done so, the right to use the library could not be limited by the social or political tastes of the board.

The principle applied was that a school board does not possess unlimited authority to remove a book once shelved, based upon a subjective evaluation of the book's quality. Constitutionally protected rights *vis-a-vis* the book are created by placing it on the shelf. A useful and instructive analogy can be seen in the teacher employment cases.

When a school board hires a teacher or selects a book its decision is almost absolute. The selection process is non-justiciable pursuant to a broad legislative intent to defer such decisions to the school board. However, once having conferred the benefit, a school board may not condition the right at the expense of constitutionally protected interests. Cases have held that even though a teacher may be arbitrarily discharged, he or she can establish a claim to reinstatement if the decision not to rehire was made by reason of his or her exercise of First Amendment freedoms. Once a teacher has established that his or her contract nonrenewal was based upon the exercise of constitutionally protected speech, the requirements of due process must be met. Further, the aggrieved party must be afforded the protections of notice and an opportunity to be heard.

2. Due Process

In keeping with the teacher analogy, it is evident that similar due process questions must be raised where a book is "fired" from a library. The court in *Chelsea* devoted a great deal of attention to the procedures employed in the book selection and withdrawal process followed by the committee. Nevertheless, the court did not consider the constitutionality of the removal procedures employed. Arguably, the committee acted in such a manner as to censor *Male and Female*. Even where such censorship is otherwise permissible, procedural safeguards such as notice and an opportunity to be heard must be followed. Issues such as the type of hearing that may be required, the burden of instituting and proving the unacceptability of the challenged materials, and a time frame within which review must be made should have been addressed by the court.

V. *The Standard of Review*

A. THE SUBSTANTIAL DISRUPTION TEST

The *Chelsea* court formulated a judicial test whereby local officials must demonstrate that a book's presence in the library poses a threat to an interest comparable to school discipline in order to justify removal of the book. This standard originated in *Tinker,* where the Supreme Court held that the test conformed to the "special characteristics of the school environment." The state bears the burden of establishing that the book did, or could reasonably be expected to, result in harm to the students. This standard is two-pronged permitting a school board to remove a book based upon either a reasonable forecast of harm or upon a *post hoc* evaluation of harm in fact. The *Chelsea* court concluded that the committee had failed to meet its burden on either prong of the test.

The *post hoc* evaluation of substantial harm is a determination that reviewing courts may make quite easily. A court may consider all the facts and circumstances surrounding the controversy, as well as expert testimony. Therefore, the extent of harm and disruption to the education and socialization processes in the school can be readily ascertained.

The problem with the test inheres in the predictive component. Under the predictive prong of the disruptive test, a threshold determination as to the reasonable likelihood of harm must be made without any concrete facts. Although courts are equipped to adjudicate controversies that are likely to occur (*i.e.*, through declaratory judgments), a court by necessity is forced to make a determination based on the same intuitive process as employed by a school board. The difficulty in applying this standard is reflected by the general trend of the courts to defer to a school board's original judgment. The *Chelsea* court found by the great weight of testimony that there had not been nor would there be any harm to the students or disruption to the learning process. The court was very careful to point out that there was only one parent who complained. Accordingly, it appears as though the students were left unaffected. Had there been other evidence of harm, such as additional complaints, the court's task would have been more difficult.

A school board's decision to remove a book necessarily involves an evaluation of the effect of its words on a student. The difficulty of predicting harm in such a situation is evident. An author of a literary work may use a given word to serve more than one function. For example, a word may be selected for its cognitive or emotive force. In attempting to evaluate the harm which might be caused by particular words, a school board may erroneously favor one of these functions to the exclusion of the other. This is something that the constitution does not sanction and has led one court to conclude that the burden of demonstrating the reasonableness of a board's forecast of disruption becomes geometrically greater when the focus is on the content of words.

It is clear that where there is a showing of actual or foreseeable harm, a court will sustain the action of a school board. However, the *Chelsea* court concluded that the school committee had not sustained its burden.

B. The Balancing Test

In applying the substantial disruption test, the *Chelsea* court balanced the interest being asserted by the state against the student's right to read. Although students' rights to be exposed to controversial thoughts and language are valuable, it is settled that childrens' constitutional rights are not necessarily co-extensive with those of adults. However, most ideas having the slightest redeeming social importance enjoy full constitutional protection where they do not encroach on more important interests.

In contrast, the state does have a legitimate interest in developing and educating young minds. This interest, however, must be unrelated to the suppression of speech where the state seeks to justify the removal of a book. In removing the book on the basis of the words contained in the poem, the school committee's interest, by implication, was related to the suppression of free expression.

VI. Conclusion

The students' right to read is premised upon two notions that are fundamental to our system of government. First, the right to receive information is necessary, if not vital, to the integrity of the decision-making process. The ideas must be exchanged in a marketplace that is uninhibited and free from government interference to assure that the information the public receives is truthful. The rights that students possess must be commensurate with their roles as future leaders of our society.

While it is clear that the right to read is a paramount interest under the First Amendment, it does not exist in a vacuum. The state has a corresponding interest in providing an education for its youth. In order for the state to fulfill its task, local school boards must possess the authority to insure that the process is carried on in a non-disruptive and efficacious manner.

The *Chelsea* court formulated a judicial standard placing the burden on local officials to establish that the removal of a book is pursuant to a substantial interest, *e.g.*, akin to avoidance of disruption in the educational process. This burden is not easily met in view of the scope of students' right to read. The marketplace rationale favored under the analytic theory of education presupposes the broad dissemination and exchange of ideas in the schools. In such an environment very few ideas, words or books can produce a significant disruption to the educative process or harm to students.

OFFICIAL CONSTRAINTS ON INDECENT WORDS[4]

It is midafternoon. A father is driving his young son home from school. The car radio is tuned to WBAI, New York, and

[4] From article entitled "New Pig in the Parlor: Official Constraints on Indecent Words," by M. Chester Nolte, professor of school administration emeritus, University of Denver; author of *How to Survive in Teaching: the Legal Dimension* (1978). *NOLPE School Law Journal.* 9:1–22. Ja. '80. Reprinted by permission.

Comedian George Carlin is speaking. "[Some of the words] you will hear are words you couldn't say on the public, ah, airwaves, um, the ones you definitely wouldn't say, ever." Then follows a monologue satirizing society's prudish attitudes toward profanity. To emphasize his point, Carlin repeats seven "dirty" words in "a variety of colloquialisms." The father, taken aback and angered by the broadcast because it has exposed his son to "trash" without warning, brings suit to bar such broadcasts from the airwaves. Admittedly the words are not obscene in the strictest legal sense, but they are "objectionable." His suit is successful.

Although they disagree over various parts of the decision, a five-justice majority of the United States Supreme Court ruled that the Federal Communications Commission, which has official control of broadcasting, can legally regulate "indecent" as well as obscene broadcasts, and that the FCC has the power to limit broadcasts of such materials during hours when children are most likely to be listening. The basis for the decision is not that the words are obscene under the *Miller* test, but rather that the "uniquely pervasive presence [of radio] in the lives of Americans" makes verbal communications different from the printed word. While all of the words are to be found in any high school library, in the case of younger children, who may not be ready to read, the intrusion of radio into the sanctity of the home (and the car) makes radio broadcasting another case.

"The individual's right to be let alone in his home or car plainly outweighs the First Amendment rights of an intruder," wrote Justice Stevens for the majority. "Pacifica's broadcast would have enlarged in an instant the vocabulary of a child who might have found 'incomprehensible' a four-letter word in print." The broadcast could, therefore, be controlled because of the "nuisance rationale." A nuisance, said Stevens, quoting Justice Sutherland, "may be merely a right thing in the wrong place—like a pig in the parlor instead of the barn. We simply hold that when the Commission finds that a pig has entered the parlor, the exercise of its regulatory power does not depend on proof that the pig is obscene."

Although the idea that local governing bodies may control

the flow of words to children is not exactly new, the *Pacifica* decision does introduce a new dimension into the issue of official censorship of textbooks and other curricular materials. Education is a state function, and legislatures almost universally allow boards of education to choose the materials to be studied, so long as state statutes and constitutional safeguards are observed. Departures from these well-worn grooves are turned over to the state courts for adjudication. *Pacifica*, however, while not fully meshing with constitutional law, does leave mundane state matters to take flight into the realm of the constitutional right to read discussed in this publication earlier.

The emergence of a *Lernfreiheit*—the student's right to read, to know, to learn and to be informed—like other constitutional freedoms, is certainly not without its limitations. But whereas in some of the challenges students are denied access to certain materials because of local board abhorrence of the language in which the materials are couched, courts have not been entirely unsympathetic to the argument that board conservatism is standing in the way of their right to learn. This article will take up this concept and develop the *Lernfreiheit* as it stands at present from the limited number of cases on that subject to date.

The four dissenting justices in *Pacifica* wrote that since the language was clearly not obscene in the legal sense—it did not appeal to a prurient interest in sex—it was protected by the First Amendment and could not be banned, since the only limits on free speech are of the obscenity genre. In one of the two dissenting opinions, Justice Brennan regarded the Court's misapplication of fundamental First Amendment principles "so patent, and the majority's attempt to impose its notions of propriety on the whole of the American people so misguided," he found himself "unable to remain silent." Accusing the majority of "acute ethnocentric myopia," Brennan argued that it permitted "the taste of the majority" to completely prevent expression protected by the First Amendment from entering the "homes of a receptive, unoffended minority." Words that the Court and the Commission find so unpalatable "may be the stuff of everyday conversation in some, if not many, of the innumerable subcultures that comprise this nation." Since the words could not be banned under the First Amendment, the minority found it unnecessary to "address the difficult and important issue" of whether the FCC could legally ban "objectionable" words from the nation's airways.

Emphasizing the "narrowness" of the decision, Justice Stevens implied that the majority might have permitted the offensive language as an occasional expletive, but that the repeated recitation of the words made the broadcast "a nuisance." In any event, the case should be seen as limited to the *facts:* the *radio* broadcast of a monologue containing the *repeated* use of *offensive language.* The ultimate effect of *FCC vs. Pacifica* on local board operation, while not yet apparent, will no doubt be limited since it deals with the spoken in contrast to the written word. Would the Court have ruled differently if the offensive words had appeared in print rather than being broadcast over the airways? There is evidence that there is at present a double standard, one for spoken, the other for the printed word. For example, the Court has upheld the power of the federal government to require radio and television stations to offer free time to groups and individuals to discuss their views on issues of public interest. Such a ruling would be clearly unconstitutional if applied to the printed media.

Miller vs. California, far from putting an end to censorship problems, is often outside the local board's grasp. Materials can be suppressed only if a) they appeal to a prurient interest in sexual matters where the average person, applying contemporary community standards would consider the materials "prurient," b) if they depict or describe, in a patently offensive way, sexual conduct specifically defined by the applicable state law, and c) if they lack, when taken as a whole, serious literary, artistic, political, or scientific value. Stung by its failure in *Roth* to deal with obscenity using a national standard, the Court modified that 1957 decision by substituting community standards as its criterion. *Miller's* net effect has been to place within the reach of local boards the wherewithal to censor local materials so long as they meet the test, which is not all that effective. Far from settling the obscenity issue, the *Miller* test has led to more litigation, more delay, and more confusion as to what is and what is not to be restricted. Boards clearly needed more leverage, which many of them claimed under the state's enumerated authority to pick and choose curricular and other materials. Increased pressures from parents and other groups have added to their woes, so that censorship in elementary and secondary schools is now at an all time high. And final legal resolution of the problem seems further away than ever.

Particularly Susceptible Individuals

One portion of the *Pacifica* decision bound to cause confusion is Justice Powell's concurrence, in which he was joined by Justice Blackmun. The separate opinion stressed the need to protect "children" from the harmful effects of the seven dirty words. "Such speech may have a deeper and more lasting negative effect on a child than on an adult," wrote Powell. "For these reasons, society may prevent the general dissemination of such speech to children leaving to parents the decisions as to what speech of this kind their children shall hear and repeat. . . . The speech from which society may attempt to shield its children is not limited to that which appeals to the youthful prurient interest. The language involved in this case is as potentially degrading and harmful to children as representations of many erotic acts."

While Powell's argument has certain persuasive merit (who wants to be caught on the wrong side of any *moral* issue?), the decision sheds little light on how local boards should judge how to proceed in dealing with the censorship issue. Can materials be chosen, for example, if they are offensive to the board, on the supposition that the board speaks for the majority of the community? How should the board seek to fit the materials to the maturity of students, given the spread of abilities in the average classroom? To what extent should the local mores of each neighborhood enter into selection of materials where several neighborhoods are included in the school district? And finally, is the concept that children are

"particularly susceptible individuals" to be given the cre-
dence that conservatives seem to think it should receive in a
world where children are more sophisticated than when the
idea originated over 100 years ago?

In *Regina vs. Hicklin,* a case that arose in England, the
court decided that materials should not be judged obscene on
the basis of what might offend the average reader, but rather
on whether it might fall into the hands of "particularly susceptible individuals." Intent of the writer/publisher was im-
material, so long as the end result was material that had a tendency to "deprave and corrupt those whose minds are open to
such immoral influence." On this basis, since the work might
fall into the hands of children, the fact that it contained any
corruption whatsoever made the entire work legally unacceptable. Thus, works were to be judged obscene if only one
page contained objectionable words. In the latter half of the
19th century, attempts were made by the courts to deal with
the writer's purpose and intent, but most rejected intent as irrelevant and sought to determine the effect of the words
themselves on the hypothetical immature individuals with
whom the material might come in contact.

A more contemporary view might be that banning materials which incite "immoral thoughts and desires in the young
and inexperienced," as one court put it, amounts to a Catch
22 predicament: how are those who are to become "experienced" ever to reach that level of sophistication if they are
precluded from reading that which may indeed "educate"
them? In its extreme, such a philosophy might even suggest
that those who want to be truly sophisticated must look elsewhere than the school to gain that status. Can the schools
teach reality through denying that it exists? The Supreme
Court has held that local school boards may not let their fief-
doms become "enclaves of totalitarianism." Apparently, the
freedom to be informed, to learn, to read, and to choose reading materials that reflect the world outside the school is not
among the constitutional rights that children, as "persons"
enjoy, since they are "particularly susceptible individuals"
and must be protected from that world at all costs.

In *Pacifica,* Justice Powell theorized that parents must fill the gap in the law by choosing the materials they wish their offspring to read. However, at least one justice has recently conceded that parents are in no position to make professional judgments concerning curricular selections. Others have held that teachers cannot be disciplined for using a teaching method resulting in the use of objectionable words "unless the State proves he was put on notice either by a regulation or otherwise that he should not use that method." Inasmuch as even the most experienced teacher's experimentation occasionally comes up short, it seems hardly likely that parents, some of whom may care little about their child's educational problems, can ever fill the gap suggested by Justice Powell in the *Pacifica* decision.

Fortunately, courts now take into account the intent of the writer in determining whether a work is obscene. Nor may isolated words be controlling: the work must be considered as a whole. Under the *Miller* test, any work, taken as a whole and having serious literary, artistic, political or scientific value is protected under the First Amendment, even though it may contain a smattering of objectionable words. Thus, not many books or magazines have been placed outside the reach of school children on the *Miller* test alone. Attempts to fit the materials to the age, size and maturity of students have met with limited success where boards are sensitive to local pressures in the society, and sometimes act (or re-act) to restrict curricular materials on the common denominator of the most conservative elements in the community setting.

Censorship in Education Increasing

Censorship is defined as the attempt to suppress materials presenting certain viewpoints or to exclude those viewpoints from library and classroom materials. According to a recent survey conducted by the Committee Against Censorship of the National Council of Teachers of English (NCTE), slightly more than 30 percent of the teachers who responded reported pressures for book censorship, compared with 20 percent in a similar survey conducted in 1966. While parents raised 78 percent of the objections to books, only 19 percent of staff members—teachers, principals, superintendents, or librarians—raised objections. In 1979, more than two dozen book-banning cases were pending in state and federal courts, where the First Amendment was being raised as a shield against the authority of local school and library boards to regulate the ideas to which elementary and high school students are exposed.

Between 1966 and 1975, the Office of Intellectual Freedom of the American Library Association reported over 900 censorship cases occurring in the nation's educational institutions. Forty of these were on the elementary level, 77 on the junior high school level, and 386 on the high school level. Sixty-four affected all levels, K-12. Schools accounted for 62 percent of all educational attacks, with public libraries and colleges and universities accounting for the remainder.

The NCTE survey above revealed that the targets of censorship in schools ranged from news magazines such as *Time*, *Newsweek*, and *U.S. News and World Report* to filmstrips dealing with drug education and sex education. Most frequently objected to among school library books were *The Catcher in the Rye*, *Of Mice and Men*, *The Grapes of Wrath*, *Go Ask Alice*, and *One Flew Over the Cuckoo's Nest*.

But there are plenty of new titles along with the old. In Cedar Rapids, Iowa, *Travels with Babar* was among 104 books banned; in Anaheim, California all of Shakespeare's works except *Hamlet* and *Romeo and Juliet*, all of Dickens' works except *Oliver Twist*, and all but one of Mark Twain's works have been declared "unsuitable" for use in English classes. In Aurora, Colorado, ten books were placed off limits to English elective classes, including some by Pulitzer prize winning writers. Attempts to reconstruct the thinking of local boards in such cases fail to reveal a consistent pattern on which to base such exclusions, inasmuch as the books and other materials were not susceptible to banning on the basis of the *Miller* obscenity test discussed above.

At least one observer has hinted that part of the censorship problem today may be due to the media explosion. Neil

Postman makes a point that no critic of the schools should overlook these days:

We are dealing with a different type of student now, one molded by "the electronic media, with the emphasis on visual imagery, immediacy, non-linearity, and fragmentation." These kids don't fit into the traditional classroom, with its emphasis on "sequence, social order, hierarchy, continuity, and deferred pleasure." It is these new kids with their new attitudes who cause even today's most intelligent and dedicated teachers to fail.

The "pig in the parlor" aspects of this new media explosion are further discussed by Postman as applied to dress codes, "which signify that school is a special place in which special kinds of behavior are required. You would not wear dungarees and a T-shirt that says 'Feel Me' when attending a church wedding. That would be considered an outrage against the tone and meaning of the situation. The school has every right and reason, I believe, to expect the same sort of consideration."

If indeed local boards are holding out against "objectionable" words in school materials, much as they did against long hair and unorthodox dress for students in the seventies, the inevitable result will be that both students and the state will gain important interests in the process. Out of the whole will surely come a clearer meaning of the student's *Lernfreiheit*—the right to learn.

In *Parker vs. Board of Education* a high school teacher challenged his dismissal in federal district court for assigning *Brave New World* to his class. His contract was not renewed and no reasons were given because he was a probationary teacher. When his suit failed he then sued the state but here too he was unsuccessful. A teacher's right to teach, said the court, is limited much as was that of *Scopes*. This caused the *Harvard Law Review* to conjecture that:

academic freedom is of questionable relevance to speech in public elementary and secondary school classrooms. The assumption of the "free marketplace of ideas" on which freedom of speech rests does not apply to school-aged children, especially in the classroom where the word of the teacher may carry great authority. It seems unwise to assume as a matter of constitutional doctrine that school children possess sufficient sophistication or experience to distinguish "truth" from "falsity." Furthermore, since one function of elementary and even secondary education is *indoctrinative*—to transmit to succeeding generations the body of knowledge and set of values shared by members of the community—some measure of public regulation of classroom speech is inherent in the very provision of public education.

The above-cited quotation, if valid, raises some interesting questions. Is the school to pass on to succeeding generations only those values that are local in character, rather than those universally accepted on a nationwide basis? Even if these could be determined, should not the educated child have knowledge of what these values are, even though they may not be practiced in his particular community? Since education is transportable—goes with the educated—should not the most isolated hamlet in which lives a child who will one day earn his living and function in a more cosmopolitan setting make him aware of values other than those of his own limited community? On the basis of these questions, both the indoctrination and the particularly susceptible individuals theories must be reexamined in the light of First Amendment considerations. If indeed there is such a right as *Lernfreiheit*—the student's right to read, to know, to be informed—then should not the law take into account that this right is separate and apart from the *Lehrfreiheit*—the teacher's right to teach? To the extent that the legal challenges being mounted seem to be shifting from the teacher's right to teach to the student's right to learn, the legal building of litigious bridges rather than walls may continue apace.

The *Harvard Law Review* article did touch on *subterfuge*. There can be cases, says the article,

in which the asserted basis for a curricular decision can be questioned by a court of law as illegitimate or as a mask for an unrevealed illegitimate motive. For example, the state should not be permitted to conceal an ideologically repressive prohibition with the subterfuge that the particular book or theory is too difficult or misleading when the evidence reveals that the same material is generally taught in other parts of the state or the nation under similar circumstances.

What this amounts to is hypocritical subterfuge—saying one thing while actually concealing another motive entirely for banning a book or magazine. As will be seen in the analyses below, the thought is not out of reach of some school boards when giving reasons for such actions on the part of the state.

Whatever its causes, censorship in public schools is on the rise, it is a fact of life, and must be dealt with. Driven to its extremities, Wood says it might lead to these results:

Robin Hood was considered communistic, Tarzan was living with Jane without benefit of clergy, and Huckleberry Finn was a racist. Ferdinand the Bull was branded pro-Franco and anti-Franco, a Communist, an anarchist, a manic-depressive, and . . . "Schizoid."

It would be ironic indeed if students had to look outside the school for information they need to survive in an environment of high media exposure. One should not underestimate the competition. Student attention is difficult to obtain and hold. If they believe that schools are places where exciting ideas are limited, they may lose that "instinct" to know reasons for certain effects or to explore into the unknown. The seductions of our media environment must yield to a school climate where nothing is hidden and where students can expect answers to their most pressing questions. Any other use for *Lernfreiheit* would be a Pyrrhic victory in the extreme.

Cases Involving Educational Censorship

Earlier cases on the subject of book banning were tried in the state courts and were apt to involve dismissal or censure of a teacher for insisting on using a certain objectionable publication. Based on state statutes, the courts tended to hold that local boards, being agencies of state government, were granted the power to determine curricular matters, and that the courts were not to second-guess them unless there was clearly some deprivation of a state-granted right. Said one judge, "It is for the lawfully elected school board, its supervisory personnel and its teachers to determine the local school's curriculum. The judicial censor is *persona non grata* in formation of public education."

A trial court injunction against the use of Kurt Vonnegut

Jr.'s *Slaughterhouse Five* had been issued on the grounds that it made reference to religious matters and also contained obscenity. The Michigan Court of Appeals concluded that there was no constitutional bar to teaching *about* religion and that the book was intended not to indoctrinate but rather to give the attitude of some religions about the World War II bombing of Dresden. To use it in this way, said the court, did not constitute an establishment of religion. "Our constitution does not commend ignorance," concluded the court in holding that the purpose of the work brought it within the protection of the First Amendment.

Perhaps the most noteworthy case was *Williams vs. Board of Educ. of the County of Kanawha,* a West Virginia case that attracted nationwide attention when the parents marched on Washington, D.C. to demonstrate against choice of materials by the board. Parental objections were to certain textbooks and supplementary materials on the grounds the choices violated their religious freedom and privacy of the family circle. To avoid such influences, the parents had placed their children in private schools. In a memorandum order, the court acknowledged that materials included in the texts might prove offensive to some parents. The First Amendment, while promising unfettered exercise of religion "does not guarantee that nothing about religion will be taught in the schools," declared the court. At the same time the court offered the well-known rationale that courts "should not intervene in the resolution of conflicts which arise in the daily operation of school systems."

In a related case not involving the printed word, a local board had banned all "political speakers" when it learned that a social studies teacher intended to permit a communist to speak (Democratic, Republican and John Birch speakers had previously spoken to the class). A federal district court quickly held that the board's action was a denial of the student's right to hear. A teacher's medium of teaching must be left as unfettered as possible, said the court, and restricted only if special circumstances, which were not present here, so dictate. A school board's "valid" interest in suppressing political expression might occur, said the court, where there might be substantial disruption of the school program, or where the topic was inappropriate for the students. Nor does fear of voter reaction, nor personal disagreement with views to be expressed, work to give the board justification for its actions. Banning all speakers was a form of prior restraint prohibited under the First Amendment. In holding for the teacher and against the board, the court said:

Today's high school students are surprisingly sophisticated, intelligent and discerning. They are far from easy prey for even the most forcefully expressed, cogent, and persuasive words. . . . A (lesson they must learn): that the power of the state is never so great that it can silence a man or woman simply because there are those who disagree. Perhaps that carries with it a second lesson: that those who enjoy the blessings of a free society must occasionally bear the burden of listening to others with whom they disagree, even to the point of outrage.

Minarcini vs. Strongsville City School District was a class action suit on behalf of children against the board, where the board refused to follow the district faculty's recommendation to purchase certain textbooks and ordered other books removed from the library. The court held that students have a First Amendment right to receive information. As to the faculty, the Sixth Circuit Court of Appeals ruled that teachers had the right to refer to the books in question. The board was ordered to replace the books in the school library, although it had the right to exercise curricular and textbook control within reason. While the board's decision not to select some textbooks over others was not arbitrary or illegal, its removal of certain books from the library constituted a violation of the Constitution as no reasons were given for the removal of the books in question.

Although the state is under no compulsion to establish and maintain a library, the Sixth Circuit Court of Appeals held that once having created such a privilege for the benefit of its students, neither the state nor the school board "can place conditions on its use which relate solely to social or political tastes of school board members." Despite the fact that *Virginia Pharmacy* pertained to adults, and came in from the commercial consumer field, the Sixth Circuit court ruled it applied equally well to the acquisition of knowledge by high school students who were denied that information through state action of the board of education. The United States Supreme Court refused to review the case.

Minarcini lacked internal consistency as well as helpful guidelines for boards as to whether children and adults are equals in receiving information. The primary weakness, however, lies in its lack of clarity and its unequal treatment of textbooks and library books. Choice of textbooks is traditionally the duty of the local board and does not ordinarily involve constitutional issues. Dissatisfaction with a certain selection does not necessarily create a constitutional question. Academic freedom should not consist of the courts' intervention to second-guess local boards of education. A more realistic approach might be to require boards to show as a matter of fact that the state has a valid interest in suppressing the printed word. Short of that test, boards should not be permitted to censor educational materials where they can show no disruption, invasion of the rights of others, or that the topic in question was inappropriate for children of that particular age or level of maturity.

School board members in Chelsea, Massachusetts, decided they didn't like *Male and Female Under 18* in their high school library. They had ordered the book removed after reading a poem "The City to a Young Girl," one of the more graphic selections from an anthology. Written by a 15-year-old high school student, the poem described in earthy terms the girl's revulsion at being treated as a sex object by men on the street. The committee chairman described the poem as "obscene," "low down dirty rotten filth, garbage, fit only for the sewer." Judge Tauro rejected this appraisal of the poem, saying in part,

Whether or not scholarly, the poem is challenging and thought-provoking. It employs vivid street language, legitimately offensive to some, but certainly not to everyone. What is at stake here is the right to read and be exposed to controversial thoughts and language—a valuable right subject to First Amendment protection.

"The most effective antidote to the poison of mindless orthodoxy is ready access to a broad sweep of ideas and philosophies. There is no danger in exposure. The danger is in mind control," wrote Judge Tauro, in holding that the school committee must pay plaintiffs' legal fees in the amount of $27,300 and must return the book to the library shelves. Removal, said Tauro, did not serve a legitimate state purpose, and constituted an infringement of First Amendment rights of both students and faculty alike. Wrote Tauro in part:

> Not every removal of a book from a school library implicates First Amendment values. But when, as here, a book is removed because its theme and language are offensive to a school committee, those aggrieved are entitled to seek court intervention. . . . The committee was under no obligation to purchase the (objectionable) materials, but it did. It is a familiar constitutional principle that a state, though having acted when not compelled, may consequently create a constitutionally protected interest (citations). . . . No substantial governmental interest was served by cutting off students' access to *Male and Female* in the library. Defendants acted because they felt *City's* language and theme might have damaging impact on the High School students. But the great weight of expert testimony presented at trial left a clear picture that *City* is a work of at least some value that would have no harmful effects on the students. . . . With the greatest of respect to such parents, their sensibilities are not the full measure of what is proper education.

The rationale that the board is not required to furnish library books, but having created such a privilege cannot place conditions related solely to social or political tastes of the board members on the use of the privilege, was prominent in the court's thinking in *Salvail vs. Nashua Board of Education,* a case arising in New Hampshire. Plaintiffs were high school students, teachers, and adult residents and taxpayers, defendants were school board members and their superintendent who had voted to remove *Ms.* Magazine from the high school library. The court held that the action was properly maintained as a class action, and that the board had failed to demonstrate a valid governmental interest sufficient to warrant removal of the magazine. The board was ordered to replace the issues they had caused to be removed and to resubscribe to the magazine, such replacement and re-subscription to be made, if necessary, by purchase out of the first sums available for library purposes.

The Nashua board had objected to the magazine's publication of ads for vibrators, contraceptives, and materials dealing with homosexuality and witchcraft. The court found, however, that it was the political overtones of the predominantly feminist publication that led to the ban on *Ms.* Magazine by the board. Such a basis for removal of a publication, said the court, "is constitutionally impermissible."

The impression is left that the board might have been successful in removing the magazine from the library if it had followed its own guidelines. Once the board has adopted guidelines, said the court, the board is required to follow them in attempts to remove a work from the shelves of the high school library. Stating that removal can be accomplished if the board can show cause, the court pointed out that "educational" considerations, obsolescence, or architectural necessity may form the legal basis for such action. Having said that, the court then held that the board had not used such objective criteria and had instead removed the magazine on the impermissible grounds of the political and social tastes of the board members.

The board's position that it was the sexually oriented advertisements to which it objected was undermined when it was pointed out that similar ads were present in other publications contained in the Nashua High School library. This led the court to conclude that political rather than sexual objections were the real grounds for the board's action in banning the magazine from the shelves.

Salvail is unique in its reliance on the *motive* as grounds for the rejection of the board's action. Ordinarily, motive is difficult if not impossible to establish, but the evidence here clearly left the court no other alternative. The lesson to be learned is that once having set up a set of guidelines, it is imperative that they be followed; failure to do so may constitute a *prima facie* basis for rejection of the board's action.

Cases Upholding Board Censorship

As might be expected, courts are divided on the issue of board of education censorship of instructional and library materials. In general, those decisions that uphold local boards in these activities tend to a) deny class actions to plaintiffs, b) hold that there is no violation of students' First Amendment rights where the board has banned certain materials from the schools, c) support the proposition that boards are given not only the right but the duty to choose instructional materials, and d) decide that boards may not bargain away the right to make instructional choices even though the board's actions are discretionary rather than ministerial. Following are some cases in which boards have been upheld in censorship activities involving curricular and library selections.

In *President's Council, Dist. 25 vs. Community School Board,* a New York City case, the decision was made to remove all copies of *Down These Mean Streets* by Piri Thomas from junior high school libraries in District 25. The Second Circuit Court of Appeals held that no constitutional issue was involved, at almost the same time that the Sixth Circuit held, in *Minarcini,* that a school board's action in removing books from the library violated the First Amendment. Since a double standard from one circuit to another is abhorrent to the law, the U.S. Supreme Court no doubt in time will be called on to mediate the difference.

Justice Douglas, in dissenting from a denial of certiorari in *President's Council,* pointed out that the right to know is protected by the First Amendment. This right, said Douglas, is consistent with evidence that the framers of the Bill of Rights meant to include both ends of the communications process within the amendment's scope. Both the sender's right to initiate a communication and the receiver's right to receive it, according to Douglas, must come within the meaning of freedom of expression.

The genesis of the right to know may go as far back as *Meyer vs. Nebraska* where the Supreme Court held that denying a student the right to study a foreign language was unconstitutional. Subsequent holdings by the same Court have strengthened the doctrine.

In 1969, Justice Marshall wrote, "It is now well established that the Constitution protects the right to receive information and ideas. . . . This right to receive information and ideas, regardless of their social worth . . . is fundamental to our free society." The question is what happens when the constitutional right comes directly into conflict with the state's right to control curricular and library materials.

Some courts, like the one in *President's Council*, solve the problem by holding that no substantial constitutional issue is at stake where a board order removes a book from the school library. Said the Second Circuit Court of Appeals, in dealing with this problem:

> Since we are dealing not with the collection of a public book store but with the library of a public junior high school, evidently some authorized person or body has to make a determination as to what the library collection will be. It is predictable that no matter what choice of books may be made by whatever segment of academe, some other person or group may well dissent. The ensuing shouts of book burning, witch hunting, and violation of academic freedom hardly elevate this intramural strife to first amendment constitutional proportions.

President's Council was distinguishable from *Epperson* because no religious issue was present and because there was no ban on teaching any theory or doctrine, as in *Epperson*. Since teachers were still free to discuss the book, their rights were not invaded by the board's ruling to outlaw the book. With parental permission, students were also free to read the book in question. Thus, the court concluded that infringement of First Amendment rights was only "miniscule."

The basic flaw in the court's decision in *President's Council* is its failure to distinguish, as the court did in *Minarcini*, between selecting this book or that from among many to place in the school library, and the act of removing a book already purchased and placed in the library because some board members feel the content of the book is objectionable. Either act of the board carries a different constitutional di-

mension. In the first instance, choosing a book for inclusion in
the library, the board clearly has that power under state statute. However, as Mr. Justice Douglas pointed out, the theory
that the students can do anything but read the book "lessens
somewhat the contention that the subject matter of the book
is not proper." The law ordinarily does not permit that to be
done indirectly which cannot be done directly, considering
such a collateral attack as unfair and unconstitutional. To
allow removal on the basis that the book is objectionable to
board members' sensitivities permits the exercise of prejudices not present in the former case where selection is usually
accompanied by selection safeguards not present when the
book is banned after having once been on the shelves. This
"absolutist" point of the First Amendment is perhaps best
characterized by Justice Douglas when he wrote:

> The First Amendment is a preferred right and is of great im-
> portance in the schools. . . . Are we sending children to school to
> be educated by the norms of the School Board or are we educating
> our youth to shed the prejudices of the past, to explore all forms of
> thought and to find solutions to our world's problems?

Some would not be so sanguine in defense of First
Amendment rights as Justice Douglas but can understand that
like all constitutional rights, the right to freedom of communication both to receive and to send messages is on a sliding
scale and can be limited on condition: that a publication is
obscene, that it contributes to the delinquency of susceptible
individuals, or that it is obsolete or takes up too much room
on the library shelf. Since these are not the usual reasons
boards ban books, the board's abhorrence of the content alone
should not be allowed to govern final selection and access in
high school libraries. That was the message in *Minarcini* despite its convoluted logic and it must remain the better rationale by which to judge removal of books from the library until
such times as the Supreme Court puts to rest the divided
courts on this issue.

Teachers should not be called on to solve the constitutionality of attempts to ban books from the curriculum. For example, in *Harris vs. Mechanicville Cent. Sch. Dist.*, insubordination charges were lodged against a teacher who refused to

confer with his principal and who violated a written agreement he had made with the administration not to use the novel, *Catcher in the Rye,* in his English classes. The lower court sustained only the first charge, and ordered the board to consider a penalty short of dismissal. The appellate court, however, reversed the court below and held that the teacher's dismissal under the circumstances was not an abuse of the board's discretion.

Four cases handed down in 1979 are all to the same effect: the board may restrict students' access to books on the basis of their own personal opinions that the books are objectionable. In *Cary vs. Board of Education, Adams-Arapahoe Co. Sch. Dist. 28-J,* the court had before it an unusual set of facts. Plaintiffs, who were teachers of English in the district, had been using certain books which were excluded from an approved list of 1,275 textbooks in 1975. The parties agreed that the books, ten in number, which were placed off limits by the board's action, were not obscene in the legal sense, that they did not represent a system of thought or philosophy, and that exclusion could not be "considered an abuse of discretion or otherwise contrary to any constitutional standards applicable to an appropriate decision-maker." Plaintiffs did, however, claim a federal question because the action of the board constituted an invasion of academic freedom. Teachers claimed that they had a protected right to select teaching materials for these elective courses on the basis of their professional judgment. The board contended that it had been given the right by the legislature to select materials and that there was no constitutional issue involved. To complicate matters, the board had negotiated with the teachers' association, and agreement was reached on a clause providing that the board "shall have the right to determine the processes, techniques, methods and means of teaching any and all subjects." The collective bargaining agreement, in the opinion of the court, was the central fact in the case. Teachers normally have professional leverage in the selection of textbooks and other materials for use in their classrooms, but this right is not unlimited. Teachers may not, for example, use their classrooms as "forums" to advance their own pet ideas. What had altered

the right, according to the district court, was the fact that
teachers as individuals had surrendered "their individual
freedom of professionalism for the security of protectionism"
by collective action and a group contract. In so doing, they
had submitted themselves to the employer-employee model
of the teacher's relationship to the school board "for everything which is within the scope of the contract and that includes the authority to control communication through the
assignment of reading material."

"But for the bargained agreement," said the court, "the
plaintiff teachers would prevail here. But because of the bargained agreement, the plaintiffs' claims must be denied. The
teacher may bargain away the freedom to communicate in
her official role much as an editorial writer who agrees to
write the views of a publisher or an actor who contracts to
speak the author's script. One can, for consideration, agree to
teach according to direction."

On appeal, the Tenth Circuit Court of Appeals affirmed
the right of the board to select textbooks and limit their ac-
cessibility to students, but with different reasoning. The
board's action in placing the books off limit was not a waiver
of the teachers' constitutional rights, said the circuit court,
but rather "it seems a cautionary clause, a reminder that the
board retains control over the techniques, method and means
of teaching the courses in question." This is a power the
board already possesses, having been given that authority by
the state legislature. After development of a history of the
problem of textbook censorship, the court quoted Justice
Black with approval in part as follows:

I am also not ready to hold that a person hired to teach school
children takes with him into the classroom a constitutional right to
teach sociological, economic, political, or religious subjects that
the school's managers do not want discussed. This Court has said
that the rights of free speech "while fundamental in our democratic society, still do not mean that everyone with opinions or
beliefs to express may address a group at any public place and at
any time." Cox vs. Louisiana, 379 U.S. 536, 554; 379 U.S. 559, 574.
I question whether it is absolutely certain, as the Court's opinion
indicates, that "academic freedom" permits a teacher to breach

his contractual agreement to teach only the subjects designated by the school authorities who hired him.

The Tenth Circuit Court in affirming the decision below in favor of the local board's decision-making powers in relation to instructional materials said:

The Supreme Court has ruled that there is no constitutional right to an education. *San Antonio Ind. Sch. Dist. vs. Rodriguez,* 411 U.S. 1, 1973. Colorado has assumed the responsibility for a public education system and provides that local school boards "shall have control of instruction." It is legitimate for the curriculum of the school district to reflect the value system and educational emphasis which are the collective will of those whose children are being educated and who are paying the costs. Since the board gave no reason for its refusal to approve these books we considered a remand to ascertain that the reasons were constitutionally permissable (but remand was not awarded).

At press time, there was no plan to appeal the decision to higher authority.

In *Zykan vs. Warsaw (Ind.) Comm. School Corp.,* a federal district court considered complaints filed by high school students about the board's limiting or prohibiting the use of certain textbooks, removing books from the library, and deleting courses from the curriculum. The court noted the lack of unanimity among the various circuits, and chose to solve the problem by following precedent set in an earlier case in the same circuit. Although not specifically on target, the earlier court had upheld dismissal of non-tenured teachers for introducing into their classroom without prior planning "objectionable" materials extolling the joys of smoking pot, nude bathing, and freaking out. There the court held for the board, on the grounds that 1) the poems and brochures, which were concocted to promote the movie *Woodstock,* had no valid educational objective, since they were not included in the teachers' lesson plans; 2) the materials were ill-suited to the age and maturity of elementary school pupils; and 3) although the board had not specifically banned *Woodstock* materials, professional judgment should have warned the teachers they were skating on thin ice. The *Zykan* court then ruled that school officials have the right to hold "opinions," about what type of citizens are good citizens, to determine what curriculum and materials will best develop good citizens, to prohibit the use of texts and library books, and to delete curricular courses—in short, to do anything they should do "as a part of the effort to shape students into good citizens."

On the subject of the student's right to learn, the court said in part:

These cases clearly demonstrate that, compared to the constitutional limits which a state has in restricting communication generally, it is a much more lax constitutional limit which school officials have in restricting communications to students. And, since the students' right to receive a constitutionally protected communication is only the reciprocal of the constitutional right to send the communication, it follows that, compared to the constitutional limit which a state has in restricting the general receipt of communications, it is a much more lax constitutional limit which school officials have in restricting students' receipt of communications. . . . There is no way school officials can make the judgments necessary except on the basis of personal moral beliefs. To allege that school officials have made decisions regarding classroom texts, library books, and curriculum courses solely on the basis of personal "social, political and moral" beliefs is insufficient to allege a violation of constitutionally protected "academic freedom."

The court then dismissed the students' complaint for lack of a constitutionally protected right on the part of the plaintiffs.

In *Bicknell vs. Vergennes Union High School Board of Directors*, local board members were challenged when they removed books from the high school library on the basis of their personal opinions that the books were "vulgar," and otherwise inappropriate for student readers. Plaintiffs contended that their rights of free speech and due process of law were violated by the board's action. The board also voted to restrict the discretion of the school librarian in the selection and acquisition of additional works for the library. The court acknowledged that students' rights were serious arguments in favor of the plaintiffs. The court agreed that "the Nation's future depends upon leaders trained through wide exposure to that robust exchange of ideas which discovers truth out of a multitude of tongues rather than through any kind of authoritative selection." Nevertheless, public education is committed to the control of state and local authorities, and "courts should not interfere in the daily operation of this enterprise." The court could not agree with the board's action, but could not find that the policies and actions directly or sharply "infringe upon the basic constitutional rights of the students." Quoting *President's Council* with approval, the court cited as "novel" the concept that a book may acquire "tenure" by shelving and cannot be removed once it has gained such a lofty status. Nor is the board's retention of books any different from its acquisition: both are at the discretion of the board and the board alone, so long as they are within the state and federal constitutional constraints in effect at the time.

Due process rights of students extend only to bona fide liberty and/or property interests created by federal or state law. Since the court could find no independent constitutional right to library books on the part of students, the petition of the plaintiffs was dismissed. As to school employees, any intrusion into constitutional rights was, if present, only "miniscule," and since librarians do not have an independent First Amendment right to control the collection of the school library, the court was inclined to uphold the board's action in its entirety.

Finally, a book banning case that attracted nationwide attention was *Pico vs. Island Trees Union Free School Dist.*, a case currently under litigation. The United States District Court for the Eastern District of New York ruled that 1) the case could not be maintained as a class action, and 2) that the First Amendment did not require the court to forbid school boards from removing books from their libraries and curricula. The facts are complicated but boil down to these: the local board removed library books from the high school library on the grounds they were "objectionable" to the members of the board; plaintiffs who were students and their parents and friends objected but were declared not to be a recognizable class of persons for whom relief could be granted by the court; and plaintiffs claimed the board's conservative philosophy of morals and traditional values was the dominant factor in the board's decision to ban the books. The issues were whether the board's action in removing or restricting access to the library books was constitutional and whether its action in removing the books from "use in the curriculum" was also constitutional. The court held that the board had acted constitutionally and within its discretionary powers in both instances.

The court held that the various causes of action reduced to one: a single cause of action under 42 U.S.C. § 1983, a deprivation of rights guaranteed under the First Amendment. The court held that *President's Council,* the only federal case to uphold similar school board restrictions on library books and in the same circuit, was controlling in the matter. Courts should find it inappropriate to intervene where school board decision-making is at work, said the court. The test of the appropriateness of the board's action was to be found in *Epperson vs. Arkansas, i.e.,* that public education is a state and local function, and courts should not intervene where no basic constitutional value is involved. Applying the *Epperson* standard, the court found no impingement "upon any basic constitutional values." Since somebody has to make the determination of what materials shall go into the library, and the state has indicated that it is for the local board to be that somebody, the courts should interfere only on those rare occasions not present here which deal sharply and directly with denial of constitutional rights.

Plaintiffs, being students, cannot speak for the teachers; apparently, no teacher in the district wanted to use the books in question. While a student under the "right to receive" doctrine may have standing to present a First Amendment academic freedom claim, before such a claim may be sustained there must be at least a real, not an imagined controversy. Here, "plaintiffs' contention that the board's action interferes with what teachers in the district want to teach, is diffuse, speculative and factually unsupported." In the light of these circumstances, there is no finding of a First Amendment violation arising out of removal of any of the books from use in the curriculum.

Conclusions

From the cases cited and other literature on the subject of book banning by local boards of education, the following facts emerge:

1. None of the books or materials which were banned by local boards were legally obscene according to the *Miller* test; in most cases, the parties agreed that the materials were short of the necessary criteria to bring them within the *Miller* definition of obscenity.

2. With the exception of the Kanawha County case, which was atypical of the cases examined, none of the grounds for objections to books was related to religious grounds; however, some cases, while lacking religious orientation, did rely on a heavy sense of moral indignation on the part of those who were in the process of banning the books from schools.

3. There were conflicting findings in at least three circuits, the First, Second and Sixth Federal Circuits specifically. Such a variety of difference may require the United States Supreme Court to settle these differences through acceptance of a case dealing with one or more of the issues contained in the cases examined in this article.

4. Two opposing and perhaps irreconcilable forces seem to be at work in the decisions examined; these may relate to state responsibility for public education vs. a national constitutional standard; to the teacher's right to teach and the student's right to know; to the collectivists' goal *pro bono publico* vs. individual First Amendment rights to freedom of expression; to adult rights vs. the rights of peculiarly susceptible individuals who must be protected from worldly things; and perhaps to the right to receive as well as to send protected messages in the school setting. Present trends in the cases examined seem to favor state's rights, the collectivistic viewpoint rather than the individual's right to receive messages, and adult rights over the rights of children. Supreme Court guidance in the way the tendencies will go is sorely needed, although a balancing of the interests may not be judicially possible to everyone's satisfaction.

5. Like all our constitutional guarantees, the right to read is not absolute, and must depend upon factors which relate directly to the feeling of the majority of persons in the community in question. So long as those feelings are implemented and controlled by means of local boards of education, the tendency seems to be that the courts will favor those boards where careful planning has led to an even-handed handling of the problem and will refuse to intervene to change a situation that has the appearance of being firmly under control of the board.

BIBLIOGRAPHY

An asterick (*) preceding a reference indicates that the article or part of it has been reprinted in this book.

BOOKS AND PAMPHLETS

Alabama Library Association. Manual on intellectual freedom. The Association. '79.

Bartlett, Larry D. and others. Selection of instructional materials: a model policy and rules. Iowa State Department of Public Instruction. '80.

Britton, Gwynneth and Lumpkin, Margaret. A consumer's guide to sex, race and career bias in public school textbooks. Britton and Associates. '77.

Davis, James E., ed. Dealing with censorship. National Council of Teachers of English. '79.

FitzGerald, Frances. America revised: history schoolbooks in the twentieth century. Little, Brown. '79.

Hatcher, Thomas C., and Erickson, Lawrence G., eds. Indoctrinate or educate? International Reading Association. '79.

*Hefley, James C. Are textbooks harming your children?: Norma and Mel Gabler take action and show you how! Mott Media. '79.

*Hung, Pham Thien. Parents protest textbooks. Freedom of Information Center Report #401. '79.

Indiana State Teachers Association. Censorship: professional improvement packet. The Association. '79.

Jenkinson, Edward B. Censors in the classroom; the mind benders. Southern Illinois University Press. '79.

Jenkinson, Edward B. "Who will control the minds of the students" in Warsaw, Indiana? Indiana Council of Teachers of English. '78.

Kofke, Crystal L. Eliminating sex bias in textbooks and education materials. Colorado University. '78.

National Education Association. Kanawha County, West Virginia: a textbook study in cultural conflict. The Association. '75.

Nelkin, Dorothy. Science textbook watchers and the politics of equal time. MIT Press. '77.

233

Oboler, Eli M. Defending intellectual freedom: the library and the censor. Greenwood Press. '80.

O'Neil, Robert M. Classrooms in the crossfire: the rights and interests of students, parents, teachers, administrators, librarians, and the community. Indiana University Press. '81.

*Parker, Franklin. The battle of the books: Kanawha County. Phi Delta Kappan Educational Foundation. '75.

U.S. Commission on Civil Rights. Fair textbooks: a resource guide. Government Printing Office. '79.

*Wisconsin State Department of Public Instruction. Division of Library Services et al. Suggestions for dealing with censorship of media center materials in schools: a Wisconsin plan. The Department. '81.

Woods, L. B. A decade of censorship in America: the threat to classrooms and libraries, 1966–1975. Scarecrow Press. '79.

PERIODICALS

American School Board Journal. 166:21–6. Je. '79. Your schools may be the next battlefield in the crusade against improper textbooks. Barbara Parker.

American School Board Journal. 166:21–6. Je. '79. Meet the textbook crusaders. Barbara Parker.

American School Board Journal. 167:14+. Mr. '80. What will parents let you teach?

American School Board Journal. 167:28–9. N. '80. How one school system learned a harsh First Amendment lesson. M. Chester Nolte.

Catholic Library World. 52:75–6. S. '80. Morality issues in the high school library. Lesley Johnson.

*Contemporary Education. 51:182–5. Summer '80. Reading materials in the public schools: selection and controversy. Carolyn P. Atkins and John L. Carline.

Crisis. 86, 6:240–3. Je./Jl. '79. Impact of Brown on textbooks. Geneva Gay.

Crisis. 86, 6:253–7. Je./Jl. '79. Revised treatment of black Americans in publications after Brown. Estelle W. Taylor.

Education Digest. 45:2–5. N. '79. Curriculum censorship in the public school. M. M. Maxson and L. L. Kraus.

Education Digest. 45:10–12. Ja. '80. Censorship in the schools. L. B. Woods.

Educational Forum. 43:392–407. My. '79. Curriculum censorship in the public school. M. M. Maxson and L. L. Kraus.

Educational Forum: 44:147–63. Ja. '80. Constitution, liberal theory, and textbook bias. Barry L. Bull.

Educational Forum. 44:165–73. Ja. '80. Impact of obscenity legislation on schools. June Edwards.

Educational Leadership. 38:139–42. N. '80. The power of the board of education to censor. Terry J. Larsen.

Educational Leadership. 38:146–9. N. '80. The New Right: threat to democracy in education. J. Charles Park.

Educational Leadership. 38:151–2. N. '80. Be prepared: a response to Charles Park. Richard H. Stewart.

English Journal. 68:7–10. D. '79. Warnings: textbooks are not made—or used—in heaven. Lois Weiner.

English Journal. 69:52–4. Ja. '80. You don't need a crystal ball to guess what's going to happen with censorship. Ken Donelson.

*English Journal. 70:58–9. Ja. '81. Freedom, censorship, schools, and libraries. Stephen Robinson.

English Journal. 70:50–3. Mr. '81. A new twist to an old problem: recent court decisions on school book censorship. June Edwards.

Graduate Woman. 75:10–13. S./O. '81. Target; public schools. Barbara Parker.

*Harper's. 260:80+. My. '80. Textbook America: the teaching of history. Walter Karp.

Harvard Educational Review. 49:361–86. Ag. '79. Ideology and United States history textbooks. Jean Anyon.

Harvard Educational Review. 50:36–46. F. '80. Sexism in teacher-education texts. Mira P. and David M. Sadker.

High School Journal. 62:311–45. My. '79. Censorship in education: symposium.

Instructor. 88, 6:24–35. Ja. '79. Censorship: the fight against it goes on. John D. Heisner.

Interchange. 9, 1:56–84. '78–'79. Justice and cultural conflict: racism, sexism, and instructional materials.

Interracial Books for Children Bulletin. 11, 8:7–9. '80. Adopting textbooks in Texas: facts and fancies. Twiss Butler.

Interracial Books for Children Bulletin. 11, 8:6. '80. Concern about content is not censorship. Robin Gordon.

*Journal of Law & Education. 10:1–15. Ja. '81. What Johnny can't read: "First Amendment rights" in the classroom. Jeffrey H. Orleans.

Journal of Law & Education. 10:23–36. Ja. '81. The right to read and school library censorship. Frances R. Niccolai.

Journal of Thought. 15:21–34. Spring '80. Alice Moore and the Kanawha County textbook controversy. Joe Kincheloe.

Learning. 8:46+. F. '80. Why don't we tell children the truth about America? Kim Marshall.

Learning. 9:36–8. O. '80. The Enfield uproar: criticism of censorship. Craig Pearsen.

Learning. 9:78–81. Mr. '81. Censorship in the schools. Nat Hentoff.

*Library Quarterly. 51:4–19. '81. Shoddy and pernicious books and youthful purity: literary and moral censorship, then and now. Kenneth L. Donelson.

Ms. p 82. S. '80. Caution—these pages may be banned in your school. L. C. Wohl.

Nation. 229:390–1. O. 27, '79. Banning books. Aryah Neier.

National Law Journal. p 1+. My. 25, '81. Censorship in the schools: national upsurge in textbook cases. Ruth Marcus.

*New England Law Review. 14:288–316. Fall '78. *Right to Read Defense Committee of Chelsea v. School Committee of the City of Chelsea:* the First Amendment comes off the shelf. Alex P. Landy.

New York Times. p B15. Mr. 27, '79. Censorship of textbooks is found on rise in schools around nation. Wayne King.

New York Times. p C1. My. 8, '79. Wave of censors hits the school. Fred M. Hechinger.

New York Times. p A19. Jl. 24, '80. Neutralism isn't neutral. Harvard N. Meyer.

New York Times. 22+. O. 14, '80. Book banning on trial.

New York Times. 16+. O. 31, '80. Parents still debating 1976 ban of books at school. John McQuiston.

New York Times. p 12+. D. 11, '80. Book-banning calls to libraries rising: complaints reported up fivefold since the election of Reagan—moves are defended.

*New York Times. XI, p 18. D. 28, '80. Is it book-burning time again? James Alvino.

New York Times. p 1+. My. 17, '81. Parents' groups purging schools of 'humanist' books and classes. Dena Kleiman.

Newsletter on Intellectual Freedom. 28:102+. S. '79. Intellectual freedom in schools: a bibliography. Gregg D. Johnson.

Newsletter on Intellectual Freedom. 28:71+. Jl. '79. 'Across-the-board' and 'bed' are dirty words? Edward B. Jenkinson.

Newsletter on Intellectual Freedom. 28:24+. Mr. '79. Patterns in the censorship of children's materials. L. B. Woods.

*Newsletter on Intellectual Freedom. 29:119+. N. '80. *Zykan v. Warsaw:* the non-decision decision. William D. North.

Newsletter on Intellectual Freedom. 29:35+. Mr. '81. Self-censorship: the proof is in the selection. Jerry Watson.

Newsweek. 96:75. N. 10, '80. The right to ban books. Aric Press, with Emily Newhall.
*NOLPE School Law Journal. 9:1–22. Ja. '80. New pig in the parlor: official constraints on indecent words. M. Chester Nolte.
Phi Delta Kappan. 61:608–12. My. '80. Preachers, politics and public education: a review of right-wing pressures against public schooling in America. J. Charles Park.
Phi Delta Kappan. 61:613–15. My. '80. The real issues in education as seen by a journalist on the far right. Barbara M. Morris.
Progressive. 44:12. Ap. '80. The schoolbook burners. Kay Keppler.
*Publishers Weekly. 216:42–4. O. 29, '79. Protest groups exert strong impact. Edward B. Jenkinson.
*Publishers Weekly. 216:44–6. O. 29, '79. Textbooks: a social responsibility. Council on Interracial Books for Children.
*Publishers Weekly. 218:32. F. 20, '81. The First Amendment: ALA's Krug: censorship attempts have tripled since Election Day. Howard Fields.
Publishers Weekly. 218:12. Ag. 7, '81. Study on school censorship finds cases on rise. John Mutter.
Review of Education. p 367–78. Fall '80. A perspective on science textbook controversies: those who depend on the Book versus those who depend on books. Jerome DeBruin.
Saturday Review. 6:24–6+. Jl. 21, '79. Book burning in the heartland: Warsaw, Ind. Stephen Arons.
Saturday Review. 7:35–7. Mr. 1, '80. What Johnny can't read. John Gardner.
*School Library Journal. 23:7. N. '76. The would-be censors of the left. Lillian N. Gerhardt.
*School Library Journal. 26:26+. F. '80. Standards and free access: equal but separate. Linda R. Silver.
School Library Journal. 27:115–17. O. '80. The controversy surrounding values education. Eli M. Oboler.
School Media Quarterly. 7:115+. Winter '79. Chelsea case decided: judge reverses censorship of school library. Judith F. Krug.
School Media Quarterly. 9:102–8. Winter '81. Self-censorship in collection development by high school library media specialists. L. B. Woods and Lucy Salvatone.
School Media Quarterly. 9:95–101. Winter '81. Book selection pressure on school library media specialists and teachers. Jerry J. Watson and Bill C. Snider.
Senior Scholastic. 113:14–16. Mr. 6, '81. Sex education: a national controversy. Sandra Gardner.

*Social Education. 43:304+. Ap. '79. Censorship: does anybody care? Anna S. Ochoa.

Texas Library Journal. p 57-9. Spring '80. The selection policy as the school library's defense against the censor. Mary Jean Livingard.

Time. 117:85-6. Ja. 19, '81. The growing battle of the books. Frank Trippett.

*Today's Education. 69:30GS-34GS. D. '80. Censorship in the schools: something old and something new. Dorothy Massie.

*Top of the News. 35:233-6. Spring '79. The enemies within: teachers and librarians as censors. Kenneth Donelson.

U.S. News & World Report. 86:51. Je. 4, '79. Censorship on rise again in schools.

*University of Detroit Journal of Urban Law. 57:523-45. Spring '80. School library censorship: First Amendment guarantees and the student's right to know. Martha L. Black.

Voice of Youth Advocates. p 52-3. F. '80. Intellectual freedom and youth rights. Dorothy M. Broderick.

Wall Street Journal. p 1+. S. 5, '79. Revised texts: school history books, striving to please all, are criticized as bland. Laurence Roste.

Wayne Law Review. 27:167-91. Fall '80. Censorship in the public school library—state, parent, and child in the constitutional area.